THE IDLER · NO.44

THE IDLER

NO. 44 MIND YOUR BUSINESS

A COLLECTION OF ESSAYS ON THE ART OF LIVING

EDITED BY TOM HODGKINSON

IDLER BOOKS

MMXI

labor omnia vicit

– Virgil

THE IDLER

NO.44 — MIND YOUR BUSINESS

Contents

NOTES ON CONTRIBUTORS   IX

LIST OF ILLUSTRATIONS   X

INTRODUCTION   I

TOM HODGKINSON *An Idler's Diary*   3

Comics

WILLIAM HOGARTH *Idleness and Industry*   14

TONY HUSBAND *Neville*   26

PETE LOVEDAY *Trials of the Green Man*   30

Conversations

BILL DRUMMOND   35

Essays

DAVID BOYLE *Small Is Splendid*   53

ROBERT WRINGHAM *From Business Plan to Escape Plan* 61

JACOB LUND FISKER *How To Retire Early*   71

SOPHIE POKLIEWSKI-KOZIELL   *Towards the Ludicrous*   85

SARAH BOAK   *Idling For Women*   97

BERNARD MARSZALEK   *Three Hours a Day*   125

ANDREW WILBUR   *The Gastronomic Underground*   133

BERNARD MANZO   *The Violence of Leisure*   143

TOBY YOUNG   *The Return of the Eton Mob*   151

LEE ROWLAND   *Karl Marx's Vision of the Free Individual*   165

N. M. GWYNNE   *Arguing: A Science and An Art*   177

WARREN DRAPER   *The Work Aesthetic*   199

MARK VERNON   *Idle Hands*   221

MATT BULLEN   *The More the Merrier*   231

ROBIN HARFORD   *Wild Food Wild Flow*   239

PAUL MILES   *Narrowboat Living*   249

WILKO JOHNSON   *Space Explorer*   257

PENNY RIMBAUD   *Birth of a Notion*   267

IDLE MARKET & ANNOUNCEMENTS   300

Notes on contributors

Sarah Boak is a musician and university lecturer who teaches popular music studies and gender theory. She is trying to write her PhD whilst bumbling about in the countryside with a woodsman and a small toddling boy. She knits badly, but with gusto.

David Boyle is a fellow at the New Economics Foundation and is the author of many books, including *Eminent Corporations*, *Blondel's Song* and *Money Matters*.

Christian Brett is a typesetter and printer, and proprietor of Bracketpress.

Matt Bullen co-writes *Family: The Web Series* with its creator Terisa Greenan. He lives in Seattle.

Warren Draper is currently replanting North Yorkshire; he has seeds in his pocket and mud on his mind. warrendraper@gmail.com

Bill Drummond is an artist, writer and musician. He is well known for the KLF among many other projects. www.penkiln-burn.com

David Galletly is a freelance artist, illustrator and graphic designer living and working in Glasgow, he has exhibited throughout the UK, Europe and the USA.

Sam Green is a London based illustrator, a recent Central St Martins graduate, whose illustrations combine detailed pencil work with digital embellishments – vividly coloured or black and white, severely contorted or startlingly realistic.

N. M. Gwynne is a retired businessman and teacher of Latin and philosophy.

Robin Harford gathers wild edible plants on a daily basis for his family. His wild food, family-friendly courses have been recommended in the BBC *Good Food Magazine*, *Guardian*, *GQ*, etc. He teaches at Eden Project, has appeared on BBC2's *Edwardian Farm*, as well as consulting about foraging with TV companies and celebrity chefs. For wild food recipes, videos, courses and more, visit http://www.eatweeds.co.uk/

Clifford Harper is an illustrator, with his roots in the anarchist movement, he has regularly illustrated many newspaper articles and columns, and is probably the sole reason some people continue to buy the *Guardian* newspaper.

William Hogarth's father opened a coffeehouse in London which proved to be a very unsuccessful venture, and in 1707 he was confined to Fleet Prison for debt. Young William on the other hand went on to be one of the sharpest satarists Britain has ever seen.

Tony Husband is a cartoonist who works for *Private Eye*, *The Times* and many more.

Wilko Johnson was the guitarist in Dr Feelgood and is a keen astronomer.

Bron Jones aka Eve Libertine is an artist and singer, and all round amazing lady.

Pete Loveday is creator of the *Russell* comics and lives in Devon.

Jacob Lund Fisker is author of *Early Retirement Extreme*. www.earlyretirementextreme.com

Nina McNamara is a graphic designer and illustrator based in Manchester.

Bernard Manzo writes for the *TLS*.

Bernard Marszalek, as an 'agent of Anarchy' in the US for Colin Ward's British journal, was one of the founders in 1964 of Chicago's Solidarity Bookshop. Currently he is associated with JASEconomy, which promotes the grassroots economy in the SF Bay area.

Paul Miles is a journalist who floats around on the canals of Britain.

Tracey Moberly is an artist and long time collaborator with Bill Drummond.

Sophie Poklewski-Koziell is Associate Editor of *Resurgence* magazine, and author of *Gathering Force: DIY Culture – Radical Action for Those Tired of Waiting*. She is currently collecting strands of writing together on childhood, creativity and choice, soon to be a blog: '21st Century Traditionalist'.

Penny Rimbaud was born in 1943. He did not study at Oxford. He does not have a dog, a wife, a flat in north London or a house in Buckingham-shire. He has been a writer throughout his life.

Lee Rowland is a psychologist and writer who taught scientific method at Oxford University, and now works with the Beckley Foundation.

Notes on contributors

Karolin Schnoor is an illustrator and designer living in London, originally hailing from Berlin, her gorgeous Nordic style – line and colour filled illustrations have graced textiles, many magazine pages, greetings cards and posters.

Alice Smith is an illustrator and designer. She is Art Editor of the *Idler* magazine, and regularly works with Bracketpress.

Mark Vernon is an journalist and writer. His latest book is *The Good Life* (Hodder). www.markvernon.com

Andrew Wilbur is a geographer at the University of Glasgow, currently finishing a PhD on back-to-the-land migration and alternative food networks in Italy. He is also the founder of Southside Foodshare, a neighbourhood food cooperative in Glasgow inspired by systems of alternative food distribution in the north of Italy.

Pete Willis is an illustrator and prolific zine-maker, he writes for *Last Hours*, is organiser of the London Zine Symposium, and runs Dead Trees & Dye zine distribution. He recently put out a new zine titled *Great Anarchists* described as 'drawn with a weirdo's hand'.

Robert Wringham is the editor of *New Escapologist*: a magazine for white-collar functionaries with escape on the brain. He currently lives the post-escape life in Montreal. www.newescapologist.co.uk

Toby Young is a columnist on the *Spectator*, pioneer of the free schools movement in the UK, and is author of *How To Lose Friends And Alienate People*.

List of illustrations

Portrait of Tom Hodgkinson Alice Smith	10	
Industry and Idleness William Hogarth	14–25	
Neville Tony Husband	26–29	
Self Delusion Costs Extra … Pete Loveday	30–31	
Portrait of Bill Drummond Tracey Moberly	34	
Small Is Splendid David Galletly	53	
Planned Obsolescence Sam Green	85	
Women Nina McNamara & Alice Smith	96–123	
Paul Lafargue Pete Willis	124	
Karl Marx Pete Willis	165	
Work Aesthetic Clifford Harper	199	
Idle Hands Bron Jones	221	
More The Merrier Alice Smith	231	
Narrowboat Living Karolin Schnoor	249	

Illustrator websites:

David Galletly	davidgalletly.com
Sam Green	sams-place.net
Clifford Harper	agraphia.co.uk
Tony Husband	tonyhusband.co.uk
Nina McNamara	ninamcnamara.com
Karolin Schnoor	karolinschnoor.com
Alice Smith	alice-smith.co.uk
Pete Willis	deadtreesanddye.com

INTRODUCTION

Tom Hodgkinson

SINCE I STARTED THE IDLER BACK IN 1993, I'VE BEEN fascinated by the idea of business and enterprise as an alternative to the slow strangulation of the nine-to-five. My embrace of small-scale entrepreneurialism has led to accusations of hypocrisy from my socialist critics. How can can you say you're an idler while you also run a business? You seem to be a little bit busy for someone who proclaims himself to be an idler. And how can you be an anti-capitalist and sell t-shirts?

The answer is that for me, idleness has always been about autonomy, creativity and responsibility. If your autonomy means that you are free to take a nap after lunch if you feel like it or that you are free to work fifteen hours if you so choose – then so be it. Idleness is an escape from slavery. It is not an opting out of life. Opting out, giving up, was formerly a considered a sin and was known as *acedia*. It became the seventh deadly sin, sloth, which is something closer to sadness or melancholy; a sort of depression. Idleness, or standing up for your right to be lazy, is an active and revolutionary position.

The problem with capitalism, said Chesterton, is that it does not create enough capitalists. In other words, most of us are wage slaves rather than independent operators. So we need to seize the means of production. We need to produce our own artefacts, food, objects and publications.

And we also need to sell our produce in the market if we are to make a living, and this is where the socialist gets himself in a pickle. He is against the supermarkets in a vague way, and against all business and commerce, which he sees as a bit dirty, but his only alternative is state-run socialism, which as any *fule kno*, is simply totalitarianism.

What the idler, paradoxically perhaps, recognises, is that it is through trade, honestly carried out, that freedom can be found. We need to set up our stall in the marketplace and sell our goods. In so doing, we make all sorts of new relationships, we enjoy ourselves and we put some good stuff out there into the world. We meet people, and we exchange ideas as well as money and goods. Trade can be a very beautiful thing.

That is why this issue of the *Idler* is devoted to business which, in another sense, is the precise opposite of idleness. The Roman word for business was *negotium*, which literally means 'not leisure'. Your *negotium* was something you had to do in order to make money. The Greek philosophers had warned against devoting too much time to your *negotium* at the expense of your *otium*, as Mark Vernon shows in his essay on the history of work.

A major feature in this issue of the *Idler* is our interview with artist, writer and musician Bill Drummond who, far from being an idler, is actually a sober Scot, a hard-working Presbyterian who considers idleness to be a waste of time. He does, however, very much approve of the idea of being a shopkeeper, and I discuss this and other matters with him in our conversation.

This *Idler* also features essays both on Karl Marx and on Paul Lafargue, his rabble-rousing son-in-law and author of *The Right to be Lazy*, which has just been republished by Charles H. Kerr. David Boyle of the New Economics Foundation praises small business, and we also have pieces on narrowboat living, the advantages of what is known as 'polyamory', or having more than one partner, and a wonderful story of star-gazing by Wilko Johnson. There are also various articles which we hope will help those who want to get out of the rat race. The whole has been beautifully packaged again by typesetter Christian Brett and artist Alice Smith.

AN IDLER'S DIARY

MAY 2010 — APRIL 2011

Tom Hodgkinson

MAY

IDLER 43: BACK TO THE LAND WAS PUBLISHED AND WENT out to the bookshops via our distributor, Central Books. We launched the issue at Rough Trade East off Brick Lane, with performances from Zodiac Youth and Asbo Kid. We have since sold about 2,000 copies, and even Waterstones has ordered it. Most seem to sell in independent bookshops, a sector which I believe can thrive following the demise of Borders and the decline of Waterstones. I went to speak at the excellent Swindon Book Festival, which is run by Matt Holland of Lower Shaw Farm, a fantastic community just off the M4. I would recommend checking out their many husbandry courses. May also saw visits to the Dark Mountain Festival in Wales where I met a grinning George Monbiot and debated the self-esteem agenda in modern education. I stayed in Llangollen as the guest of Jay Griffiths and Penny Rimbaud. Then to an event at How The Light Gets In, an excellent new philosophy festival at Hay, where I was set against Will Hutton and Douglas Murray to argue against the work ethic. In between all these events I made slow progress on my husbandry book, *Brave Old World*.

JUNE

Graham Burnett and I spent the weekend at Dial House in Essex running our 'Ditch the Day Job' course. We had eight takers and enjoyed a very interesting weekend. I was a little worried later because we heard that the parents of one of the course participants had been furious with her, and by extension, us: surely the last thing she should be doing in a recession was trying to find out how *not* to get a job? June 13th and 14th saw the Lynton and Lynmouth Music Festival, my local music festival in North Devon. This was the eighth year of this fantastic free festival. Once again we had a long, sunny weekend, but the festival was marred by the invasion of a gang of louts who broke into one of the camps and beat up two students. The main culprits, two North Devon yobs called Rothery and O'Driscoll, have now been put behind bars. But the incident has damaged the festival, perhaps irreparably, and it has been cancelled for 2011. This is a shame as a free festival, one which is put on simply for the sake of it and not to make money, is a rarity these days. We trooped off to the gigantic Glastonbury at the end of June, quite a different beast from our Lynton event. I gave a talk in the Free University of Glastonbury, which sits in the Park field, probably the most civilized area. The weather was gorgeous, and the highlights were the House of Fairy Tales and a talk on composting loos. Glastonbury can hardly claim to be eco-friendly though: it leaves an enormous pile of rubbish behind. As we drove out, I felt a surge of puritanical disapproval for all those people who buy tents and folding chairs from supermarkets on the way to down to Glastonbury, get massively wrecked all weekend, and then leave their camp behind for someone else to clear up.

JULY

We held our second 'Simple Living' course with the School of Life, and taught a bit of vegetable growing as well as a lot of merriment. We also swum in a beautiful sandy cove near our house which we had never discovered before, but whose existence was revealed to us by

Wild Swimmer Dan Start. The following weekend Graham Burnett held a second 'Ditch the Day Job' course at the Sustainability Centre in Hampshire, a Permaculture place, and had another fine time with fifteen course attendants, although I have to say that I am finding the permaculture approach to gardening can tend towards the messy. At home, my own veg patch thrived thanks to a simplified system of two large beds (not raised), the excellent Grow Your Own Vegetables by Joy Larkcom, seeds from the Real Seed Catalogue and a lot of hard work. I read Virgil's farming poem *The Georgics* again for my new book, *Brave Old World*, and I am struck by the line: *labor omnia vicit*, or 'hard work conquered everything'. This is certainly true for gardening, and probably for life in general, but how to reconcile this with the more Epicurean tendencies of the *Idler*? The end of July saw us take an ambitious project to the Port Eliot Festival: the Idler's Academy. This was our first school, and we ran a course of about twenty lectures covering sewing, Latin, scything, Virgil, cocktail-making, star-gazing and the latest research into frogs. Bill Drummond, our woodwork teacher, spent the weekend making a bed (after all, there's nothing wrong in being good with your hands). We set up a tuck shop and bookstall at the back of our tent, and had a very excellent time indeed.

AUGUST

While on holiday in France, Victoria and I start to think about the possibility of opening the Idler Academy full time. Over the weeks that follow, we start to make plans and ask advice. Would it be crazy to open an independent bookshop and café with a busy programme of talks? We start to look at shop rents in London, and investigate Bloomsbury, Covent Garden, EC1 and Notting Hill. Our trendy friends say we are mad not to think about opening in Old Street. Uncle Bill Drummond approves of the idea because it will get me out of bed. Parents sound a note of caution.

SEPTEMBER

I set up a stall at the Porlock Arts Festival selling my books. We are in the village hall. I man my table for three hours without any sales, then pop out to get some Fairy Liquid. I find out when I return that Margaret Drabble and Michael Holroyd had been looking at my stall very closely but had left because there was no one there. Such are the tragedies of life! I begin to immerse myself in the strange and unfamiliar world of spreadsheets and business plans. We need to do many, many sums if we are to make our idea work. On 30th September, having hit on Notting Hill, home of Rough Trade and Record and Tape Exchange, as our preferred location, we went to see Mr Barnard, the estate agent. Young Mr Lowry took us to see a vacant property at 81 Westbourne Park Road. It was a gorgeous Georgian shop with a basement and small garden, just a few doors down from Celia Birtwell, and opposite The Westbourne pub and the West London Buddhist Centre. 'It's perfect!' we said. That night we went to 39 Bedford Street for the launch party of Rachel Johnson's book about working on *The Lady*, and told various journos about our idea. The reaction was warm and positive. Then began four months of negotiations and bureaucracy of a fairly stressful kind. Not the least of the whole thing was the fact that having condemned usury, I now found that I was forced to embrace it, as we needed to borrow money to get the whole thing going. I received a very charming fan letter from the wonderful Emma Thompson.

OCTOBER

On the 1st October I went to visit Emma Thompson, who plied me with fine white wine and canapés. She said she would be delighted to open our shop. I did a ukulele-based talk at England's Lane Bookshop in Hampstead. I took Arthur up to London to see serious young indie band These New Puritans at the Barbican. They are accompanied by a children's choir, and an assistant drummer smashes a huge block of ice on stage and amplifies the resulting sound. We met the most excellent

Jessica Huth who agrees to be shop manager. At home I continued with Latin lessons, gardening and trying to finish my book, which looking horribly unfinishable.

NOVEMBER

I meet Dominic West at a party in London. A charming man and an *Idler* fan. He says he will do a reading at our shop. Victoria and I visit an interesting local home schooling group. I have been thinking very hard about home schooling for years now, but it looks like we'll never get round to it, because, I'm afraid, it seems too much like hard work. Our idea instead is that we will do a lot with the kids at home. Still, it's an interesting day, and I have enormous respect for parents who decide to home school. I give a talk about starting your own fanzine, and I'm told that many of the children in the group then followed up the idea. Book still a mess.

DECEMBER

We were completely snowed in over Christmas and New Year. We did very little beyond keeping warm, playing games and planning events for the shop. We had bought two enormous turkeys from local small-holders, with the intention of taking them up to a giant family Christmas. Instead we jointed them and froze them, and ate turkey for about two months. Victoria came back from a shoot with ducks and pheasants, which we plucked, gutted and froze. Maybe I was doing it wrong, but the plucking process was time-consuming and difficult. Would it have been easier just to buy the pheasants from the butcher? Yes. Still, we filled a freezer full of excellent game at a cost of precisely nought pounds. We had Wwoofers to stay for two weeks which was an excellent experience. They dug and manured the vegetable patch, made parsnip wine, piled logs and tidied the garden. Just before Christmas, the editor of the *Independent on Sunday* rang to offer me a column, I gratefully accepted and we celebrated with a few real ales.

JANUARY

The kids missed a week of school as a result of the snow. We kept the house cosy with roaring log fires in the wood-burning stoves. This year the log supply held out beautifully and we had a steady supply of dry wood to burn. We went sledging and trudged down to the pub occasionally for a brandy. On the 17th I went up to London for a performance at 5x15, the literary event organized by Rosie Boycott and her daughter Daisy Leitch, which took place at the Tabernacle. I had agreed to do three songs on the ukulele. I was the last on the bill, and sat through the four fifteen-minute talks from the other writers, all of which were excellent. I have never been so nervous in my life. There were 300 people in the audience, consisting of what you might call the *haute bohème* of Notting Hill. Afterwards we hooked up with the excellent Mary Killen and ate a dinner at Rosie's place. Back at home we go out of our minds with stress about the shop. The shopfitters – the brilliant Octink, and can I take this opportunity to send a big shout out to Will, Tim and Clarke – have already made a start, but there are problems with our loan. It's all to do with having been living on a low income and not having borrowed over the last few years. If I'd been massively in debt, then it would have been easy to borrow more. To make matters worse, I find that the company that runs the *Idler*, Idle Ltd, has been the victim of a scam. A group of chancers in Kent formed a company called Innovative Deck Lifting Equipment Ltd (IDLE Ltd) and scammed three companies out of a total of £13,000. The companies then left County Court Judgements logged against my Idle Ltd. It was back in 2007, but these were serious black marks against my good name. I spent a few days immersed in a nightmare of bureaucracy, trying to get these judgements lifted, and thanks to the Federation of Small Businesses for their good advice in this matter. Over this period, Victoria and I can hardly speak for fear and worry. The words 'stressed' and 'depressed' come up, and Arthur gets them muddled and says: 'Mummy, are you still distressed?'

FEBRUARY

Now began one of the busiest periods of my life. Victoria and I work from eight in the morning till ten at night every day on the shop, only pausing to throw a crust of bread to our children. I finally finish my book. At last a loan comes through so we are able to pay the shopfitters. We are helped with the shop and the whole project very much by architect Tom Allen who designs the shelves. Victoria chooses the paint colour and floor stain. And on 24th February, we throw a party to launch the shop. Emma T makes a fantastic speech, and Chris Goodwin of the Lute Society leads the merry throng in a Latin singalong of 'How Much Is That Doggy In The Window?'

MARCH

The shop opens for business on 1st March, and the opening night is packed to the rafters with pupils for Mark Vernon's 'Introduction to Ancient Philosophy'. In fact, people call the shop during the afternoon pleading to be allowed in. That first week we also have Harry Mount giving a Latin lesson and Charles Hazlewood giving a singing lesson. A great start. But now begins my own transformation from idler to shopkeeper, and I find that I can sympathize with Basil Fawlty. It's the catering. You become paralysed by the number of *things to do*. And while you try to be polite to tricky customers, a voice inside you wants to bellow: 'Your coffee was a bit cold? COLD? Do you know this coffee comes from Monmouth, the finest coffee importers in London? Do you know how much thought and work has gone into that coffee? Now GET OUT!' But you don't, and hence the tension. Victoria and I do a few days each in the shop before returning home and swapping over. This seems to work all right. One week at home Roy the bee man comes to check on Victoria's bees and hooray! They have survived the winter and are buzzing happily.

APRIL

A whole host of volunteers pop up and offer their help. They are the charming and intelligent Heathcote Ruthven, Madaline Morley, Lily Laflin, Hepizibah Winsor-Clive and Nicki Minus, and I realize that we have our prefects. Head Boy is Alexis Self. I also realize that the wonderful thing about being in a shop is that it is so very democratic. It is an open space. Anyone can wander in. Those who can't afford the lectures volunteer to help instead, or contribute in some other way. We meet some fantastic people. The locals are very supportive and are an interesting lot. The downside is the pressure to meet our considerable overheads, but on the other hand, the Puritan in me reckons this is no bad thing, as it keeps us on our toes and free of complacency. In mid-April I go on the Today Programme to defend bank holidays, and this leads to a piece in *The Sun* on the same subject, and an appearance on Sky News. Great fun. Well, as I write at the close of April 2011, the shop has been open for two months. We have put on 25 events and sold hundreds of coffees and books. We have created our own free space, an autonomous zone, and already people are meeting other people there, and things are happening. Above all, we've been introduced to an absolute mass of good things happening out there: people are making things, doing things, creating things and enjoying themselves, and trying to create independent livelihoods. The wonderful weather in April adds to my sense of hope and possibility.

Portrait of Tom Hodgkinson by Alice Smith

COMICS

PLATE I

The Fellow 'Prentices at their Looms

The Drunkard shall come to
Poverty, & drowsiness shall
cloath a Man with rags

PROVERBS XXIII:21

The hand of the diligent
maketh rich

PROVERBS X:4

PLATE 2

The Industrious 'Prentice performing the Duty of a Christian

O! How I love thy Law it is my
meditation all day

PSALM CXIX:97

PLATE 3

The Idle 'Prentice at Play in the Church Yard, during Divine Service

Judgments are prepared for scorners
& stripes for the back of Fools

PROVERBS XIX:29

PLATE 4

The Industrious 'Prentice a Favourite, and entrusted by his Master

Well done good and faithfull
servant thou hast been faithfull
over a few things, I will make thee
Ruler over many things

MATTHEW XXV:21

PLATE 5

The Idle 'Prentice turn'd away, and sent to Sea

A foolish son is the heaviness
of his Mother

PROVERBS X:I

PLATE 6

The Industrious 'Prentice out of his Time, & Married to his Master's Daughter

The Virtuous Woman is a
Crown to her Husband

PROVERBS XII:4

PLATE 7

The Idle 'Prentice return'd from Sea, & in a Garret with common Prostitute

The Sound of a Shaken Leaf
shall Chace him
LEVITICUS XXVI:30

PLATE 8

The Industrious 'Prentice grown rich, & Sheriff of London

With all thy getting get understanding
Exalt her, & she shall promote thee: she
shall bring thee to honour, when
thou dost Embrace her

PROVERBS IV:7–8

PLATE 9

The Idle 'Prentice betrayed (by his Whore), & taken in a Night-Cellar
with his Accomplice

The Adulteress will hunt for
the precious life
PROVERBS VI:26

PLATE 10

The Industrious 'Prentice Alderman of London, the Idle one brought
before him & Impeach'd by his Accomplice

The Wicked is snar'd in the
work of his own hands
PSALM IX:16

Thou shall do no unrighteousness
in Judgement
LEVITICUS XIX:15

The Idle 'Prentice Executed at Tyburn

When fear cometh as desolation, and their
destruction cometh as a Whirlwind; when
distress cometh upon them, they shall
call upon God, but he will not answer

PROVERBS 1:27–28

PLATE 12

The Industrious 'Prentice Lord-Mayor of London

Length of days is in her right hand, and
in her left hand Riches and Honour

PROVERBS III:16

Industry and Idleness, engravings first published September 1747.

TO BE DISCONTINUED...

CONVERSATIONS

Bill Drummond standing in the Penkiln Burn clutching salmon and bluebells
photograph by Tracey Moberly

GO FOR IT!

A CONVERSATION WITH
BILL DRUMMOND

Tom Hodgkinson

BILL DRUMMOND HAS BEEN A MAJOR INFLUENCE ON ME since the late Eighties. All his projects – Echo and the Bunny-men, the Jams, graffiti campaigns, the KLF, *Chill Out, The Manual*, the K Foundation, burning a million quid and now The 17 – have showed courage, spirit and a sense of autonomy. Drummond got on with it.

I went to interview Bill and Jimmy Cauty in 1991 for the *Guardian*. It was around the time when the ambient house movement was start-ing, and this intrigued me. The KLF had just released the excellent *Chill Out* album. At around the same time, I read their book *The Manual: How To Have a Number One The Easy Way*. This excellent title sold itself as a guide to go from being on the dole to having a number one hit single in the British charts in six months, but really it was about being creative and doing your own thing. I remember thinking about how the KLF approached life and wondering: why doesn't everybody do this? *The Manual*, and the activities of the KLF generally, were among my inspirations to set up the *Idler* magazine.

Later I went to a Shoreditch pub to see the pair giving a screening of the film about burning the money. I asked Bill if he would do an inter-view for the *Idler*. 'No,' he said. 'We're not idlers.' I began to realize that far from being a fun-loving prankster, Bill was in actual fact a unsmiling Presbyterian Scot with a strong work ethic. The perceived louche public school hedonism of the *Idler* was anathema to him.

Bill did eventually become a contributor to the *Idler*, writing the 'Bad Advice' column with Mark Manning. I think he had realized that we were not just Oxbridge dilettantes and that there was a serious mission behind the magazine. A couple of years ago, we took our families on a trip to Lundy Island, and spent many hours wandering around the cliffs and moors discussing usury, which, as a Puritan, Bill defended.

The interview that follows took place in the newly opened Idler Academy in London.

★

TH When we were on Lundy Island, we talked about the fact that in the Catholic Church up until about 1500, usury was very heavily disapproved of. The idea was that you were committing the sin of sloth, if you were the usurer, because you weren't doing anything creative. You were just sitting around doing nothing. By virtue of time passing you were making money. And secondly you are not allowed to sell time because it doesn't belong to you, it belongs to God. Also they felt that it exploited the poor. They had a more providential attitude towards life: that misfortune had been placed there by God and it was not for someone else to profit from it. The person who needs the money should be an object of charity. But commercial loans did happen for businesses.

BD And they were okayed by the Catholic Church?

TH I believe so ... you had the Medicis, for example. As in Islam today: Muslims still do mortgages, even though they are supposed to be against usury, or *riba*. Do you think that sort of climate would have stifled enterprise, or encouraged it? In setting up this shop, we've had to borrow money.

BD Everything that's happened in Europe since the Renaissance, couldn't have happened if people couldn't rent money, or weren't allowed to rent out the money they had.

TH What has happened?

BD Well, I'm not going to put a value judgement on it, but ... the West grew. The West became the dominant culture in the world as free enterprise blossomed.

TH   Wasn't it the dominant culture before then? Rome?

BD   It was dominant in Europe but no, not compared to the Chinese. You couldn't fund an expedition to the Spice Islands or wherever it might be without these methods. Now, you said you shouldn't rent time, but time is part of growing. The time I spend building a chair, that's what you buy when you buy that chair, that time in my life.

TH   Now when we first met many years ago, I asked if you'd like to do an interview for the *Idler*. And you said, 'No, we're not idlers.' Does this mean that you would approve of the dynamic hard-working culture that came after 1500 more than the luxurious, Providence-based medieval version of Christianity?

BD   You're taking it for granted that that's what society was like before. I wouldn't know whether it was like that or not. I don't have particular opinions about the past. I'm not a historian, but I don't mind having a strong work ethic. When I think of idling, I think: who would want to do that? It's the fastest route to depression. Life is short enough as it is, it's getting shorter by the day, and there's lots of things I want to do. Now, I'm aware, as I've watched the *Idler* evolve and change, that you as chief idler have had to squeeze things in and slightly change it to make it work. And you're one of the least idle people I've met. Lots of people have pointed this out to you: you celebrate idleness, but really … as a student or a post-student you might have been an idle person, spending time down the pub and smoking your cigarettes. But that isn't how you operate now. So you've changed the definition of what being an idler is over the past 15 or 20 years.

TH   Well, this is what is often thought, but if you look at issue one, I actually say, this is not about slobbing around and giving up, it's about doing your own thing. Idleness and entrepreneurialism are in fact very closely related. Idleness in the workplace is an expression of defiance, and the will towards liberty. If you are working for a big corporation, doing a job that you hate, and which you find boring, which is the reality for a lot of people, then slacking off, skiving, is a way of taking back some power for yourself. But when released from that prison, the guy who was previously the idler in the office – because he couldn't stand to be confined in that way, or told what to do – can be quite dynamic. So it has always been about: what's the alternative to the nine-to-five? Being idle is about taking responsibility.

BD But that's not taking responsibility, that's skiving off. That's somehow thinking you've won something; but you've won nothing. Because you're still a slave. One of the problems I've always had with the rebel, is that the rebel spends most of his time kicking against the thing he's rebelling against, instead of walking around that thing, walking away from it, and getting on with whatever it is he wants to be doing. So: don't skive off. Leave the job. Make your own thing happen. As you've done, Tom.

TH Well, John Nicholson calls skiving hypocrisy.

BD Of course it's hypocrisy.

TH It's the first step, though, to freedom.

BD It's *not* the first step to freedom. It's the first step to not taking responsibility for your own life. As soon as you get locked into that thing of blaming somebody else for your own predicament, you are entrapping yourself, enslaving yourself. I know you're not actually in bonded slavery, but as soon as you're an adult, you have to take total responsibility for your life. And take total responsibility for everyone else's life in a sense as well, because we have to live together.

TH Sartre says that the free man has the burden of the whole world on his shoulders.

BD Absolutely. We are totally free. Now, it's a contradiction, because since God created the universe, everything has been mapped out. But we have to ignore that, and make the decision: we are totally free. We have to take complete responsibility. Part of that freedom is to come up with a society that works, and a society that works is always evolving, always changing, so the morals that we use to make that society work, change. What we think is okay now, will be seen as immoral in a hundred years' time.

TH The suspicion of the usurer, though, is still here today: it's called banker-bashing.

BD I think that's a real weakness of people. In the Eighties it was Margaret Thatcher or the South Africans we hated, and now it's the bankers. That's blaming somebody else.

TH And we're actually complicit in the situation anyway.

BD Of course we are! When you blame the banker, you give up something in yourself. We should be thinking: right, the financial system hasn't worked. What we thought was good for the previous 20 years, has changed. It needs to be more regulated. It was good to deregulate the City, but now we have to reign it back. It's harder now: we have a global economy, so it's almost impossible for a national government to do that. But to go back to your word usury. If we take out a loan, and we think we've got some free money, it's our responsibility. If you go out and drink loads, you get drunk. And you might do some bad things when you're drunk. But it's your responsibility.

TH I noticed that people read my first book and said, 'Well, it's all right for you, being idle. I've got to pay this mortgage.' But I said: 'You took on the mortgage knowing the deal. You wanted to live in a bigger house so you took on a mortgage. You can't later complain about it.'

BD I've made lots of mistakes and got myself in all sorts of scrapes in the past, and still do. But I know, at every point, I created the situation. And as soon as I think somebody else has created the situation, I'm giving away my own freedom.

TH Do people actually want to to be free, in that case? There's something comfortable about being a semi-slave. If you're in prison, life can be easy. There's no responsibility. Your meals are made.

BD And guys who leave the Services: you take away that structure and they fall to bits. Or people who have worked in the public sector all their life: they go on strike every so often for more money... there's a pension at the end ... it's comfortable. Of course it's comfortable. The contradiction is that we are individuals, and we have to work as a group to exist as a species. We need each other. So there will always be that in-between area.

TH I think that's what you put across in *The Manual*. Yes, we accept our complicity in the situation that we've created, and you can't throw all the blame at the bankers or the headmaster or your parents. But at the same time, you can recognize injustice and protest against it.

BD You do something about it, you don't just protest against it; you don't just go on a march. We can all sit and shout at the TV and read newspapers. The only thing that counts at the end of your life, is *what you've done*. You may have all sorts of opinions. But if you haven't *done* anything, none of that counts. And that's what's wrong with pubs. Because alcohol encourages people not to do things.

TH It's true that the pub is the handmaiden of work. It's the consolation prize. It's the reward. But it *is* a pleasure: six o'clock, pint, complain about the boss. I used to enjoy that. It's a surface pleasure, like fast food, but it is kind of fun. Everyone has these great ideas in the pub. Then you forget them the next day when you have to go back into the office ... but going back to the *Idler*: the whole point from the beginning has been to encourage people to take responsibility and do their own thing.

BD Yes. Which I obviously agree with.

TH But at the same time, reflection, contemplation, prayer, meditation, reading, walks in the country, a long meal taken over a few hours: these are idle pleasure which it is worth defending.

BD OK. But the point I want to get back to, is that a lot of anti-Semitism is based on what you were talking about at the beginning. Christians may have traditionally blamed the Jews for killing Jesus, but because they weren't allowed to have land, they developed other crafts, such as working with gold, diamonds, and money. They could build up their wealth not in land, but in money.

TH The Jews were allowed to lend money, because they were not Christians.

BD But the Christians resented the fact that they owed the Jews loads of money. We have had world wars based on this. The real reason that Hitler was able to get a whole chunk of Europe behind him was because they owed loads of money to the Jews.

TH The Brits and the *Daily Mail* were fans of Hitler at certain points.

BD And I'm sure a lot of that was based on ... Jews had no allegiance to a state. They could move around, and that was resented ... I think when we talked about usury before, the word 'freedom' was being bandied around. One man's freedom is another man's slavery. The way I would put it is this: if I have this chair, and you want to sit in it, I have the right to rent you that chair by the hour, and you have the right to pay me. If I have £100 and you need £100 to get your business going, then why can't I rent you that money? I don't see that as a major problem.

TH But don't you see it as a major problem when people are deceived, encouraged to borrow more than they can afford, go into debt, with the result that they get seriously depressed? They get a debt that they can't afford to pay back, for example with a motor car.

BD Yes, and that's why we need laws, that's why we need rules, that's why the City needs to be regulated. But that doesn't mean to say that me renting you £100 is fundamentally wrong. I'll rent you the money for a week and it will cost you £10, just like if I rent you the chair for a week.

TH There's a company called Wonga which lends money at very high rates of interest. Surely that's wrong?

BD Of course it's wrong. But the fundamental thing of renting money is not wrong. There should be laws that govern how money is rented, in the same way that when you rent property, there are laws. In the same way, there isn't something fundamentally evil in the renting of money. We have to be aware of our weakness as human beings. But we have to be grown up as well.

TH But surely usury is a trick whereby the rich steal from the poor?

BD Almost the very opposite. Wealth, until recently, was measured in land. That's where wealth was. What borrowing money meant was that people without any land could make something happen. If they hadn't been allowed to rent that money, they wouldn't have had the money to buy land. I would have had to bang you over the head with a club and steal the land. This way, I don't have to do that.

TH But actually land ownership was conceived of quite differently in the manorial system, where you had rights over land, and you might be able to use land for your whole life, but you didn't exactly own it in the sense that you could sell it, or build on it and sell it for more, as property developers do today.

BD Obviously the way that you own land has evolved over the centuries. There would have been a time when a tribe owned that land. At a certain point, we were no longer hunter-gatherers, we were farmers, so we had to have fixed land. And when you get two cultures that meet each other for the first time and have different ways of dealing with land ... Once the white man hit North America, he had a completely different approach to that of the Native Americans who were hunter-gatherers, the majority of them, and the tribe owned the land.

TH   That clash is well portrayed in *Little House on the Prairie*. Actually the Ingalls made some silly decisions: they had fantastic energy and optimism, but they built their house in the wrong place. The Native Americans lived quite lightly, with great knowledge of their environment. The Puritans came in and said, 'We're going to build a road and do our thing, with a huge amount of effort.' Then they got it all wrong and had to build another house.

BD   But you're romanticizing the Native Americans as having it right, and the Puritans as having it wrong. There is not one wrong or right. There is an evolution, and I don't mean evolving into something that's better ...

TH   Some of the Catholic intellectuals in the Twenties, like Chesterton and Belloc, had the idea of Distributism, the idea being that each family would have its acre of land. There is freedom in land, because you can grow your own food and keep animals. Chesterton said that the problem with capitalism is that there are not enough capitalists. Most people are working *for* the system. There are not enough small businesspeople. So what they were trying to do was to give freedom through the more equal distribution of land. It was called Peasant Proprietorship. Everyone should have their own allotment or acre of land on which they can grow stuff and have some measure of independence. Is that not a sensible scheme?

BD   I don't know about that. What I do know is what they did in the Soviet Union with the *dachas* was almost exactly the same.

TH   I think the *dacha* pre-dated the Soviet Union, but the Soviets definitely kept it going.

BD   They had so much land. Moscow was surrounded by all this unused land. Every family got the same amount. And going back to what you were saying, it is the human condition that some of us have more get-up-and-go than others. Some are entrepreneurial and some are not.

TH   If you think about, for example, a band, there is the kind of person who enjoys being the roadie. He doesn't want to be in the band. George Harrison said that about Mal Evans, The Beatles' roadie. He enjoyed helping people and being supportive. I can't go up to him and say, 'Quit The Beatles, start your own business, and be entrepreneurial.' On the other hand, I think that a lot of people do want to be encouraged to be entrepreneurial. And I think that's what you were getting at in *The Manual*. That's how I read it, anyway.

BD   That's exactly it.

TH   Although it was specifically about the music business, it could be applied to any area of life.

BD   The music business thing to me was just an excuse. My main thing is: don't wait to be asked. Don't wait to be given permission. Don't wait for somebody else to validate you. Get up and go and do it. Which does sound horribly close to some horrible American self-help book. Once I became aware of that whole genre, I thought: is that all that all of that was? Which was a bit of a downer for me personally. But I still stick by it. Don't wait for a major record company down in London.

TH   And that is what punk was supposed to be about.

BD   Punk though suffered as much from putting icons up there. I see that as what fascism is. We have our Johnny Rottens, and what's he called, from The Clash …

TH   Joe Strummer.

BD   And our Joe Strummers up there on pedestals. I do that, too, I put things up on pedestals.

TH   It's natural, isn't it?

BD   It's also natural to tear them down.

TH   I've noticed that with my own readers. They read my books and like them, and then later they go on to forums and give me some real abuse.

BD   They shouldn't give you abuse. They shouldn't be on forums, they should be out doing stuff.

TH   Well, that's why I closed down the *Idler* forum. They seemed to be a load of whingeing procrastinators. The medium itself, the forum, seems to encourage whingeing and procrastinating. It's like Facebook which is a short-term solution to loneliness in the office.

BD I don't do Facebook. I don't know whether it's a generation thing.

TH Twitter?

BD I don't do that, either. I've got too much in my life. Too much going on. What's obvious to state, if I'm having a go at our culture, is that all it's interested in doing – and this happened with music in the twentieth century – is turning us into consumers. You don't have to make it any more: we'll have the experts, we'll have the geniuses, we'll have the good-looking ones making it.

TH That's what rock 'n' roll is.

BD Yeah, and that's my big downer. I know that you with your ukulele, are trying to break that down. And what I do with The 17 is another way of breaking it down.

TH The problem is though that there are levels of ability. John Lennon is a much better songwriter than I am. He's the master carpenter.

BD That doesn't matter. I mean, I find it hard to believe, but there may be people out there who are better at doing sex than me! But imagine if, the trick had been done, from now on, you don't have to do sex. All you people, we've got this tiny group who will do the sex for you, and you just watch them, and buy into that. That's what happened with music in the twentieth century. It was taken away from everybody.

TH We all used to sing all day long. And more old-fashioned cultures today still do.

BD Of course they do. And I've done enough travelling around the world, even though I'm anti-travel …

TH Why are you anti-travel?

BD Because travel's just escapism. Wherever you go, you're there. All that happens is that the more you travel, the dumber your mind grows, because you don't notice the changes and the differences of where you're at, where you are … but going back to music, it's been taken away from the people, and people have to take it back.

TH Are the TV talent shows an expression of people trying to take it back, or are they just an extension of the whole thing?

BD They're just an extension of the whole thing, because all you have to do is sit there and watch. I guess I'm against anything where somebody else is doing it for you. You go and see a film, and people are stealing cars or taking risks, and all you're doing is sitting in a dark room watching this. And I think: no, no, you get out of that cinema now, and steal a car. That's why I think football hooligans are better than regular football supporters. All a football supporter is doing is paying his money to watch other guys playing football. So he's getting his highs and lows from what other people are doing. The football hooligan is getting his highs and lows out of beating people up. So he's actually doing something.

TH   [shocked liberal silence] Erm ... singing does happen in football stadiums.

BD   It does.

TH   That is a case of a real collective singsong, and that's wonderful in a way.

BD   It's fantastic.

TH   I can see the attraction: singing in a vast group and watching the amazing skills of the football players. Everyone in the world wants to watch David Beckham on a big screen, even the pigmies of Southern Africa. There is something godlike about these football stars.

BD   I still say that it's a weakness of us as a species, and that's why we get the Hitlers and the Stalins. This may just be a typical Dad-thing, but I said to my eleven-year-old son on Sunday: what makes you feel better? Hitting a six, scoring a goal, or having a thing bought for you? Obviously, it's actually hitting a six. It's when you've done something yourself.

TH   All children seem to want to do though is to watch television and be bought things. Go to entertainment parks. Be entertained.

BD   I'm as bad a parent as anybody else so I will use the television.

TH   Going back to football: the origins of football were an outlet for violence. It was always being banned by the Corporation of Chester for being too violent. It was done on Shrove Tuesday, and was a big blow-out. People also used to go around killing cocks. It was a huge outlet for all this aggression and energy before Lent started.

BD   I like football, if you're playing it. That's what more of us should be doing. I don't know what you do when you're a bit older and you can't play these things.

TH   Play darts.

BD   I love darts. And pool.

TH   Pool and darts are surely complete idler's pastimes.

BD   [long silence] Then I hate pool! No, I've got a pool table at home. I've got no room for it. When I was young, it was snooker. But snooker's too hard.

TH   I did used to love watching snooker and darts on television. That is fun. I think you can be a bit too hard on people, Bill.

BD   I'm always harder on myself.

TH   Which brings me back to the matter of this edition of the *Idler*. It is the business issue. I don't see a contradiction between idling and starting a business. They're actually closely related. I'm actually quite knackered today as we've been working so hard to set up this shop.

BD   More of us should be shopkeepers. I think being a shopkeeper is a very, very good thing to be.

TH   A nation of shopkeepers now seems like quite a fantastic thing. We're actually a nation of semi-slaves, which is much worse. I think of those pictures of the Victorian draper standing proudly outside his shop and I feel like that now.

BD   It's fantastic. One of the most fundamental requirements of the human condition is for our lives to have meaning. That's what religion does. Running a shop gives your life meaning.

TH   Trade: this again is where I would part company with socialism. I quite often get the comment: you say 'You're an anti-capitalist, but you're selling t-shirts on your website!' But I see trade as a great thing. It produces an engagement with another human being. We've only been here ten days, and we've met some wonderful people. Things are happening already, and that's because we've set up a stall in the market. That's what I mean by: what's wrong with capitalism is that there aren't enough capitalists.

BD   For whatever reason, we in Britain, and especially the white population, have lost that entrepreneurial spirit.

TH   Yes, because you see it in the immigrants.

BD   Some races are more entrepreneurial than other races. The Turkish people around where I live are really entrepreneurial. They make things happen. And we seem to have lost that.

TH Why have we lost that, what's happened? Have our rulers deliberately tried to create a situation where you've got quite stupid people coming out of school, not well educated, and not very capable either? They've been prepared for a job, a boring job in the economy. In other words, to be a slave. That's the central purpose of education today.

BD I wouldn't say there was a golden age of education. I know that when I was at secondary school, I was on a conveyor belt. I was supposed to get an apprenticeship at the steelworks. Factory fodder.

TH Actually, William Cobbett said the same in the 1820s.

BD What I think is so much better now about education, is that then, it was more about imparting knowledge. It wasn't teaching people how to think. And now they are taught far more how to think, and question. That does mean you've got to put up with all the attitude.

TH Doesn't that lead to the children at school thinking: 'Just because he's the headmaster, he thinks he can tell me what to do?' Again, this new system produces incapable people, and also whingers. Although I admit that I'm going on research and anecdote rather than direct experience: you actually have two daughters at London state secondary schools. Would they know where to put the apostrophe?

BD They would. And the school they are at, they will defend it to the hilt. There's been a war between their school and the Toby Young Free School on the Spectator site. There's been a war between teachers at my daughters' school and him, and he looks like a fool. It looks like he has no idea what is actually going on within education.

TH I think it's a noble pursuit he's engaged with. He wants to start an academic school: why not?

BD But he's standing in judgement on other schools, without really understanding what they're doing. And in the same way, as much as I find Starkey entertaining, on the Jamie Oliver show, the kids are right: they can think faster than he can.

TH Isn't this the system that's created the lazy white people that you mentioned? Lots of self-assurance, but not much knowledge?

BD Is knowledge what is needed now?

TH The point of grammar is that it does teach you how to think clearly, and to detect when you're being manipulated or bamboozled by advertising for example. Or politicians. Cobbett was against state and private schools, but he wrote an English grammar because he wanted people to be able to understand when they were being hoodwinked.

BD Well, these are hunches. Even though I was really rubbish at English, I'm a total stickler, and I can see that bad emails lead to confusion. But I know that it's more that, I'm the problem.

TH My Mum went to the grammar school in the Fifties, and this was her total saviour. She knows her Milton and she would be incapable of putting the apostrophe in the wrong place, because it was drummed into her. Moving back to the business thing, one problem is that if you're told you're vaguely creative, an artist or a writer or a musician, then you shovel the responsibility for your finances onto somebody else. Somehow it's seen as uncool to have a filing system, with invoices paid, invoices unpaid and so on, VAT, bookkeeping. But I notice that before the Industrial Revolution, bookkeeping and accounts were taught as a matter of course to the gentlefolk. So what I'm trying to say is that it's not square to take responsibility for your own finances. But the romantic poet is meant not to concern himself with dirty commerce.

BD We should all take responsibility. My experience in the music business shows that bands – and especially lead singers, they're the worst – create a power base out of not knowing what's going on. They loathe and despise their manager and record company and look down on them, but they're addicted to them, and the manager can exploit this weakness.

TH That could be a win-win situation, couldn't it?

BD That's the trade-off! But yes, everyone should be given responsibility. Maybe everyone should be given £1,000 when they leave school and told: 'That's it. You can either go and blow all that on drugs now, or you can set up your own business.' That sounds like one of Jesus's parables, doesn't it?

TH Is there any point in doing anything, though? My actions don't seem to have any effect on anyone else. Sometimes I think, 'What's the point?'

BD If you think that, you're wrong. Of course they do. Maybe your books won't change the world. But you've still got to keep going.

You've got to keep opening that shut door and adding up your columns. What I think is good about what you're doing is that we should be making our culture ourselves. I'm totally against the Arts Council.

TH I did look at grants once. But there are so many strings attached.

BD You have to make work that ticks their boxes. But with your shop, you sell some books, sell some coffees, sell some cakes, sell some tickets. And you're free of that control. The greatest culture of the twentieth century hasn't been culture that's been state-sponsored, whether it's The Beatles, or Hollywood.

TH I find that I can't get myself in a lather about these cuts! I try.

BD I love the cuts.

★

That's because Bill is a responsible man who thinks that life is supposed to be hard. And I have to agree, to an extent: Virgil said that Jove sharpened men's wits by making life hard, and the cuts will sharpen our wits and ultimately make us stronger and less dependent on the state. I have spent twenty years searching for the easy life and now I know: it doesn't exist. Even living on a farm and writing for four hours a day is hard work. As Virgil wrote, *labor omnia vicit*, hard work conquered everything!

ESSAYS

David Galletly

SMALL IS SPLENDID

David Boyle

Y OU DON'T GET VISITS BY THE POPE VERY OFTEN. IN
fact, between the departure of Adrian IV (the only English
pope) and the visit of John Paul II, we had to wait 823 years.
'He doesn't come here every day,' said Claire Richard, 11, in Aberdeen.
'It's not even like once a year.'

So when they do come, it gives everyone the opportunity to get
things off their chests. It might be Peter Tatchell complaining that the
Pope believes all the wrong things. Or Richard Dawkins complaining
that he believes anything at all, but it doesn't really matter what the
complaint is. Deep within the breasts of most of the English beats a
long-standing suspicion of Popery.

We have been through Catholic Emancipation, only about two
centuries ago, but it hasn't changed. A fear of obscure, mumbling
ritual and priestcraft is imbibed in our mother's milk.

Nor is this anything really to do with the Reformation, or the
marital troubles of Henry VIII. Way back in the Middle Ages, back
beyond the Synod of Whitby, the English have felt frustrated and
irritated by the very existence of the Pope.

In fact the role of Rome and the role of Brussels seem to follow
parallel paths in the English political psyche: ultramontane authority,
obscure regulations, privileged cardinals. And let's face it, the
European Union is a Roman Catholic project if ever there was one.

But I have a theory about this. At root, what really offends the
English about the Catholic Church is not the ritual, nor even the
authority, though that doesn't help, but its sheer size. There is something about large, over-mighty institutions which offends the English.

It has done right back to the medieval period when the Catholic Church was really the only one.

All the other institutions were human-scale. You knew the local priest, abbot, squire, sergeant or bailiff yourself. You wouldn't need a league table to judge their performance. When abbeys grew too large, the English hated them too for their hypocrisy, laziness and privileges.

These days we abolish quangos just as Henry VIII abolished the monasteries, and forget for a moment that he stole their wealth and left the poor untaught and the sick untended. Our own public service debates are motivated by some of these very same medieval emotions. All political issues are at root theological, said Cardinal Manning – and they are.

I don't necessarily share the antipathy to the poor Catholics, but I do feel that, when we first took up our cudgels against large institutions (probably when Boadicea first led the Iceni against the Roman Empire) the English got it about right.

We all know that small institutions have to rely less on bureaucracy, systems and processes and can therefore be more flexible and more human. We know there is more attention to detail in small institutions. We know that public clocks are always wrong, and railway station gardens concreted over, when the ruling institutions are too big.

These are emotional, nostalgic arguments, but they have an important kernel of truth.

During the hottest week of May 2008 my mother-in-law arrived at her council-run college in Croydon to find that the central heating was on. It was sticky and sweltering. During every spare moment, she set about the long business of tracking down somebody who had sufficient authority to turn off the radiators.

The principal of the college wasn't responsible. Nor were those responsible for the college at the local authority. Most of them not only had no power over their own heating; they also had no idea who had a familiar experience in centralized public services.

Towards the end of the day, she discovered the right person. It was a man with a laptop, somewhere in the council building which also housed the education officers. He was persuaded to act, and at the click of a mouse the radiators went off. Many people I know have similar experiences, often in schools, so I don't believe this is actually very unusual. The reason is the same: the institutions are too big for the human dimension to work.

But the real point is that smaller units are more likely to let humans use their unique skills effectively, building relationships with each other, summing each other up. It also means they can pay attention to detail, as nobody was doing in the case of the Croydon radiators.

Of course, this sounds a bit glib. You can imagine companies, factories, schools, hospitals or doctors' surgeries that are just *too* small, and rely too much on one individual. We all know communities that are too small, inward-looking or actually in-bred. What we have to do here is to strike a balance so that institutions stay human-scale.

Schools are the sharpest point of this argument, although politicians insist on limiting the issue to the size of classes. Most research into small schools over the past generation challenges the idea that schools are better when they are bigger.

The push for big schools began in the US after the successful Soviet launch of the Sputnik spacecraft. Educationalists persuaded themselves that somehow only huge schools could produce enough scientists to compete with the USSR. It is one of the peculiar ways that Soviet thinking filtered into the West.

The first challenge to it came from Roger Barker, describing himself as an environmental psychologist, who set up a statistical research centre in a small town in Kansas after the Second World War and researched the local schools to within an inch of their lives.

It was his 1964 book *Big School, Small School*, with his colleague Paul Gump, which revealed that despite what you might expect there were more activities outside the classroom in the smaller schools than there were in the bigger schools. There were more pupils involved in them in the smaller schools, between three and twenty times more in fact. He also found children were more tolerant of each other in small schools.

This was precisely the opposite of what the big school advocates had suggested: big schools were supposed to mean more choice and opportunity. It wasn't so. Nor was this a research anomaly. Most research has been carried out in the US, rather than the UK, but it consistently shows that small schools (300–800 pupils at secondary level) have better results, better behaviour, less truancy and vandalism and better relationships than bigger schools.

They show better achievement by pupils from ethnic minorities and from very poor families. If you take away the funding anomalies which privilege bigger institutions, they don't cost any more to run.

But why should smaller schools work better? There is some consensus among researchers about this. The answer is that small schools make transformational human relationships possible. Teachers can know pupils and vice versa.

'Those of us who were researchers saw the damage caused by face-lessness and namelessness,' said the Brown University educationalist Ted Sizer, who ran a five-year investigation into factory schooling in the 1970s. 'You cannot teach a child well unless you know that child well.'

Frightening evidence of this came in June 2008, when the *Times Educational Supplement* reported that 21 per cent of Year 8 pupils said they had never spoken to a teacher.

'Talk to the children, if you can,' one school volunteer I know was told by the headteacher on their first visit. 'Nobody talks to them these days.' That is evidence for a lot of peculiar things about our society, but also the scale of organisations, and schools in particular.

The real problem is that thinking has been dominated for most of the past century by those who believe in the economies of scale in industrial processes, and that these can somehow be applied to absolutely everything.

By the end of the twentieth century, they believed it with such fervour that no other opinion was possible. Our schools and public services were rebuilt on the industrial model, with hefty fees to IT companies to install software that controlled every response of the frontline staff (the A&E software at King's College Hospital requires nurses to go through 22 pages of questions before they can treat anybody).

Even when clear evidence emerges that big institutions are, in fact, less effective or productive than small ones, a strange blindness descends on those who weigh the evidence.

Those awkward little facts that wouldn't quite go away were at least swept firmly under the carpet. Like the peculiar phenomenon, first noted two centuries ago by the radical reformer William Cobbett, but confirmed since. Why is it that ten farms of a hundred acres each produce more than one farm of a thousand acres and why is it more varied?

Nobel economist Amartya Sen has also shown that small family farms are more productive than big industrial ones. Economies of scale? Hardly. The personal touch, attention to detail, the effectiveness of human-scale housekeeping over other economic systems? It isn't quite clear, but the same thing works in other areas of production too.

Big organizations mean different kinds of behaviour, but also different kinds of people. They have more imperial people at the top, who are paid vastly more (how else can Mark Thompson justify his £834,000 salary as director-general of the BBC?).

They also tend to have more docile people lower down. The founder of Delta Consulting David Nadler has written about working for the telecoms giant AT&T. When they began looking to recruit more entrepreneurs, they found that people like that don't tend to work for companies like AT&T.

It is hardly surprising, in those circumstances, that big organizations cost more to run than small ones. A series of studies by the think-tank Reform and others found that the smallest police forces are the most effective in the UK, catching more criminals for their population than the big ones.

Another recent study showed that American hospitals cost more to run per patient the bigger they get, and it doesn't make any difference if those hospitals are non-profits or profit-making.

These are the costs of scale in the public sector. But there is some evidence of the costs of size in the private sector too. When the business writer Robert Waterman says that the key to business success is building relationships with customers, suppliers and employees that are exceptionally hard for competitors to duplicate, you know things will have to shift. Because size gets in the way of that.

There is evidence that the bigger companies get and the more impersonal then the less innovative they are able to be, which is why so many pharmaceutical companies are outsourcing their research to small research start-ups. In fact, this trend seems to have been going on for most of the twentieth century. Half a century ago, the General Electric finance company chairman T. K. Quinn put it like this:

> Not a single distinctively new electric home appliance has ever been created by one of the giant concerns. Not the first washing machine, electric range, dryer, iron or ironer, electric lamp, refrigerator radio, toaster, fan, heating pad, razor, lawn mower, freezer, air conditioner, vacuum cleaner, dishwasher or grill. The record of the giants is one of moving in, buying out, and absorbing after the fact.

It is true that two musicians invented Kodachrome film in a bathroom. Google was invented by two computer nerds in a university student digs. Big organizations are not creative. So why do they stay big? Largely because the salaries and share options are more lucrative and the earnings available for people organizing the mergers are out of all proportion to their benefits.

The accountants KPMG studied the result of mergers and acquisitions (a mega-industry worth $2.2 trillion) in 1999 and found that shareholders lose out in more than 80 per cent of all cross-border mergers. They found that only 17 per cent of all mergers added value to the combined company, while as many as 53 per cent actually destroyed shareholder value.

So why do they happen? Because the rewards to those individuals who make them happen are absolutely huge. This is the crux of the problem. Managers of big corporations are paid inordinately more than managers of small ones. Managers of big schools, hospitals and police forces get paid much more, and have more status than managers of small ones.

That must be why, despite all the evidence that they cost more and are less effective, schools are still getting bigger on both sides of the Atlantic. The number of British schools over 2,000 pupils has tripled in the last decade. As I write, a new school is opening in Nottingham with more than 3,500 pupils. Some schools in New York City have a terrifying 5,000 in them.

It is why only two per cent of UK charities now hoover up two-thirds of the funding. It is also why UK hospitals are gobbling up each other and why despite all the evidence we seem likely to see mergers of police forces. It is a terrifying testament to the power of self-interest over effectiveness.

It also seems likely that the UK government will force more public sector organizations to share back-office services, and create more monstrous, faceless systems. These will cost hugely more than they did when you could speak to experts direct and they could tackle your problem and get it right once and for all.

But those who defend these corporate monsters don't usually do so in terms of their salaries and benefits. They say they make economies of scale possible.

Ever since Frederick Winslow Taylor and Henry Ford began to split people's jobs into their constituent parts and run assembly lines past them, we have had the idea that creating big organizations can be cheaper than small ones. It implies that one big institution should have fewer costs than a handful of small ones.

You can see why this should seem to be so. If you merge organizations, you can cut out some of the duplication. You can sack some of the duplicate marketing managers. You only need one accounts department.

But what you also get are the extra costs of bigness, like the radiators in Croydon, and all the other inefficiencies of a bigger management infrastructure, more rules, more monitoring, more paperwork, more databases and more IT support.

That is why, despite the commitment of Whitehall and the big consultancies, the idea of economies of scale is not working any more. 'Beyond very small volumes [it] is a concept that should be discarded,' says Professor of Accountancy professor Tom Johnson.

Economies of scale work well in assembly lines when parts and products are standardized. That is why it was such a breakthrough for Henry Ford. But even car assembly plants have moved away from the idea. Toyota tries to reduce its batches right down to one at a time. It is the flowthrough they want, not the huge scale.

But service industries, dealing with human beings, can't standardize.

When they try to, they find so many exceptions which are so difficult to deal with that the savings start to evaporate. This is the sad story of all those shared back-office services and call centres that we now live with.

The lesson of all this is not that small is always going to be more effective than big, but that – because it allows human beings to work effectively and build relationships – it often is.

The economist E. F. Schumacher is often credited with coining the phrase 'small is beautiful'. It was the title of his most successful book, after all. In fact, it was his publisher Anthony Blond who came up with the phrase and Schumacher never liked it much. He wanted the right scale for the task, eminently sensible but also eminently twistable by self-interested political forces.

So let's stop being so balanced about these things. I suggest that all those angry English campaigners forget about the poor Pope, for all his multiplicity of shortcomings, and start going for the real enemy: the big institutions, their inhuman systems, their sclerotic hierarchies and their staggering waste.

If we can shift all that Protestant energy, from Henry VIII to Dawkins, that creative English disdain for the big and useless, and set it to work on our own institutions before the government merges them all into one big cost-cutting institution run by dumb software, then maybe we can really change things for the better.

FROM BUSINESS PLAN
TO ESCAPE PLAN

HOW COTTAGE INDUSTRY CAN
SAVE YOU FROM SERVITUDE

Robert Wringham

IN 1992, A YOUNG AMERICAN CALLED CHRISTOPHER McCandless changed his name to Alexander Supertramp, donated his savings to charity and set off for the Alaskan wilderness in pursuit of rustic solitude. After four months, he died of starvation.

Not for me, thanks! The wise idler – the person who has discovered the joys of the hammock – knows that life is worth living. Fill it with lengthy breakfasts, afternoon strolls, library patronage and evening merriment. Homelessness and martyrdom may be noble but a cushioned seat at a fireplace with some decent pipe tobacco is a far more sensible use of free will.

As Jean-Paul Sartre points out, free will doesn't happen in a vacuum: there are certain realities we must resolve if we're to embrace a Supertrampian will to freedom without starving to death in the attempt. One of them is money. To avoid the polar fates of meaningless employment and shivering-in-the-darkness poverty, we must become money-savvy. For better or worse, we live in a world where money is required for survival and dignity.

*

EMPLOYMENT IS PRAGMATISM

If we want to make money, our first mistake would be to go job-hunting. Employment, writes Robert Kiyosaki in his book, *Rich Dad, Poor Dad*, is a short-term solution to a long-term problem.

The long-term problem is money. Until the day we die (hopefully at a ripe old age, filled with brandy and of an exotic clap) we will need money.

The short-term solution is to seek employment. Even a well-paid job only allows us to forget about the money problem for a month or two. Through work, we temporarily escape the indignity of poverty but fall into the other indignity of mindless submission. Moreover, it becomes increasingly difficult to focus on a permanent solution and, all the while, our youth is ticking away and our creative dreams are decaying. Employment keeps the wolf from the door but at an exorbitant cost. We're talking about our youth and dreams here: nothing is worth that sacrifice.

Employment is pragmatism. It's like continuing to walk against a powerful conveyor belt instead of stepping off and finding the emergency-stop button.

THE LONG-TERM SOLUTIONS

It's not unheard of for people to step off this conveyor belt and to address the problem once and for all. If employment (taking a job) is a short-term solution, what are the idler-compatible long-term solutions?

One is financial education. Know how to save and invest. Know the difference between an asset and a liability (an asset being something that generates money and a liability being something that costs you money — your house, contrary to popular opinion, is probably a liability). Financial eduction is perhaps the most appropriate and efficient course of action to solve the long-term problem. Learn how to invest money made through a day job so that you can retire from it sooner rather than later without depending on a pension scheme. Excellent companions to this strategy are Jacob Lund Fisker's website, www.earlyretirementextreme.com and Alvin Hall's book, *Money for Life*.

Another long-term solution is to run your own cottage industry. I always hesitate to say 'small business' because the term is needlessly modest: a cottage industry has the potential for huge scope but will always be managed from your cosy centre of operations. Ricky Gervais, for example, describes himself as a cottage industry: from a small London office he wrote and sold 30 thirty film and sitcom scripts, recorded and distributed the most downloaded and lucrative podcast in the world to date and made his way into the *Time 100* list of the world's most influential people. Whether or not you enjoy Gervais' work, this is quite the organizational achievement for one portly comedian and a laptop.

In his 1974 economic treatise, *Small is Beautiful: economics as if people mattered*, E. F. Schumacher writes: 'the ideal from the point of view of the employer is to have output without employees, and the ideal from the point of view of the employee is to have income without employment.' There's a lot of truth here, hence the rift between the managerial and worker castes. Through cottage industry, it is possible to embrace both of Schumacher's ideals by quitting your job and setting up business alone. *You* can have output without the employees. *You* can have income without a job.

The somewhat-glib advice to 'find what you enjoy and let money catch up with you' is understandably hard to accept by those who've been trapped in white-collar professions for a long time, but this is surely the best advice for someone starting a cottage industry: to what could you most stand to dedicate your time? What excites you?

A third option is to create an automated business capable of generating an optimum income (whatever you need to live comfortably) without your having to tend to many business matters yourself. These businesses involve identifying a niche market, finding someone with a product to sell to it and setting up a virtual shopfront and online advertising campaign. All you're doing is matching a product with a market and once your advertising campaign proves successful, you can sit back and allow the process to continue on its own. It's like getting a plate spinning and checking occasionally to ensure momentum is kept. An automated company takes a lot of time and an injection of cash to get started, but if successful will solve the money problem once and for all with very little maintenance. Even if it takes a year to figure out, this is a better use of time than 50 years of employment. If you need advice on how to concoct an automated company, try *The 4-hour Workweek* by Timothy Ferris in which he describes such a self-operating machine as a 'muse'.

BUY YOUR FREEDOM

Like a Roman slave, it is possible to buy one's freedom: initially just enough freedom to figure things out before embarking on one of the aforementioned 'long-term solution' projects.

What follows is a short escape plan originally published in the third issue of *New Escapologist*, fine-tuned for the sophisticated modern day hominid. It looks simple but deceptively so, informed by rational business techniques such as 'downsizing', 'liquidation' and 'geoarbitrage'. When employed, it is nigh on impossible to find the time and energy to formulate an escape plan. This is probably why most people don't recognize that escape is even an option. The aim of this escape plan is to buy yourself the time and energy with which to develop a long-term solution.

You want to flee a life of white-collar servitude. Fortunately, being paid to sit in front of a computer is a healthy circumstance from which to start plotting your escape. It is from here that you might begin.

1. Ensure you are paid at least £355 per week. This is the average weekly wage of a UK worker. To settle for less is to squander yourself. If you must sell a portion of your youth for money, make sure it is at the going rate. If your weekly income is significantly less than this sum, your first task is to get promoted, to secure a pay rise or to get a better job elsewhere.

2. Save money. You will need moderately healthy financial reserves to fund the first weeks or months of your escape. Aim to save a useful sum of money. I recommend at least £5,000, though the more you save, the more comfortable you can be for a while. This sum is your

escape fund. This will be harder to achieve if you're in debt or subscribe to unnecessary services.

In order to reach your target more quickly, sell unnecessary assets. Convert unwieldy possessions into mobile, 'liquid' cash. You may only want to do this for high-value goods: selling individual DVDs is time-consuming and seldom lucrative.

3. Use your job as a career gym. Like the convict who uses the prison gym to get in shape, get as much experience as you can and as many flavours as possible: do favours for people, run meetings, attend training courses, generate ideas, talk to the boss, talk to the cleaners, manage a budget, write reports, deliver presentations, make the tea. Record all of this on your CV.

As anyone with an office job knows, most of your time at work is spent skiving or doing useless shit. There's even a word for it: presenteeism. Use some of this time to maximize your skill set. This will provide a safety net: you need to make yourself re-employable in case your escape plan fails.

4. Cull your expenses. It's probably obvious that your income must be greater than your outgoings. Bills can be avoided if you gradually eliminate your dependencies on the services for which you pay. Get rid of your car and become a pedestrian. Get rid of your mobile phone by telling people to use your house phone or email instead. Get rid of any other false liberty that only results in bills. You will soon find an optimum outgoing: the true cost of living. It will be much less than it was before your elimination process and will usually be the sum of your rent, food, house phone, council or municipal tax and electricity. Let us call this sum Cost of Living, for it will come into play again later.

5. Quit your job. This is the end of your career. Have a warm, dark beer to celebrate.

6. Give your house or apartment keys back to the landlord. Put your stuff into storage (I can vouch for a company called SafeStore, but there are lots of others). Cancel all Direct Debits, except for the one paying for your storage. Up until now, everything has been pro- logue. This is the real beginning of your escape.

7. Take your *escape fund* and fly to somewhere vibrant and cheap. The official best cities in which to find this combination are Zürich, Vienna, Vancouver, Geneva, Auckland, Frankfurt, Sydney, Munich and Dusseldorf. I can also personally vouch for Berlin and Montreal. Rent a cheap apartment there. Immigrant-heavy areas (such as Kreutzberg in Berlin and Saint-Henri in Montreal) are culturally alive and financially inexpensive. They have good food, public transport and are popular with the creative classes.

Use half of your *escape fund* to enjoy a long and restful vacation. Explore the city; relax cheaply or for free in parks, museums or libraries; make friends; invite old friends to visit; eat, drink and read. Enjoy yourself and vigorously celebrate your escape.

8. Invent a cottage industry. Use the rest of your time here – however much time your *escape fund* allows – to invent a way to ensure you'll never have to go back to work. Remind yourself of why you wanted to escape in the first place: the drudgery, the early mornings, the mindless submission, the waiting on pay cheques. Never forget the conditions from which you are escaping. Think up a cottage indus- try for yourself. It must be either (a) fully automated, requiring little work on your behalf or (b) fun. In either event, the income generated by your cottage industry must be equal to your *Cost of Living*.

Don't try too hard. Through your period of inactivity, you will probably discover over a poolside margarita what you want to do. As explained above, this could be a cottage industry, an automated com- pany or an investment plan. We will discuss the advantages of each of these models presently. You may also want to consider diversifying your plan by merging these models.

9. Put your plan in motion from your apartment or from a cosy space in a public library. When the money starts to come in, you will have found yourself a vocation. You have escaped.

Try it. The worst case scenario is that your cottage industry fails and you have to go back to office drudgery, tail between your legs. If this happens, you will at least have enjoyed an extended vacation, lived abroad, tried and failed at entrepreneurship. This is better than what you'd have been doing otherwise. You'll have some interesting items to put on your CV and some great stories for the pub. Best of all, there's nothing to stop you from trying the whole thing again.

HONING YOUR BUSINESS SKILLS

In *Small is Beautiful*, Schumacher opines that 'the man of order is typically the accountant and, generally, the administrator, while the man of creative freedom is the entrepreneur. One requires intelligence and is conductive to efficiency; while freedom calls from, and opens the door to, innovation.'

Who is more free and innovative than the idler? The idler can avoid the fate of the accountant or the administrator simply by obeying his nature. There's no reason, however, that an idler can't also be a 'man of order,' tending to his own administrative duties. Doing so is to remain fiscally and organizationally hygienic. Here are a few business skills, conventional and otherwise, that can help the idler in maintaining his or her cottage industry:

1. Become a Bohemian
The less money you spend, the less you have to work. This should ring true to both the employee and the entrepreneur. The Bohemian doesn't fill her life with frivolous tat: with a strong will, she proofs herself against artificial desires. She lives with the bare minimum and

enjoys the simple pleasures of reading, meditation, cookery, sewing, socializing and artistic pursuits. The Bohemian is not one for over-consumption and it is for this reason that she doesn't submit to much in the way of labour.

Especially in the early days of your business – when your base of clients or customers is small – it's a good idea not to put too much stress upon your money-making machine. The less you are forced to rely on it for withdrawals, the less effort will have to go into its survival.

Reject the usual consumer distractions. Instead of driving, become a pedestrian. Lose your mobile phone, gym membership and other expensive commitments. Instead of going to expensive city bars, throw a party and rejoice in home-brew and the jug band. Reduce your exposure to advertising by reading library books instead of glossy magazines or fatuous websites. Pool your resources with other wild-haired Bohos.

Embrace the simple pleasures of Bohemia. Start a sketch book, learn the bongos, go for walks, team up with a loved one to make your way through the *Karma Sutra*. None of these brilliant things require money so all help your cottage industry to prosper. Indirectly, your business can benefit from time spent writing saucy limericks.

2. Define your business projects

The white-collar world has introduced us to 'project management'. Some organizational psychologists are against project management because it creates paperwork for employers and a decline in job security for employees (because they can be hired for a limited-duration project and fired upon its completion). This may be true, but the technique of having a system of self-contained projects with well-defined outcomes and end-dates is a huge organizational boon. A skeletal, non-bureaucratic project management technique would look something like this:

Visualize (or draw) a vine of delicious fruit. Each fruit is a desired product of your cottage industry. Some of them may be tangible ('write a book', 'build a wall', 'generate £1,000') while others will be less tangible achievements ('simplify banking operations', 'learn

French'). For each fruit, denote a 'ripening date': it is your job to nourish this fruit so that it will fall from the vine on this date.

The advantage of this approach is that your achievements will visually stack up. You'll see the fruits of your industry become finished, diverse outcomes. This is a great way to manage your company and provides the kind of satisfaction seldom experienced by an employee. This is the antidote to the fruitless Groundhog Days of worker life.

3. Learn to balance the books

'Don't spend more than you earn' is a golden rule. Keeping records of your earnings and expenditures will allow you to keep track of this. Maintaining a 'profit and loss account' and a 'balance sheet' will allow you to take your business seriously. Such techniques are also easy-peasy-pudding-and-pie to master. Consult YouTube for free, ten-minute tutorials on both.

4. Promote

The Internet has belched a lot of trivial tot and downright ugliness into the world: the inanity of LOLcats, the ugliness of MySpace, the tedium of forum flame wars. But for all of this, the Internet has cut the need for complicated advertising strategies or even a physical shopfront for small businesses.

Instead of a shop, set up an online shopfront. You might want to foster the skills to do this yourself or pay a web designer to do it on your behalf. Personally, I cheat by employing a webmaster to build my sites and to repair them when they break, but there is value in learning to do it yourself: the ability to build an elegant website is quite empowering and could even provide an alternative business or sideline in the future. If you're testing the water, set up a cheap template shopfront using a service like shopify.com.

You can also take to old-fashioned marketing media such as distributing printed fliers in your local area.

5. Know your friends

Recognize that everyone has a skill or an area of expertise. A friend may speak a useful language, have a Rolodex of untapped industry contacts or hold practical know-how from which your projects can benefit. Naturally, you'll be given opportunity to pay them back by introducing your own skills and wisdom to the social pool.

DESTROY YOUR RESISTANCE WITH 'FEAR SETTING'

We often have business ideas (or ideas to improve our health or expand our minds) but we don't implement them. The reason is resistance: an internally-generated force that makes you procrastinate or defer from achieving something of personal or social worth.

There are many techniques for overcoming personal resistance to embarking on a business endeavour, some of which are discussed intelligently in *The War of Art* by Steven Pressfield. This is recommended reading.

For the benefit of this essay however, let us look at a simple exercise pioneered by magical, dancing business Gonk, Tim Ferris called 'Fear Setting'. Imagine the absolute worst case scenario that could result from your foolhardy escape plan and ask yourself how you would recover if it failed. You'd probably just go back to work in a similar job to the one you left. This would be a defeat and a return to square one but it's not so terrible as worst case scenarios go: it wouldn't cost you a limb or your roguish good looks. You can always recover from a defeat and you will have learned something and had fun in the process.

You can embrace the spirit of Alexander Supertramp without suffering his fate. Ask yourself: what are you afraid of?

HOW TO RETIRE EARLY

Jacob Lund Fisker

IRETIRED FROM MY CAREER AS A PHYSICIST WHEN I WAS 33
years old. I'm now financially independent and can support myself
for the rest of my life – or the next 120 years, whichever is shorter.
I didn't win the lottery; I didn't get lucky in the real estate boom; I
didn't discover some superior investment in stocks; I didn't start a
successful business while being lucky enough to sell out at the right
time; nor did I earn an outsized salary. In fact during my working
years my income was comparable to that of a long-haul trucker.
However, instead of spending my income like a typical wage earner, I
saved and invested it so that I'm now able to derive a living income
from my investments. Essentially, I spent my working years saving
enough money to establish my own patronage or trust fund. These
days I can do whatever I want, whenever I want (within reason), and
you could do the same. It's not complicated to do this, but it isn't easy
either. It's similar to how following a diet or training to be able to lift a
weight as heavy as yourself from the ground up and over your head
isn't complicated. But it's certainly not easy; it requires a degree of
dedication and persistence that many don't possess. Achieving financial
independence is similar. Many would rather not think and worry
about how much money they spend. Ironically they consequentially
end up spending their entire life struggling with their finances tied to a
job in order to make money. It's possible to avoid this, and in this essay
I'll try to make the case that this is possible and point you in the right
direction to get started.

The world is governed by a set of laws. Fundamental to everything
are the laws of physics – I used to do this for a living – but there are
also laws of biology, chemistry, geology and so on. What these laws

have in common is that we can't violate them. It's the way the universe works. They are laws of nature. Similarly, there are laws of ecology which explain how systems interact. Humans and the environment is one such system. Here the laws describe how humans affect the environment and how the environment affects humans and what happens if one destroys the other or vice versa. Since we are conscientious beings, we can control our behaviour to some extent. In this regard we are unlike a herd of deer on an island without predators who will happily eat all the shrubbery and consequently die of starvation; or are we? Moving on. How humans behave towards each other is determined by cultural laws. These cultural laws are divided into legal laws, economic laws, and moral laws. I think it's fair to say that most human behaviour these days is governed by economic laws that is, the world is run by money. How much money one has or makes determines one's position in society to a far greater extent than it has done at any time in history. This is good news, because money is your ticket to freedom. You don't need to have been born into an aristocracy; you don't need to join or work your way up the political class system; you simply need to accumulate a certain amount of money relative to your spending, and to do this you need to understand why and how. Here's how it works. Depending on your role in society, money flows in different ways. If anything this determines your position in a class system. In general, people may be aware of such a class system but they aren't aware that they can deliberately choose their class by changing their behaviour; in particular, they aren't aware of what that behaviour should be. The following figure shows the cash flow for a working consumer. Here you go to work to earn a wage. You then take that wage to the shopping centre and spend it on stuff after which you bring the stuff home to consume. Insofar as you need to buy this stuff to live, you need to work to live. Here, stuff is a general descriptor for expenses.

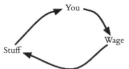

The cash flow of someone who works for a living.

It's those expenses that keep people tied to their jobs. The term wage slave is often used. People are no longer slaves to other people. Rather, they are slaves to their need for wages. Wage addict is perhaps a better term. Many believe that more stuff results in more happiness than better stuff. Due to this belief they need to work even harder to satisfy their wants. Buying a lot of stuff results in waste as seen in this figure. Waste should here be seen as superfluous consumption. These are the things that end up discarded and unused in people's attics, garages and closets. It's the subscriptions to magazines that don't get read; the cable channels that go unwatched; the leftover food on the plate; the tools that never get used, and so on.

The cash flow of someone who works for a living and generates a lot of waste.

One feature of consumer culture is that people are often convinced that they're entitled to stuff they haven't earned yet and thus lack the money to buy. This is where consumer debt enters the picture. Consumer debt is the idea that your present self should be allowed to enjoy itself and that your future self will somehow make up for both the debt and the interest by working harder or smarter or whatever. This is distinctly different from business debt which follows the idea that earnings grow faster if the business borrows money to invest in increased production thus avoiding having to wait for a profit to show. Of course this carries some risk too, but in almost all cases, a business will be able to earn some money using the money they borrowed. Conversely, with very few exceptions such as student loans for an increasingly limited amount of vocations, consumer debt is almost certainly a net loss to you. It almost never increases future earnings. The cash flow for a person with consumer debt who lives above his means looks like the following figure. A temporary boost in the amount of stuff beyond what he can otherwise afford is facilitated by borrowing money. There is a subsequent long-term loss of wealth to other people in the form of interest.

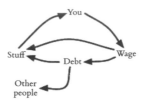

The cash flow for a person with consumer debt.

Some of the wages are now diverted into paying off debt and paying interest to other people. However, it's possible to buy more stuff than is otherwise affordable from the increased cash flow by using credit.

This party can be extended as long as one is able to borrow more and more money. Once this is no longer possible, the party stops and one must now deal with the hangover of living below one's means and seeing a substantial fraction of one's wages going to other people. While the pleasure of living above one's means is quickly forgotten once that is no longer possible, debt isn't so easily forgotten. Since there's a lender for each borrower – money doesn't appear out of nowhere, that is, unless you're a bank – it becomes a simple matter of symmetry to conclude that if your present self saves the money instead of spending it and invests it or lends it out, your future self should be able to relax and work less while enjoying the same standard of living.

The cash flow of someone who is working and living below their means ('sacrificing') in order to save and invest their money for a better standard of living in the future.

The figure above shows how this works. A worker chooses to 'sacrifice' – that is, give up something currently for future gains – and save money to invest. While this is described in financial terms and currently done using the financial system, there's a much simpler way to think about it. Suppose Paul is capable of plucking X amount of berries each day. He plucks enough berries to work only five days a

week. He spends the weekend eating the surplus berries he plucked the
other days while relaxing on the beach. Suppose Peter also plucks
berries. Rather than relaxing, he spends his weekends fashioning a
picking stick. Using the stick he can now pluck twice as many berries
each day, thus he only needs to work half as much as before. Rather
than making his own stick Paul asks to borrow Peter's stick. Peter
agrees to lend Paul his stick in return for some of the berries Paul picks.
While Paul is doing all the picking with the stick, Peter did some work
making the stick and thus he should be compensated as well, hence the
payment of profit or interest. Fashioning another stick, Peter now has
two sticks. If he keeps making sticks, he will eventually be able to quit
plucking berries completely and just lend out his sticks. Some have
moral issues charging interest – that is, demanding a cut of the berries
plucked in return for lending out the picking stick. In the light of the
discussion above, I don't. Especially since the financial system means
that I don't even need any kind of creative talents or skills in terms of
creating new technology or machines. I can simply save berries or
money and pay someone (invest it) to invent it and I will get my return.
The markets have been sufficiently democratized to bring them within
the reach of anyone willing to save money rather than buying stuff.
If I have saved and invested enough, my cash flow will eventually look
like the following. I no longer need to work for a living. My invested
savings, my assets, now pay for all my stuff.

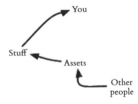

Financially independent and no longer working for money.

All it required was some 'sacrifice' of some 'stuff' by my past self.
I'm not talking about giving up a fun and meaningful life, but I am
talking giving up waste and a lot of consumption and replacing it with
more meaningful and, dare I say, more inspiring activities. That way

we could all live a life of leisure only working a handful of years before we retire to a life with more meaning to it than recreational shopping and moving into ever bigger homes. So why haven't we all been doing this? There are no natural laws preventing it. In fact, due to technological advances, the economy is now twice as efficient as it was 50 years ago. Back then it was widely predicted that increased productivity would result in a more leisurely pace of life with a reduced working week. However, it turned out that most people were more interested in shopping and increasing the squarefootage of their homes than in relaxing and so the productivity was turned into consumer products rather than leisure. Since this attitude is so widespread and in many ways so ingrained in our culture, it's often perceived to be the only choice. But it isn't. It may be that it's not mentioned explicitly in the cultural laws, but there are no economic or legal laws that forbid financial independence. You only have to deal with the traditional moral 'laws' which states that 'he who dies with the most toys wins'; that we should all 'shop 'til we drop'; and that 'being busy' is a virtue. However, it's quite possible to say no to spending one's best years working simply in order to shop and buy more homes or work more than one needs; in fact it would probably be better for the planet if people dialled back their consumption a notch or ten. As it is, recreational consumption is creating an ecological disaster as we're busy turning a diminishing amount of natural resources into an increasing amount of pollution. Hopefully, the moral laws will change to reflect this reality before it's too late. The financial independence made possible by savings is very easy to understand. Imagine saving 25% of your income. If you save a quarter of your income and work 4 years, you can take the next year off living on your savings. This scales: Work 4 weeks, take the next week off. Work 12 years and take the next 3 years off and so on. If you save half your income, the equation changes: Work 1 year and take 1 year off and so on. If you save 75% interesting things start happening. Work 1 year and take the next 3 years off. Work 4 years and take the next 16 years off. I made a little table illustrating this principle for different savings rates. Note that for savings rates beyond 75% things really start taking off.

If you work with a savings rate of r% for one year	You need to work this many years to take one year off
1%	99
5%	19
10%	9
15%	5.66
20%	4
25%	3
30%	2.33
40%	1.5
50%	1
	You can take this many years off before you need to work again
50%	1
60%	1.5
75%	3
80%	4
90%	9

Table showing leisure time versus savings rate.

As it turns out, you don't need to save cash to cover all your future expenses. You can invest the money or lend it out. This allows you to get away with somewhat less in terms of accumulation. Historically speaking, investments have returned about 3% in real terms for most of the history of mankind. This fact can be counted on insofar that commerce doesn't break down completely – so far this has only happened during the period we know as the Dark Ages. If we are due for a repeat of that period, you probably have bigger things to worry about than market returns: buy guns and ammo. The government won't bail you out, because the government is very likely defunct at this point in the same way the Roman Empire was effectively gone at the turn of the previous millennium. Overall, this is very likely not something you need to worry about. I'm just mentioning it to illustrate how dependable the 3% real return rate is. With 3% returns, you simply need to save 33 years of annual living expenses. Even if you expect to live substantially longer than that, 3% of about 33 years of expenses is about 1 year of expenses. Therefore, it will cover you in perpetuity, which is more than most mortals need. Now 33 years or more worth of expenses saved sounds like a lot especially considering how many are barely capable of saving 6 months' worth of expenses to carry them over in case of a job loss. There is only one way to save more. It's the trite old story about earning more or spending less, the difference being the savings. Since we're talking substantial amounts of savings, the only robust method in doing so is spending less. For most people it's a lot easier to reduce their expenses to less than a quarter of their after-tax income, thus making it possible to reach financial independence in less than a decade, than it is to quadruple their after-tax income. Hence, what I'm about to present isn't a get-rich-quick scheme; it's more of a get-poor-quick scheme. Some think that spending less means living less. This is mainly a problem for those who have outsourced most parts of their life: entertainment, health, childcare, cooking, clothing, investing, etc. They no longer know how to live; they only know how to make money to pay for their living, hence 'making a living.' Learning how to live can be as frustrating as any education, but it's hardly a sacrifice and it's quite empowering. In order to get started it's crucial to have certain rudimentary financial skills.

First and foremost, you must have a budget. Without an understanding of where the money is going and buying things without considering the impact on the bank account, it will be difficult to live on your savings. It's no matter if this budget exists solely in your mind, but it must exist somewhere. If you have a significant other then a budget is especially important to get on the same page, figuratively speaking. There are two kinds of budgets: The normative budget, where you allocate money into different spending categories; and the descriptive budget, where you track your spending retroactively. While it works for some, I don't like the normative budget; the chance of treating unspent money at the end of the month as mad money to be spent rather than as savings is too tempting. Instead I just track my spending from time to time. There are many software tools to do this, but you can also use a #2 pencil and the back of an envelope. No need to keep meticulous records, unless you're into that sort of thing.

With the budget done, calculate the true cost of every budget category. If you need to save and invest an amount corresponding to 33 times your annual expenses to become financial independent (see above), then you need 33 × 12 times your monthly expense or roughly 400 times the monthly cost of a budget category to self-finance and have it paid for by investment returns instead of work. If you pay 1,000 per month (I'm keeping prices unit-less for the sake of internationalization) on your home you need to save 400,000 for early retirement to keep paying for your home. If you pay 400 for food, that's 160,000, and so on. Add all these numbers together for the total price, that's your current 'number'. This number will now be reduced. Some expenses are trivial to deal with. Maybe you got talked into paying 'just 2.50 in fees per month' for some irrelevant service you never use. Are you really going to save up 1,000 to keep paying for that for the rest of your life? Get rid of it. You may also want to consider whether 'unlimited texting for an extra 25 per month' is really worth saving 10,000 for? Eliminate expenses one-by-one accordingly. You will likely find that your biggest expenses are you home, your transportation and your food, most likely in that order. The biggest impact on your bottom line and your chances of retiring within the next decade will come from changing these. However, these are also the most difficult to change for most people because they are a big part of people's habits and lifestyle. For example, many consider moving one of the most stressful things they can do. The reason is that their home is full of stuff which requires weeks to organize, pack and unpack. Personally, I can have all my stuff packed within two hours or about the same time it takes me to pack for a long vacation. I don't have a lot of stuff. I only own what I use regularly. To further reduce cost, I make sure that whatever I use regularly has the most optimal quality in terms of cost and durability. Sometimes this means paying more upfront, but it pays off in the long run.

Many people own tremendous amounts of stuff. If you can't remember where you put something, you have too much stuff. If you accidentally bought something which you forgot you owned already, even worse. Try not to own things which aren't used monthly – seasonal things like a winter jacket being an obvious exception. Here are two tips for figuring out what you actually use: 1) Put all your stuff in moving boxes and mark them with today's date. Then seal them up. Open them again if you need something; then reseal and write a new date. If a box remains sealed for more than a year, sell or donate the contents. You don't need them. 2) Instead of dealing with boxes, put the stuff you just used in a designated place. For example, put your recently worn clothes on the left-hand side of the clothes rack. After a while the clothes you never wear will have diffused to the right and you can get rid of them. Instead of putting plates and utensils back in the drawers, leave them in the corner of the kitchen table. After a month, get rid of anything still in the cupboards. I consider everything I own for sale. I try not to hang on to something just in case I'm going to use it some day. That day may never come and meanwhile it's keeping me from doing things. By selling things again I tend only to acquire things I know have a good resale value, that is, not junk, and thanks to eBay and the likes, the whole world becomes my library. This way I don't become attached to my stuff. The effective cost then becomes the difference between cost and sales price divided by the number of months I hang onto the thing. If I multiply this by 400, I get my financial cost. To make this number as small as possible I prefer to buy things used to ensure that they have already taken the depreciation hit from 'driving it off the lot'. I also aim for higher quality things that keep their value. Finally, I try not to trade in and out of stuff too spontaneously. I carefully consider the bottom line for most purchases much like a profitable business. Consequentially, in the long run, I pay almost nothing for furniture, tools, appliances or bicycles. Clothes I either get really cheap or I hang onto until they wear out – this can be a very long time, my pressure cooker is 10 years old and my jacket is more than 13 years old. Buying and selling things used has the added benefit of increasing the usefulness of a thing. It's a form of serial ownership that reduces resource waste. You don't need to buy and sell things to reduce waste. Swapping and bartering are equally valid as are lending and borrowing.

Owning a lot of things makes it necessary to have a large home with many rooms to organize and warehouse rarely used things. Each extra room increases not only your housing cost but also your heating and electric bills, since most people for some reason prefer to store their stuff at room temperature. Conversely, having only the things you need, you can stop paying for several of these rooms. Two people living together only need one room, not five. If you move into a small home, not only will you significantly reduce costs, you will also spend less time maintaining and cleaning it. Consider creative and untraditional living arrangements: camping trailers, boats, garden sheds, attics, caretaking, couchsurfing, converted garages, converted hotels, studio apartments or even regular houses. You could sublet rooms to other people. If you don't like people, you can sublet for storage of other people's stuff. Be creative! Having successfully got rid of your excess stuff, packing up and moving should be quick and easy. After that you only need to send out change of address forms to the relevant places (I keep a list) most of which can be done online. When you move consider the location. If you can find a place to live that doesn't necessitate owning and operating a car, you can eliminate what is typically people's second-largest expense. The easiest way to find a convenient location is to use Google maps or similar along with a search engine for real estate or rentals – you can also do this with an old-fashioned map and the newspaper. Find the distance between your new home and your place of work and check if shopping exists within walking distance (2 miles/3 km). Depending on how fit you are, keep the distance between work and the prospective home under 4 miles/ 6 km if you are going to cycle. Also consider how buses or subways can extend your range. If, for example, there's a bus stop half a mile from work and another 1 mile away from home and they connect, this solution will work as well. The goal here is to turn the ownership of a motorized vehicle into a thing of the past. Back then driving a car was a leisure activity: every weekend people would drive their cars to the countryside and enjoy nature. These days people have moved into the former countryside, now suburbs, and sit in backed-up traffic every day because everybody else got the same idea. Just because you don't own a car doesn't mean you can't rent one and drive around for special occasions, if that's your thing. Instead of commuting by car, either walk or ride a bicycle, or combine those with public transport if you have to. Walking or cycling will also provide simultaneous and free exercise. Just add bodyweight exercises, like burpees and one-armed pushups, then cancel the gym membership.

Of course moving well is just one component of a healthy life (and reduced health care bills), eating right is the other one. It's getting difficult to eat well. Supermarkets are full of frozen preprocessed food which is rich in salt and additives for extra taste and colour and hydro-genated fat for increased shelf-storage life. Sometimes people get inspired to cook for themselves and rightly so. They pick out a recipe, make a shopping list, and then spend half an hour at the supermarket hunting for ingredients. In general, this approach is about as cost-effective as preprocessed foods yet takes much longer. It's better to learn the principles of cooking. This way you head to the supermarket, find whatever produce or meat is on sale and proceed to invent a recipe based on what's on sale plus the staples in your cupboard – keep a supply of rice, beans and pasta. Progressing from the novice level of purchasing ready-made products and services to the technical level of following recipes, tips and step-by-step guides and from that onto the master level of no longer needing recipes or how-to guides requires a fundamental change in personal habits and values. As anyone would know, changing habits is difficult, but changing one's values is even more difficult. Many consumers have turned their life into a passive sequence of purchases and their identity into the job title they hold to make that living. Shopping serves as recreation, therapy, entertain-ment, as well as status. Working serves as self-identify, meaning, an outlet for personal ambition, as well as something to do. Abruptly rebuilding one's self-image outside the career and consumer frame-works takes time and effort.

Cooking is a useful and important first project, but in time the transition from novice to master should be expanded to other parts of your life: repairing and maintaining vehicles (if any), appliances, clothing, etc. and building furniture, electronics and even housing. You get the best economy by picking up skills which are useful to yourself but which may also be useful to many others. For example, I have taken up bicycle repair. Other no-brainers include beer brewing, cabinet making, gardening and home maintenance. This may seem overwhelming, but in many ways self-sufficiency and adopting a Do It Yourself ethic is like learning to swim. Beginners, who struggle to stay afloat, wrongfully conclude that those who swim lap after lap must be living a hard and uncomfortable life. Of course this is far from the case. Who is struggling more? Someone whose toilet backs up on a Sunday and has to wait until Tuesday for the plumber and pay 200 for 15 minutes of work or someone who can fix it himself immediately for less than 10. The question is rhetorical. Of course there is much more to learn about living on your own terms than what can be covered in an essay like this, but in general a person with skills can do more with less. Eventually you should be able to reduce costs by about 80% compared to the median household while finding both meaning in the form of the things you do rather than the things you buy and status in the form of the competence you gain and the community connections you make instead of the title your employer bestows upon you. As explained above these savings can be turned into investments allowing you to become financially independent and reach the point where you no longer need to work for a living in about the same time most people spend on getting a university degree. Of course, the savings can also be used to pay off debt if you got entangled by poor choices in the past; it can be used to fund a start-up business without having to take on debt to support your cost of living before making a profit; it could be used to start a family; you could start a foundation; or whatever else you can imagine. In either case, unlike most consumers, you can now make a deliberate choice as to what you want to spend your life on, because now you know there is a choice.

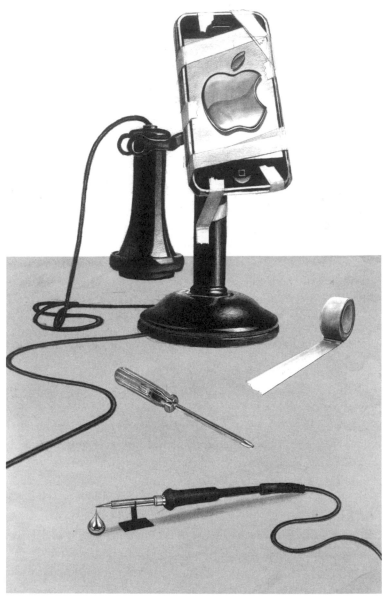

Sam Green

SLIDE TOWARDS THE LUDICROUS

THE MADNESS OF PLANNED OBSOLESCENCE

Sophie Pokliewski-Koziell

M Y EYES WERE TO BE OPENED WITH THE PURCHASE OF
an MP3 player. Fed up with CDs whose music jumped with
the slightest scratch, I felt it was time to enter the age of
digital music and downloads. One lifetime purchase would surely do
the trick or so I thought. However, I found to my frustration that MP3
players are only built to last 18 months, as they have been designed to
only allow a certain number of battery recharges. So, what about
taking the battery out and replacing it? Not possible to do it yourself
Madam, but it's possible for us to do it for you for around the forty
pound mark, but for that price, Madam, it's hardly worthy it when we
can sell you the newest model for seventy pounds. I've suddenly
realized that I have a seemingly naïve belief that things should last, or
be easily repaired, but as I've found out, times have been a-changing.

So a new phrase has come into my vocabulary, 'planned obsolescence', which describes the phenomenon of consumer goods designed
to either fail (death dating) or deliberately to go out of fashion (psychological obsolescence). There is also another type of obsolescence,
'functional obsolescence', which is of a more natural type, when a
product is not desired anymore because the next model generated is of
far higher efficiency and capability. This often happens during great
leaps forward in technological research, for instance in computing
when integrated circuits (microchips) were being developed in the
1960s. At this time anything that had just come off the conveyor belt

was instantly obsolescent, as the rate of change of the size and complexity of circuits was phenomenal. A great example of this is when American astronauts boarding Apollo's last flight in 1975 carried with them pocket calculators that were several times more powerful than the capsule's onboard computer, designed less than a decade before. Whereas functional obsolescence seems like a natural progression, deliberately planned obsolescence seems much more pernicious, even sinister.

Sadly for us, deliberately planned obsolescence is not a conspiracy theory but a well documented practice. The phrase, actually coined in 1932, was brought into the public domain by an American industrial designer called Brooks Stevens in the 1950s. Its origins date back to the post-war excesses of manufacturing in the US. The whole country had geared up for mass production of cars, fridges and furnishings and after a decade or so, the immediate needs of the population had been fulfilled. In a nutshell, no one really needed anything else. But the stuff was still rolling off the production lines, and the manufacturers realized they had a problem on their hands.

The solution came from the car industry, which had solved their own saturated market problem in the mid-1920s. At this time General Motors had successfully lured consumers away from the Ford Model T car designed for durability and longevity and introduced style as a major marketing ploy. It seemed that the populace were fed up with the unchanging black Ford, and General Motors' new coloured cars with extra lights, low slung chassis and stylish tail fins won an immediate following. Every year, another model appeared, rendering the owners of the previous one feeling slightly behind the pack. Psychological obsolescence was born. It proved to be a highly successful consumer motivator. The American public were slowly being re-educated away from their forebears' nose for quality and durability, towards a penchant for style, regardless of what was beneath the bonnet. Of course, the whole point was that there wasn't much change beneath the bonnet. The engineers must have felt a little peeved, as the designers and marketing department took over. Not much mileage in developing and advertizing a new spark plug, when it was so much easier to add another tail light, or change the shade of the upholstery.

Thus, in the space of a few decades, Henry Ford's great vision of building 'a car for the great multitude [that] will be constructed of the best materials, by the best men to be hired, after the simplest designs that modern engineering can devise,' had been tarnished by the problem of over-production. Instead, cynicism had entered the world of car-making. Harley Earl, a custom car designer in 1955, spelt it out in black and white, our big job is to hasten obsolescence. In 1934 the average car ownership span was five years: now it is two years. When it is one year, we will have a perfect score. Once the emphasis grew on psychological obsolescence and superficial style changes, durability and quality naturally started to fall off. In fact, these values were a positive deterrent to the repeat purchase cycle. If chrome didn't look so good after a couple of years, well that just added to the impetus for the consumer to get the newest model. It's not that cars were deliberately made to break, just that the emphasis had shifted from longevity to style.

The 1950s was the era when consumerism was born in the US, and it was born from the problem of over-production and the need to keep the economy going. Suddenly planned obsolescence and its associated reduction in product quality was infectious; it swept through women's fashion, the domestic appliance and furnishings industry and later into men's clothing. As Victor Lebow, a marketing consultant, crudely summed up at the time, 'Our enormously productive economy demands that we make consumption our way of life, that we convert the buying and use of goods into rituals, that we seek our spiritual satisfactions, our ego satisfactions, in consumption. We need things consumed, burned up, worn out, replaced and discarded at an ever increasing rate.' And where America led, Europe and the rest of the world followed.

Of course there were critics along the way, and engineers who were more than uncomfortable with the notion of shirking on quality of the mechanism but concentrating on the colour. Then there were the consumers who were fed up with shoddy goods which fell to pieces when their guarantees expired. Repair men were soon up to their eyes in work. The manufacturers didn't wait long to take up this new avenue of revenue and soon most companies had service departments, busy charging householders for fixing the poor quality goods that they'd bought from the same company in the first place. Today, this has mushroomed into a huge insurance industry, which must be seen by the pre-war generation as a curious development: you buy a product, and expecting it to break in the near future are happy to pay the manufacturer instalments of money towards its repair!

Then somewhere along the line, we gave up repairing most goods, as back at the shop they'd shake their heads and say that it was cheaper to buy a new one. This is today's predicament. Repairs are costly due to high labour rates, and manufacturers have little enthusiasm for supplying parts for old models. Hand in hand is the increase in complexity of products; so many buttons, dials and controls, so much in-built electronics, that your average repair guy, be they in an electrical shop, or garage, can do little but scratch their heads. Indeed, after drying up the issuing of instruction manuals, manufacturers simply decided to prevent the repair of certain goods. Maybe decide is too strong a word, and too simplistic an interpretation – the larger picture is more of a very competitive market driven mostly by price, rather than quality, and the availability of numerous new engineering processes such as plastic moulding and plastic soldering. The combination of these factors leads away from the old nuts and bolts model of easy disassembly to sealed units and unreachable parts. Hence, when a baring goes in the motor of a washing machine, you can't get into it to fix it – the parts are non-removable, so off it goes to the dump.

Replacing items that haven't broken down yet is not always an ecological disaster. Take my aunt's fridge. It was a large cream Electrolux, and stood stoutly in the corner of her kitchen, like a benign giant, for over 50 years. Yes, 50 years, I've double checked! Long after everyone had updated their kitchens with American-style fridges with their fancy crushed ice dispensers, her fridge kept humming. The reality is though, that in terms of energy efficiency it was right at the bottom of the graph compared to latest fridges to come off the production lines. So, when people trade in an old fuel-guzzling car, or inefficient chest freezer, for an updated version, then that makes sense. It's when we're buying new goods to replace those that haven't worn out yet, that the slide towards the ludicrous begins.

So where are we now? Apart from some small voices of dissent, we've been hoodwinked into increasingly rapid loops of planned obsolescence. We've got fashion that changes its spots so fast, you're out of date as soon as you leave the shop. But thanks to bottom-end stores you can buy clothes that almost spare you the bother of washing them – they fall to bits so quickly. The pinnacle of children's toys' obsolescence has got to be the free gift stuck on the front of the *Tweenies* or *Dr Who* magazine. Made to last an hour, at the most, just enough distraction time to allow a parent to drive to the next shop. Fair enough, some people cry, there's room for cheap clothes, and ephemeral toys – don't be such a puritan. Point taken, but what is interesting about this steady creep of planned obsolescence is that it has now universally become the way the game is played. There's little option for most of us. If you don't want to spend your life shopping, you have to search hard, and go out of your way and price range to find quality products.

Luckily a few companies go against the trend, but they are in the minority, and usually in a pretty exclusive price bracket. Miele, for instance, has not joined the trend for cheap white goods, but sells products that are designed for longevity and reparability. They are a good few hundred pounds more expensive than the basic high-street models, and most people won't accept or can't afford those prices. As the price of a basic washing machine has dropped by nearly 70 per cent in 30 years we've got used to paying the cheaper prices, and balk at the higher price bracket. Interestingly however, if you adjust for inflation you'll find that today's Miele costing £687 equates to a price of £95 in 1973 the cost of a basic (but well-made) Hoover washing machine.

Advocates of planned obsolescence point to it being a prime factor in innovation. They say that if products were more durable, and people slower to buy replacements, then production would slow down, the economy would suffer, and so would the rate of change of design and technology. However, in the case of washing machines, where is the innovation of the past years? Not much change I would say, yet many of them still suffer the same faults their predecessors had as well as new ones created by using cheaper production methods and lesser quality parts.

What's really wrong with this new mindset? For some, shopping is a planned pleasure, and new things are to be coverted, cosseted, admired and then disposed of. If the producers are giving us the newer and better model, surely we should take them up on their offer? Why should a mobile phone last more than five years if we plan to get the newest version for Christmas? The answer in spiritual terms includes perpetual dissatisfaction, envy and unhappiness. The American theologian Reinhold Neibuhr's interpretation of the situation is as apt as when he wrote it 50 years ago, 'The productive power of our industry threatens to make our culture subordinate to our economy more goods and services may lead to a tremendous pressure upon the consumer to adopt more and more luxurious living standards for the sake of keeping the economy healthy it can become a threat to the serenity of life.' Hear, hear! Victor J. Papanek, a designer and educator in the 1970s, extrapolated things a step further: when people are persuaded, advertised, propagandized and victimized into throwing away their cars every three years, their clothes twice yearly, their high fidelity sets every few years, their houses every five years, then we may consider most other things fully obsolete. Throwing away may soon lead us to feel that marriages (and other personal relationships) are throw-away items as well and on a global scale countries, and indeed subcontinents are disposable like Kleenex. The impact of our throw-away culture on our relationships, culture and soul is surely significant, and maybe in ways that we don't fully understand now.

In terms of the effects of our use it/bin it culture, the ecological implications lie mostly in resource use and waste. The most powerful example of accelerating planned obsolescence and the ecological havoc it causes is in the electronics industry. At one end, there is a continued boom in electronics equipment – from video game consoles and mobile phones to laptops and digital audio players (iPods and MP3s). Obsolescence is taken for granted by consumers and peddled fast by advertisers. Larger memories, quicker processing, new software, miniaturization and above all, fashion, combine to make a thriving industry with a large turnover. At the other end is the electronic waste stream which, in the US, is growing at 2–3 times the rate of any other waste source. In Europe alone, 100 million phones are disposed of each year. As American architect, William McDonough, aptly summed up, everything is designed for you to throw away when you are finished with it. But where is away? Of course, away does not really exist. Away has gone away.

With electronic waste (e-waste), there has never been a safe 'away'. It is notorious for its content of highly toxic chemicals such as lead, cadmium, mercury, beryllium, Brominated Flame Retardants and polychlorinated biphenyls (PCBs). This type of waste is clearly non-compostable, but for decades we've been burying our heads in the sand, and chucking it in landfill by the loadful, or even worse, incinerating it. The ecological consequences of these actions are the leaching of heavy metals (landfill), and the production of carcinogenic dioxins (incineration). The small size of some e-waste belies its potential harm: in the US, e-waste only represents 2 per cent of the waste stream yet an estimated 70 per cent of heavy metals in landfills come from discarded electronics.

The other solution has been to export e-waste out of sight and mind, to India or China for dismantling and recycling. However, this is far from ideal as countries receiving e-waste often have weak environmental legislation with the result that informal recycling yards have sprung up across Asia and Africa. Recycling in this case means low-paid migrant workers, working without protective clothing, extracting copper, lead and other precious metals from the remnants of mobile phones using primitive open-air smelters. This informal recycling obviously creates massive environmental pollution and damages the health of workers and residents in the area.

Solutions to e-waste do exist, such as reuse and refurbishment (especially of computers), company take-back programmes and ever-tightening legislation especially in the EU. However, e-waste is highly complex and difficult to handle due to its composition and increasing miniaturization. It is often intentionally designed not to be easily disassembled – in the case of Apple iPod – thus recycling becomes labour intensive and therefore expensive. Company take-back programmes rely on the awareness of consumers and their willingness to take the initiative. So far, results haven't looked promising. Nokia, the market leader in mobile phones, recycles just 2 per cent of the phones it sells.

Also the small size of much of this lifestyle technology and the lack of consumer awareness, means that many people will throw their old mobile phone or iPod into the dustbin. So although there is a growing attempt on a government and council level to deal with e-waste responsibly, it can easily slip into the conventional waste stream and evade recycling. Of the estimated 8.7 million tonnes of e-waste created annually in the EU a massive 6.6 million tonnes of e-waste is not recycled.

So what of the future? Maybe there'll be a kickback against planned obsolescence and people will shout enough but somehow I doubt it. We're now into the third generation of people brought up on the compelling buy-consume-buy cycle and there are few folk left who remember or value durability and longevity. The avid consumers of tomorrow, our children, will not know any differently: unless of course we teach them. It always interests me how of the three environmental Rs taught in schools Reduce, Reuse, Recycle there is very little spoken of Reuse and Reduce almost seems a dirty word. Reduce threatens the economy and our jobs or so we believe. Instead, recycling is hailed as the great fix-it mechanism. Litter-picking is turned into school art. Waste has been transformed and looks pretty. Everyone is happy. But the truth about recycling is that salves a guilty conscience but allows the waste to continue. As *The Ecologist* journalist Simon Fairlie says, recycling offers business an environmental excuse for instant obsolescence. Also recycling has its own ecological footprint of energy use and pollution: the stuff has to be collected, sorted and processed. Overall, surely it would be better if there was less of it in the first place.

Manufacturers and designers can be encouraged through legislation and government policy to change their ways. They can be gradually moved in the direction of producing goods which are more robust, easier to recycle, possible to repair, and have the potential to be upgraded. But, without the consumer's interest and commitment to ensuring longevity of their products, it might not amount to much. At the moment *a quarter to a third of all discarded products are still functioning*. That's incredible! What does that say about us? That the majority of us want to consume, we crave change and novelty, and we aren't really interested in longevity? Or is it that we fall out of love with our possessions before they're ready to give up the ghost? And why would this happen? Is it all about keeping up with the Joneses or is there another element to it? Is it the perhaps the fault of the object we bought? As Jonathan Chapman, an academic looking at these issues, aptly sums up, 'waste is a symptom of a failed subject/object relationship.'

Interesting discussions have been taking place amongst designers about the question of meaningful attachment. Industrial designers find it easy to address issues of increased durability and resilience, but overlook the emotional element of the relationship between person and product. This is especially true with electronic items. In fact, the emotional side of design may be more critical to a product's longevity than its practical elements. Have you ever noticed that if you fix something, even if crudely, you lend it more character? By spending time with it, putting energy into it, you somehow forge a relationship with it? This getting fond of objects might be the key to slowing down the consumption cycle. Here's a test describe your television. All I come up with is a screen with buttons. I've starting to realize that we don't handle electronic items much. We just press a button or turn it on remotely and job done: we expect it to work. Maybe electronics leave us cold. I do see people showing off their new mobile phone or iPad, but it always turns out to be more like a crush than a deep love affair, because within a year they're thinking about another model. It seems that when our suitcases get battered and scratched, or our jeans faded, that is a positive and sought-after sign of use – a badge of honour. But a few scratches on our shiny new iPad, and we're feeling distressed too. So maybe the future is to relook at the design of electronics from an emotional attachment point of view. How can you personalize mass-produced electronics? Would there be a market for half-way products, which are ones that are partially built, but the owner finishes off, and thus individualizes?

I once spent time in the highlands of Guyana, South America, with a tribe called the Patamona. Not much consumption going on there, as expected, but a lot of creativity and making. There seemed to be a lot of time spent hanging out, which would be equivalent to our leisure time. But whilst our industrialized society spends their free time overwhelmingly involved in consumption and shopping, it is evident that pre-industrialized societies would have spent their time making. Now, if you actually made your own houses, clothes, bowls, baskets, spoons and saddles, then you would probably feel pretty attached to them. Making an object is surely at the crux of personalizing it and having a relationship with it. The likelihood of wanting to throw it away after a few years is small because a large investment of time and thought would have gone into it. Repair would be the favoured option, giving the object yet more character and personal history.

Bringing this thinking into a modern-day context, what can we do now to beat the appalling waste created by psychological obsolescence? How can we slow down our rapacious appetites and unhitch ourselves from a never-ending cycle of unnecessary consumption? Well, try and make as much as you can yourself, and if you can't make it, personalize it. Build, repair, create and rebel! Feel secure in last year's dress. Clean your shoes. Wear your mother's clothes. Dare to be different. Don't throw away something that works. Don't let your appetite for consumption be stimulated! Resist! Ignore advertising, and above all try and reduce your children's exposure to it. There is no such thing as sustainable consumption, don't be hoodwinked. Yes, there are more ecological forms of products being developed, for instance the new electronic circuit boards of the future may be developed from the field of transmaterials and made from soybeans and chicken feathers. This is all very positive, but the worry is that we may be convinced to carry on consuming because it is 'good for the economy, and for the environment as well.'

Consumerism is at the heart of psychological obsolescence, so we address consumerism itself. Consumerism has become a way of life for many people. Why? Jonathan Chapman offers some interesting clues, 'As natural as breathing, the drive to consume could be described as symptomatic of a stimulus-seeking species dwelling in a homogenized world in which the prevailing experience of everyday life comes with the majority of problems already solved and decisions already made.' So consumerism may have become a way of life in modern life, because it is the only way that we feel alive. Is there a link between societies living in more diverse and challenging environments being less driven by attachment to possessions? Perhaps when people are busy living in a creative way they don't need shopping to define them. But what about the economy? At times of disaster – an international terrorism incident, a recession – we're told to keep our heads down and shop. For what? For the economy, stupid. The economy is still king. We are conditioned to believe that the economy must grow or we will all perish. Interestingly our finite planet doesn't get a look in on this fuzzy logic. It is high time to deconstruct our destructive economic paradigm and redefine economic growth in the context of human and planetary well-being. Plenty of work and thought have already been put into this, but it is now time for political and social will to put it into action. Until then, psychological obsolescence will continue to be a powerful tool to stimulate purchases in a saturated market, and planned obsolescence through reduced product longevity will become an accepted way of ensuring repeat purchases.

FREEDOM?

Me Time Satisfying
Disinfecting Fulfilling
Mothering Inequality
Cleaning Underpaid
Housewife Exhausting

Home Work
Career

Bijou Apartment Big Home
Porsche Volvo
Childless Children
Misfit Maternal

Family

Chaos
Balance
Habitual Safety

Pyschology

Beautiful
Well Behaved

Disaster!

Reliable Dominating
Boring Exciting
Lots of Sex Not Enough
Good Man Bad Man

Bra size
Smiling
Available
Twinkling
Radiant

Charm

Spinster Plastic
Bin Liner Designer
Ageing Facelift
Bags Botox
Lines Smooth
Natural Enhanced

Beauty

Grooming

Stooped
Backbrace
Backache **Poise**
Elegance
Stilettos

Free-Thinker
Live Fast
Religion Die Young
Regardless
Follower

Hungry Fulfilled
Obese
Voluptuous
Best Friends
No Friends **Friends**
Friends

Figure Hourglass
Athletic
Skeletal

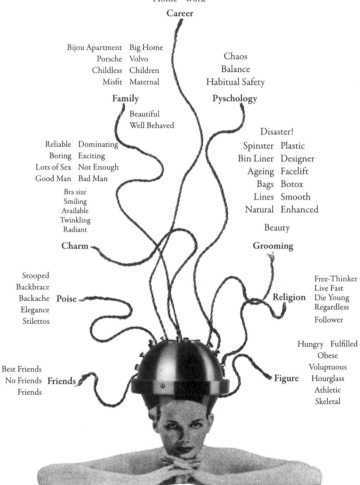

The Personal Success Chart

IDLING FOR WOMEN

Sarah Boak

IN TERMS OF PRACTICAL IDLING, ONE COULD ARGUE THAT
loafing around is no different for women than it is for men.
Daydreaming, hedonism and pleasure-seeking are seemingly
genderless pursuits that are available to all of us. Indeed, when we look
at contemporary culture as reflected by television commercials, we're
bombarded with images of women enjoying themselves; taking some
much needed 'me-time' to sit and read the latest celebrity magazines,
enjoying a sensual shower with the most fragrant of shampoos,
indulging in chocolates, glasses of wine and other 'naughty but nice'
treats. However, there is a sinister flipside that is implied every time
these adverts appear. Women are only able to do these pleasurable
things on short and fleeting breaks from their real business – that of
being a 21st-century superwoman.

In between these adverts for female indulgence we see the old 1950s
ideal of domesticity rolled out time and time again. Women's place –
according to the advertisers – is still firmly in the kitchen, doing the
dishes and making everything shipshape in the house. The adverts
show us what we're supposed to believe – that men are utterly domes-
tically inept, can't remember anything and rely entirely on women to
organize their lives. The marketers are shrewd in telling us that it's
the women that are firmly in control here. This plays to any feminist
sensibilities that we may have. The man cannot figure out how on
earth his wife makes the house smell nice, or look so very clean, and
she is pleased with the control and authority that this offers. It's a real
feminist victory, being able to use a plug-in air freshener.

So now the house is in full female control, the woman can tackle the
real time-consuming task. She must eradicate ALL traces of dirt, grub

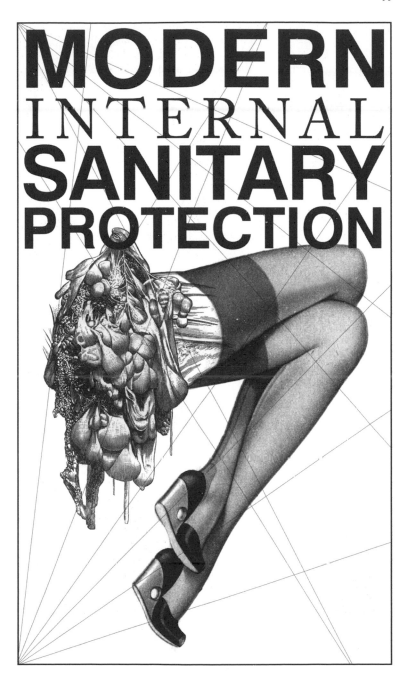

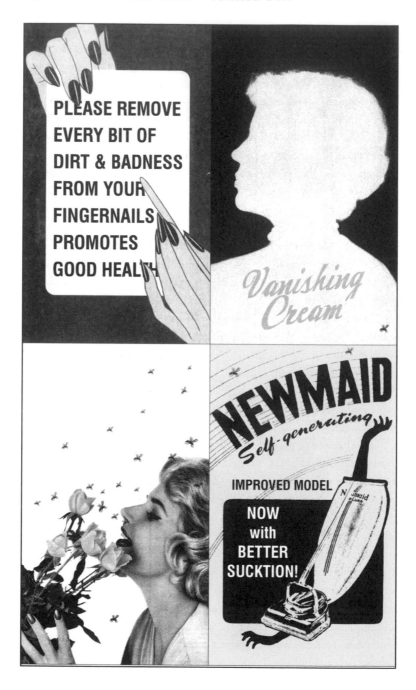

and grime around the house. With umpteen new products to help her, her foremost time drain is the problem of removing 99.9 per cent of germs from all surfaces, in order to protect her family. The very cornerstone of femininity is at stake here. The female nurturer and mother figure has a duty to her family, to protect them from pain and illness. The guilt-inducing adverts make women feel that if they don't spend this time scrubbing and squirting, wiping and scouring, they are in some way less of a wife/partner/mother.

These adverts show us that domesticity is not the only aim for the 'weaker sex'. Women must also be groomed to within an inch of their lives, to compete in this 21st-century world of female beauty and youthfulness. Celebrity icons are plastered across the media. Impossibly thin and unnaturally beautiful, they are sculpted goddesses that most women couldn't even imagine looking like. But then we don't have teams of stylists, make-up artists and personal trainers working round the clock for us. And as for ageing, well, this is seen as the most pernicious disease that must be 'fought' and 'reversed', by all women. The 'signs of ageing' are the equivalent of a death sentence for the 21st-century superwoman. We must remain youthful at all costs; even if we lose our sanity, and our sense of perspective. But fear not! We can now carve ourselves up, inject toxins into our faces, implant, staple and stretch ourselves to fit into this commercially created ideal of femininity.

Now that we're groomed and sculpted, with our organized and germ-free family homes, all that is left for women to do is enter the wonderful world of work. After all, this is the 21st century, and we are in a world of equality – right? Again, the celebrity icons pave the way for us, showing that you too can be a nurturing woman, fulfilled by having a brood of contented children, whilst scaling the career heights and achieving success in numerous industries. Not only does Celebrity X have a film career, but also runs a successful clothing line, produces perfume and is now trying her hand at singing. And of course she still finds time to look immaculate. For the rest of us mere mortals, the paycheque doesn't quite cover the army of staff to help us achieve all these goals. Instead, we sit in airless offices, doing something that with luck we at least find a little bit interesting, but watching the clock tick

down those 37+ hours knowing we still have the kids to bath/the dinner to make/the house to clean. In the corporate world, there isn't really much time for idling, for either men or for women. Our bosses are finding more and more ways in which to measure us, and our 'productivity', to make sure we're up to scratch and on target. So women, who according to the Fawcett Society are still paid 17 per cent less than their male counterparts for equivalent work, not only lose out on a monetary front but also lose out in terms of freedom. Our time is squeezed by the world of work, just like our menfolk's, but we're measured and accountable both in the home and in the workplace. Where is the freedom to loaf?

The *Idler* magazine has previously come in for some flack for being a little male-centric, and possibly – dare I say it – 'laddish' in content at times. But at the heart of the *Idler* is an anarchic philosophy, based on questioning 'the system'. Capitalism, commercialism, corporate dominance, governance, 'the man'... whatever you want to call it. This system that we live under is not equal in the slightest, and doesn't allow for a proper understanding of community. Despite the promises of feminism, through which much amazing work has been achieved, women still get the raw end of the deal in our communities. Community, for me, is at the heart of an idle way of life, and is where women really can have an impact. Despite the constraints of domesticity, some of the roles that women have been encouraged to undertake in that sphere – those of nurturing and caring, facilitating and peacekeeping – are actually at the heart of strong communities. I believe these 'female traits' aren't actually naturally female, but are what society has encouraged women to do and to be. People are much more complex than a series of reducing stereotypes. No, these 'female traits' can apply to us all. Women can perhaps help strengthen our communities by fostering these traits in our families and localities, across both men and women. And why? Well, a successful community is an idle one. This gives us time – something that women nowadays argue they don't have much of.

Our community ties give much scope for idling. In chatting with our neighbours to find out how we can pool resources, drinking tea with friends while the kids play together, sharing a veg plot, we are

Be *Sociable*

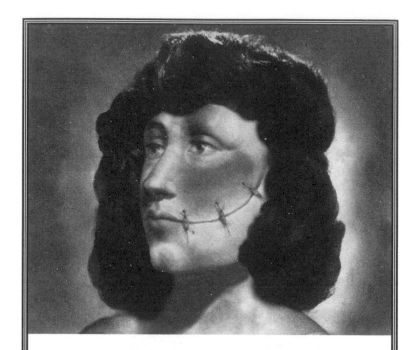

DANGER!

Women's Suffrage Would Double the Irresponsible Vote

It is a MENACE to The Home, Men's Employment and to All Business

Yes ☐   No ☒

actually saving time and slowing down a little. No longer do we trawl the aisles of Tesco's alone, dragging our tantrumming toddlers behind us, but we come together to share breadmaking, veg growing, and thus share our time burden. But what about this blessed resource that many women talk about   'me time'? The concept of 'me-time' is a horrible one, whose idler pretentions are actually far from the truth. Surely, under an idle philosophy, *all* our time should be orientated to what matters most to oneself? The problem is that what matters most to ourselves – under the system – is all skewed. The ego actually is something that should exist in dialogue with other egos: in community. What should matter most to us is working with other people to secure the best and most pleasurable conditions for living. It is the culture of commercialism and of capitalism that feeds a misleading understanding of ego, and separates us out into competing units of personality. We fight for resources individually, rather than combine them collectively. A idle person bakes two loaves and gives one to her neighbour, knowing that her neighbour will help fix her bicycle, or make her a lasagne. This is 'me-time' proper. Orientating ourselves to what matters most to us; our families, good times and sharing.

This collectivity has a female feel to it. The original understanding of feminine traits may be a stereotypical, generalized one, but I think women should embrace these traits irrespective of their source. They are entirely positive and can be reclaimed from their negative, demeaning origins. Hell, let's all get back in the kitchen! Let's bake some cakes, brew up some beer, turn up the stereo and enjoy ourselves – men, women, children, dogs, cats, the lot. No more singular slaving over a pot! The thing is that true idleness, in my mind, is a caring idleness, and in that way this article is just as relevant for men as it is for women. Let's create the conditions for idleness for all the people we love and live with, irrespective of gender. It's great if our menfolk manage to find more time to piss about and dream and think lofty thoughts whilst drinking beer. But using the Buddhist philosophy of 'mindfulness', we must think about the cost of our own actions on the people around us. If we are brutally honest, some of our idling can, at times, come at a price to those who we care about. It's time to find ways around these

issues and try to reduce the societal pressure on women to clean, to be groomed and to be everything to everybody.

What strategies can we put in place to make a woman's life a more idle one? Coming together in communities is certainly at the heart of this project. But for women, I think there is a specific need for time to idle alone. Virginia Woolf argued that all women should have 'a room of one's own' to be able to write fiction, but of course her argument extended much further than the idea of writing. A woman needs a space away from the expectations of others – and here, I include the massive pressure and competition between women themselves, something that can be a terrible burden. Women need physical space, in order to achieve some mental space. I would always have considered myself a city girl, loving the hustle and bustle of the cities in which I lived. But I fell in love with a woodsman, and so had to move to the countryside. And there, a wonderful thing happened. I found idleness. The noise of the city, and the noise of all of those competing expectations somehow quieted. I had physical space to myself – fields and paths and woodlands – and my mind responded accordingly, opening up into daydreams and reveries, fictions and fantasies. I could read. I could walk. I could let my mind go wherever it would. And I felt that without the prying eyes of the city, I was free to be whomever I chose.

If we don't have the luxury of the space of the country, at least we need to find city spaces for women to lounge, to read and to ponder. Let's orientate our cities around pleasure and pontification. There's often quite a practical element to idling – the sharing of domestic resources and tasks to help us go about our lives – but, as Tom Hodgkinson's books show, the intellectual and thinking element of the idler is really key. So in our cities, we do have some places to go for intellectual succour. Places like the The School of Life in London where we can be prescribed, not pills or potions, but reading and ideas. Feeling low? Don't scrub your sink – immerse yourself in books! But here is the issue. Where are all the women idlers? In the canon of idle writings, there are many by men. The female role models are yet to be championed, and maybe yet to be discovered. We need more women writers, eccentrics, creatives, thinkers, idlers. We need a more visible female presence to be inspired by. Ultimately, this all comes back to

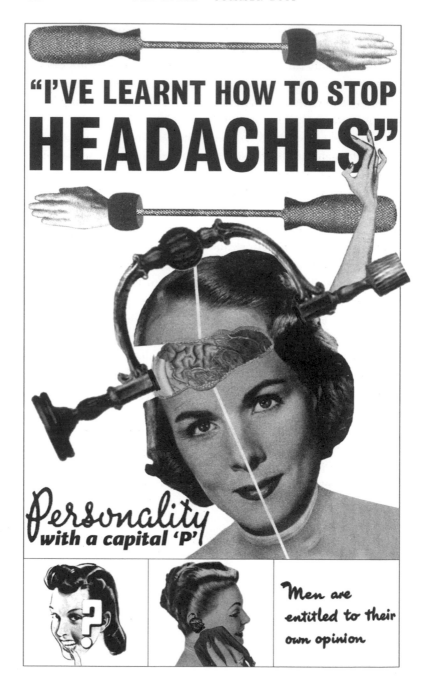

the idea of orientating ourselves to the most important things. Sod the germs – isn't reading Kerouac or Cixous or Mitford more crucial to our lives and our sanities? The cleanliness brigade have made us lose sight of the hierarchy of what's important. Too busy scrubbing the floors, we've lost sight of the stars above us. At the end of my life, I don't want to be known as a woman who did a lot of cleaning. I want to be known as a woman of passions, of intellect, big thoughts and silly overblown moments. But most of all, as a woman who wasn't afraid to think.

And what happens when a woman thinks? She becomes creative. And this is where we, as women, have a *huge* resource to tap into. Women across the ages have engaged in practical and creative pursuits. From quilt-making to knitting, baking and music-making, women have expressed themselves through various crafts, and fortunately for us these are making a comeback, with a modern twist. Women are rediscovering knitting, and the pleasure of an idle chitchat across the click-clack of needles, with groups such as 'Stitch 'n' Bitch' which can now be found in even the most provincial of towns. What I particularly like about 'Stitch 'n' Bitch' is that this isn't twee, old-fashioned type knitting – though there is pleasure in that type too. This is a politicized, funky, slightly radical type of knitting. Knit yourself a tongue-in-cheek bustier, knit 'Fuck the System' into a cushion, knit a spiky neck collar to give yourself a bit of comfortable yet punk style. This isn't just knitting a scarf or a sweater – it's about expression. And it comes together in communities of women. The world of work and the domestic sphere often find us separated off into 'types' of women, organized in age groups and interests. But in these knitting groups, all ages and types of women can mingle. When that happens, we find the most unlikely and the most pleasurable friendships grow.

This DIY creative attitude is exploding and is well facilitated by the internet, where women are blogging about their creative pursuits, sharing patterns, ideas and encouragement. And unlike television – where we have one way of living being expounded, to the expense of all others – these blogs show a myriad of ways of life, with many idle politics and persuasions being found. Lots of women around the world are exploring ways to slow down their family life, and are finding that

creativity is at the heart of this. This creativity strengthens our family ties across generations too. I have spent lots of happy evenings finding out all my mum knows about quilting, baking and crafting, and those times together are really precious times that can't be bought and can't be rushed.

Let's return to one of our original problems – that of the sculpted, groomed and eternally youthful woman. How do we rid ourselves of this massively pervasive stereotype? One obvious way is to change our viewing and reading habits. Steering clear of women's magazines and turning off the telly massively cuts down the amount of exposure we have to this fallacy of beauty. When we situate ourselves in our communities, rather than in single isolation, it reminds us of the variety of beauty. When we spend time outside, in nature, we realize that beauty comes in many forms. Beauty is multiple, not singular, as the media would have us believe. Beauty is also of all ages. We do have some strong women role models, particularly older women in the public eye – such as Judi Dench, or Susan Sarandon – who are not personal-trained and plasticized to within an inch of their lives. However, much of the media promotion of 'natural' or 'real' beauty is still linked into the promotion of anti-ageing skincare, or make-up, or the pursuit of 'youthfulness'. I think that what we need to return to is the concept of glamour. There is nothing forced, or pressured about glamour. Glamour is indulgence. Glamour is fabulous. Glamour is thinking 'fuck it to the make-up this morning, I'm having an extra half hour in bed' and shoving on some sunglasses. Glamour drinks champagne, eats chocolate by the ton and loves voluptuousness. Glamour is not stingy or calorie-counting. I hope also, that glamour can be applicable at any age, in any type of clothing, and is about enjoying the charade and dress-up of being a woman.

Now what this glamorous, thinking, creative woman, needs is a release from work. Let's face it, as all us idlers know, work is a tedious thing. I'm not talking about part-time, flexible, doing the stuff you like that isn't really work, work. I'm talking about full-time, corporate wage slavery, which us women are supposed to be thankful for being liberated into. I worked my way up this awful ladder, labouring – quite literally – under the pretence that intelligent women should just keep

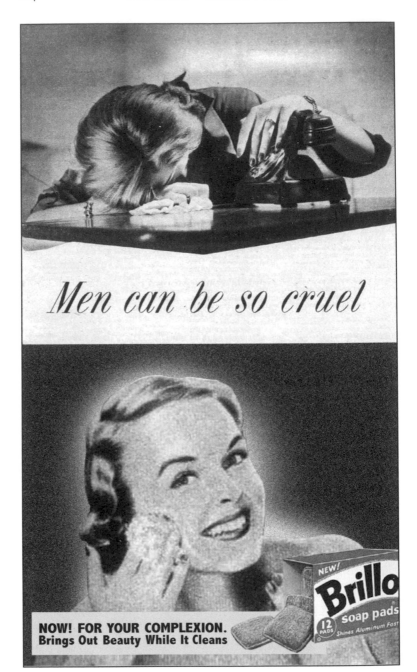

climbing and climbing, until they reach that pinnacle of 'senior management'. What a load of toss. You get paid to listen to people whingeing about how much they hate their jobs, and how little they're getting paid, and even when you try to nurture talent it's unappreciated and sullied by office politics. But many women have already made a break for freedom, and we need to use those women as role models. Women who are mothers often work part-time, flexibly, or not at all, in order to find space and time to do what they feel is most important to them. But we don't have to be mothers to do this. I started working part-time years before I became a mother, because I wanted to play music more. I loved that time idling about with friends, singing and playing and writing music, and I put that above my work life. It's financially a really difficult thing to do, to give up the stability of a regular wage, and particularly if we subscribe to the 'want, want, want' mentality of consumer culture. For women it means maybe rethinking those trinkets that we're supposed to value. Again, the house-proud attitude may have to shift a bit. Our houses don't have to look like they came out of *Elle Decoration* magazine. We need to embrace a bit of 'wonkiness' in our lives. There is more beauty in charity shop finds, stuff handed down through families or via the wonderful and system-challenging Freecycle, things that have been made by hand, than there will ever be in the mass-marketed tat that is supposed to be beautiful. Some of these things are 'wonky', have bits missing, are made with love (and not necessarily massive talent), but this is where the beauty lies. Many women I know think like this deep down, but we just get a bit waylaid by the sparkliness of the new and the bright lights of the shopping centres.

When the idler becomes a mama, all hell breaks loose. Children are devilishly life-changing, and at first it seems hard to imagine where the idle life can be found in the midst of all of these infantile demands. But I think that motherhood offers plenty of opportunity for the true idler, starting right away with the pregnancy. If ever an opportunity were presented for serious lounging, snoozing and eating, this is it. Although the early days of pregnancy can be bilious and sick-making, the dormouse-like state is perfect for loungers and much happy sofa snoozing was spent in my first trimester. Then, once the nausea passes,

[MARRIED LIPS]

[UNMARRIED LIPS]

...for smooth lips,
DON'T BOTHER!

To Safeguard Health it is NOT necessary To DISINFECT ONCE A WEEK

So they don't like Your ★Trifle?

She is 44!
Can you believe it?

HEART PAINS never trouble me now!

Are <u>you</u> Brimming with **HEALTH** and **ENERGY**

To be perfectly FAIR

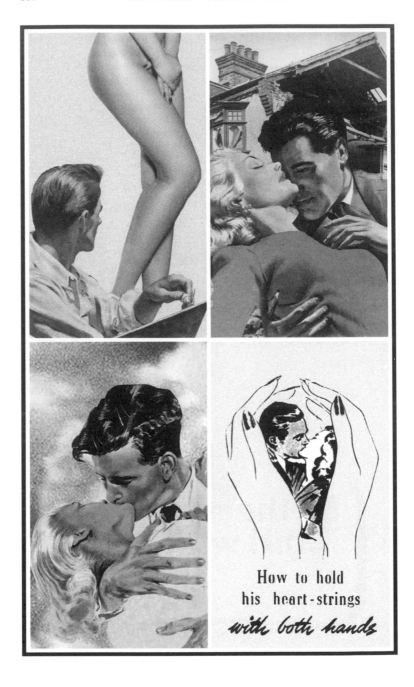

you have plenty of opportunity to meet with other mums-to-be and eat your own body weight in cake. Once you're in the latter stages of pregnancy, moving around is really just a drag, and fusing your body to a sofa/bed/beanbag is practically a prerequisite. That coupled with the fact that you can't actually get out of the chair you're in, and you're in idle heaven. And pregnancy sex gives you a perfect opportunity to let your partner do all the 'work' whilst you recline in ecstasy.

Idling in its true sense is bound up with both creativity and politics, thus the idle mama is both a creative mama and a political one. The system medicalizes the female body and likes to intervene in childbirth from the offset. We are encouraged to ignore our own intuition about our bodies, and to give over control to medical staff. The norm is to give birth in hospitals, where we can be 'monitored' and checked throughout the birth process. For a first-time mother, who is naturally nervous about the unknown process of childbirth, this is reassuring. The other option – of a midwife assisted home birth – is a very scary one, where the thought of something 'going wrong' is too much to bear. But the medicalization of childbirth is a new thing – women traditionally gave birth in their homes. Statistically speaking, women who have their babies in hospitals are more likely to have 'interventions' in the process, such as forcep births or caesarean delivery. Home births rely on fewer drugs, which is a much better start for both baby and mama. In hospital births, women are often encouraged to lie on their backs and not to move around, particularly if they are attached to monitors, drips, or have had epidurals that remove the option of movement. The idle mama can opt for a home birth and move around freely, in the comfort of her own surroundings. There is nothing better than giving birth to your baby in your own bedroom, then sitting up in your bed having a nice cuppa and a slice of toast. I love telling my son about how he was made in this bed, in this house, and he was born right here too. There's none of the stress of staying in a ward, having to pack up everything and go home. The idle way is just to stay in bed! And this can go on for as long as you want. Women are starting to talk about 'babymoons', like the related word 'honeymoon', which is a period of days spent in bed with your baby and your partner, and

just chilling out. Let all your visitors come up to the bedroom and meet you there in your pyjamas!

When the baby becomes a toddler, then a child, the tantrums may start and disciplining has to kick in. However, there are also many opportunities for the idle mama, in her quest for a more idle life. The real antidote to work, I find, is play. Engage with your inner child. Spend time dancing about like a loon, draw big colourful crayon drawings, splash about in puddles and dig holes in the mud. This is all great fun, is intensely idle as it's not work at all, and also – an added bonus – is educational for your child. My two-year-old and I have created a great dance routine, where we do gentle ballet moves (made up by myself, from the pretend school of ballet) then spend a period of time lying on the floor looking at each other whilst occasionally flipping our legs in the air. I like that our dance is both fun and restful. He's getting the idle vibe from an early age. There is so much fun to be had mucking about, and this sort of play allows both you and your sprogs to be really creative, which means that for the idle mama it's really a must.

So let's embrace our feminine traits of nurturing and caring, and come together in our communities to find a more idle way for the ladies. No more slavery to fashion, cleanliness or domesticity. Let's shepherd in a new era of idle glamour, mucking about with the children, lofty thinking and a female anti-work ethic. And hopefully, amongst the *Idler* pages, we'll start to hear more voices from the idling superwomen.

Poised Perfection
Deliciously Aloof...

But She Can't be Beautiful without Beautiful Hair

IMPORTANT:

Make Yourself Look Lovely

Illustrations on pages 96–123 by Nina McNamara & Alice Smith

Pete Willis

THREE HOURS A DAY

PAUL LAFARGUE AND THE RIGHT TO BE LAZY

Bernard Marszalek

IT IS WIDELY KNOWN THAT THE MOST POPULAR MARXIST essay is the *Communist Manifesto*. But which text ranks second in popularity? Few know that the answer is *The Right to be Lazy* and that the author was Paul Lafargue, Karl Marx's son-in-law.

Despite the popularity of this non-conformist Marxist essay, Lafargue's historic obscurity led Leslie Derfler, his American biographer (his two-volume history is the definitive work), to research Lafargue's legacy in France. Derfler found that though Lafargue was the co-founder of the first French Marxist party, *Parti Ouvrier* and the first Marxist member of the Chamber of Deputies, monuments to his accomplishment are few, and nowhere near the quantity memorializing Jules Guesde, the co-founder of *Parti Ouvrier*. No grand boulevards, no large statues, no squares or new townships are named after Lafargue. Was this due to discrimination against Lafargue's Jewish heritage? Or was it that heritage combined with his Black and Red lineages that aborted significant civic commemoration?

Lafargue never hid his multiple racial origins, and was recorded as saying that of all his bloodlines, he was most proud of his African heritage. He was probably referring to the pride he felt as a descendent of the black slaves who participated in that incredible 1804 revolution in Haiti that created a black republic.

Or maybe the French bourgeoisie – who after all must approve all monuments – frowned on his birth on Cuba soil? But most likely Lafargue's caustic wit prevented any constituency to rally to his banner. Certainly this essay was never popular with the Church of

Marxism (that collection of scholars who resembled the monks of the Scholastic schools in all ways but their dress).

Most Marxists, traditionalists wed to a condescending view of the working class, felt uncomfortable with these words from *The Right to be Lazy*:

> A strange delusion possesses the working classes of the nations where capitalist civilization holds its sway. This delusion drags in its train the individual and social woes which for two centuries have tortured sad humanity. This delusion is the love of work, pushed even to the exhaustion of the vital force of the individual and his [sic] progeny.
>
> In capitalist society work is the cause of all intellectual degeneracy, of all organic deformity.

There is no way to prove that this essay was popular with those who were the butt of Lafargue's wit, but then who else was reading it, if not the workers to which it was directed?

Lafargue's family moved from Cuba to Bordeaux while Paul was still a child. He remained in France until his college days, when he got suspended from medical school for participation in student demonstrations and emigrated to England to finish his studies. Lafargue gravitated to the Marx household, as did so many other exiles, for the political salon that it was – the centre for a new international movement. Soon though he adopted another role than that of the emigré, when he became the suitor of Karl's middle daughter, Laura.

In 1868, with his degree and with Laura Marx as a new companion for life Paul returned to Paris to practice medicine and promote the French section of the International. Various legalities created obstacles to a remunerative medical practice and in 1870 when the Prussians occupied the suburbs of Paris, where the Lafargues lived, they fled to Paul's family home in Bordeaux. The following year the people of Paris seized the city and called for a national revolution and the Lafargues, though eager to return to the capital, were requested to stay in Bordeaux to organize provincial support for the Commune.

After the attack and slaughter of the Communards, police harass-
ment increased countrywide and Paul and Laura narrowly escaped jail
by fleeing to Spain. A year in Spain unsuccessfully attempting to
undermine the anarchist influence in the International preceded their
return to London, where they dedicated ten years busily propagandiz-
ing for the nascent Marxist movement in Europe. In 1882, they
returned to Paris as an amnesty for the Communards was granted and
political activity began to accelerate.

The Lafargues saw their mission as popularizing Marxist theory
in France and to that end Paul and Laura translated, published and
authored essays whenever they weren't agitating within the electoral
arena. Creating an explicitly Marxist presence in French politics, for
many years influenced by Proudhon or Blanqui, seemed at times an
insurmountable task. However, as manufacturing came to increasingly
dominate the French economy and as workers in the new industrial
centers responded to the exhortations of the socialists to organize,
Lafargue and Guesde were convinced that the time was right to create
the explicitly Marxist *Parti Ouvrier*.

In 1889, after seven years of agitation, Lafargue won a seat as the first
Marxist elected to the Chamber of Deputies. His emphasis on organizing while in the Chamber meant that he used his status as a Deputy to
expand the influence of socialism beyond his immediate constituency.
As a result, an opportunist accused Lafargue of ignoring the more
practical concerns of his electors and captured his seat at the next
election.

The manic-depressive nature of 19th Century electoral politics, a
venture new to the socialist participants, with its pyrrhic victories and
its crushing defeats (sounds familiar?) left all who participated
exhausted, if not bitter and resigned. Lafargue himself, more an intellectual than a party organizer, maintained his equilibrium and never
descended to the petty vindictiveness so readily apparent even in the
early history of socialist politics. And though he argued against the
anarchists after his youthful exposure to Proudhonism, toward the end
of his life he hesitantly endorsed syndicalism as a legitimate organizing
strategy.

When juxtaposed to electoral politics and its easily co-opted programs, the day-in-day-out nature of on-the-job organizing may have seemed for Lafargue more promising for lasting social change. Of course, with the incorporation of trade unions into state structures, as auxiliaries to political parties for instance, that approach proved problematic.

Lafargue chose the title of his most popular essay as a rebuttal to the call for the 'Right to Work' by reformist socialists, whose idea of agitation was based on the typical paternalistic, lowest common denominator premise adopted by political opportunists. Not much seems to have changed in the way of slogans since the nineteenth-century, but work has been transformed dramatically, in ways that wage slaves then could never imagine. However, as a recent academic study of happiness at work revealed (to the astonishment of the researchers we presume), one basic fact remains constant through the centuries – work sucks.

Lafargue's approach to the subject upset those socialists who, more influenced by the corrosive intellectual effects of Christianity than they wished to recognize, sought to elevate the heroic productivity (and sacrifice) of the workers as compared to the leech-like (slothful) behaviour of the bosses. The development of the work ethic, as it has came to be known, served so-called socialists as much as the ruling class.

There is no doubt that erecting gravity-defying structures, for instance, brought pride to the workers at the birth of the industrial age. These were real accomplishments even if one must question the larger issues – the actual oppressive conditions under which the work was done. In other words, the fruit of one's labour can be a source of self-esteem, especially by those who demonstrate considerable skill, and yet that sense of self-worth offers little reprieve from the everyday humiliations of order-taking.

Workers must cultivate a kind of schizoid perspective so that their sense of pride can be maintained in spite of the abuse and incompetence of the order-givers. Solidarity on the job often takes the form of resistance to authority, but societal temptations for individualistic solutions limit the longevity of these defensive postures. To collectively protect one's integrity for the long term melts away with the seductive siren call of self-employment.

We all sell our labour, in a passive sense, as essentially commodities; those who seek to be 'their own bosses' attempt to transcend their passivity to become active participants in the marketplace. For all the benefits of attaining a modicum of control over their work-lives, the stress of constantly seeking work and maintaining a commodious relationship with clients has, however, its own drawbacks. Only an insignificant minority of the highly skilled, or just plain lucky, attain the status of master, or the role of Artist, and thus secure a livelihood based on a reputation among the rich. We might call this the 'William Morris Escape'.

The illusions of self-employment are pervasive, and the toxic notion that ownership means freedom becomes the remedy *de jure* to co-opt those disaffected by workplace misery, to build community assets in poor neighbourhoods (a trendy elixir among community organizers in the US) and to devolve state services to the formerly state-financed staff (a current UK prescription).

Several years ago George W. Bush rolled out his 'Ownership Society' programme – basically a smokescreen for tax cuts for the rich – which drew an instant, near apoplectic, response from the promoters of Employee Stock Option Plans (ESOPs – a system of limited employee buy-ins) who rushed to a press conference to decry the Bush programme and declare that they were the true advocates of an ownership society.

Owning shares in the company you work for (without the voting rights that come with stock ownership), sometimes called 'owning your job', is like sailing a small vessel in the open seas – you are at the mercy of the squalls – in the former case, kicked up by the fury of the marketplace. Stock ownership, flexible employment and any number of other ameliorative schemes are all measures taken to contain the growing frustrations of working.

Lafargue while hardly advocating capitalism with a 'human face' by introducing palliatives, as today conjured up by Human Resources consultants, did see that mechanization could temporize the horrors of long hours of toil. The workers should directly benefit from industrial technology, Lafargue argued, by reducing their work hours, instead of working harder or, worse, fired when their job was automated.

A good workingwoman makes with her needles only five meshes a minute, while certain circular knitting machines make 30,000 in the same time. Every minute of the machine is thus equivalent to a hundred hours of the workingwoman's labour, or again, every minute of the machine's labour gives the workingwoman ten days of rest.

Lafargue, though concerned with the issues of work as degrading, exploitative toil, had a more profound agenda:

Thus far my task has been easy; I had but to describe real evils well known, alas, by all of us; but to convince the proletariat that the ethics inculcated into it is wicked, that the unbridled work to which it has given itself up for the last hundred years is the most terrible scourge that has ever struck humanity, that work will become a mere condiment to the pleasures of idleness, a beneficial exercise to the human organism, a passion useful to the social organism only when wisely regulated and limited to three hours a day; this is an arduous task beyond my strength.

More explicitly, not unlike Nietzsche writing at the same time, he calls for a revolt against Christianity and liberal politics:

... to arrive at the realization of its strength the proletariat must trample under foot the prejudices of Christian ethics, economic ethics and free-thought ethics. It must return to its natural instincts, it must proclaim the Rights of Laziness, a thousand times more noble and more sacred that the anaemic Rights of Man concocted by the metaphysical lawyers of the bourgeois revolution. It [the proletariat] must accustom itself to working but three hours a day, reserving the rest of the day and night for leisure and feasting.

Lafargue proposes that the proletariat reverse perspective on work – not that we serve work, but work serve us.

What can this mean? Work is so basic to our lives that to suggest a

life where work is a 'condiment to the pleasures of idleness' is to invite
ridicule, if not more extreme verbal abuse. Possibly, more than the
capitalists and their politicians, who will respond in predictable ways
to any attack on work, workers, who fear for their futures without
employment, could be repelled by what they might interpret as an
assault on their survival by the privileged. It is informative however
that when the rich plead for economic relief from whatever govern-
mental abuse they imagine victimizes them, they call for tax relief, or
subsidies, or some other economic privilege. They essentially plead for
money. And what do the workers call for? Jobs!

It is obvious that we are living in a time when work is not only a
major source of stress and frustration, but also disappearing; financial
ministers of all the rich countries having nothing more to contribute as
a policy solution than a shrug of their shoulders. So what is more
utopian? Continued reliance on neo-liberal pseudo-solutions, like
workfare, or a perspective that separates jobs from income?

We face a troika of catastrophes involving declining resources,
climate change and a financial system run amuck, yet despite these
impeding catastrophes, smiling faces appear on the nightly news spinning fantasies as reality. One wonders whether the Spin Doctors will
ever realize that they have convinced no one that 'we are on road to
recovery.' If this isn't a time for revolutionary solutions, then when
will that time arrive?

Lafargue correctly analysed the difficulty of creating change when
he wrote over a century and a quarter ago, that providing the analysis
and critique is easy, but to formulate a strategy to implement the
reversal of perspective is another matter. In his time all socialists had
expectations based on a limited perspective circumscribed by national-
ism, miscalculations of reformist potentials on both a political and
economic level and under-appreciations of human malleability. On
this last point, a rigid and self-serving Social Darwinism that defined
human behaviour as competitive has been refuted by research from
neuroscience labs and early childhood development centres. This new
science reinforces the view that we humans are a co-operative and
empathetic species.

These findings explain some of the frustrations of employment

where our basic nature is suppressed; and more, it explains our eager-
ness to join volunteers, despite the lack of monetary compensation, for
what can be an exhausting effort. The 'instincts' Lafargue hoped
would inform our actions may be more valid than he imagined from
his readings in anthropology. By reversing perspective to enlarge our
capacities for emotional reciprocity we tap into a notion of interper-
sonal abundance. The strategy that informs Lafargue's vision is not
simply a matter of will power, it entails a daily practice of strengthen-
ing our desire to live differently. If employed, subversions of authority
make for a wonderful game to enliven the necrophilic dreariness of
work. For those unrestricted by employment, then the world becomes
a stage for dissident diversions – the imagination the only limitation to
our fun.

No strategy to solidify one's reversal of perspective as second nature
can long satisfy based on individual actions; collective measures create
a culture, if only a rebellious mini-culture, of pleasure. All around, but
usually under the radar of the mass media, the elements of a new
culture percolate projects in urban agriculture, alternative transportation and energy, community art, and an endless list of endeavours in
the field of social justice that make concrete a vision of a society where
human needs are addressed.

As isolated developments these may seem inadequate given the
catastrophes we face. With so little time to create a viable way of life to
sustain us, the enormity of the odds for change can overwhelm. But
to succumb to depression and immobility is to be dominated by the
perspective of power, a version of the work ethic, where our sacrifice
seems meaningless in the larger scheme of things.

Ours is a game of focus where one eye looks beyond the horizon
while the other rests at hand on the joy of creation with others who
reflect our quests. And like any game the attraction can be compulsive
and so small beginnings grow and spin-offs occur and news spreads of
worthwhile deeds to be emulated and adapted to other innovative uses.
There is no other life to live but one that embodies here and now how
we wish to live tomorrow.

THE GASTRONOMIC UNDERGROUND

Italy's *mercatini clandestini*

Andrew Wilbur

YOU RECEIVE YOUR INVITATION IN THE POST. PHOTO-copied, cheaply produced, usually with hand-drawn maps. The information is bare and functional: date, time, location and an intimation of who might be there. If you've received an invitation then there's a good chance that you know what to expect. You're known by the organizers, effectively an insider already. The venue never stays the same and months may pass between events. Nobody wants to be officially associated with what's happening so everyone has to take a share of the responsibility – and the potential consequences. For all the secrecy and cautiousness, participants in Italy's *mercatini clandestini* have to force a laugh at the absurdity of all these measures. They are, after all, simply trading food.

There are secret economies everywhere in Italy, where decades of pervasive bureaucracy, Mafia extortion, political corruption and misguided tax regimes have created marginal trading structures and finance channels that circumvent the official economy with remarkable creativity. The most recent comprehensive estimates put Italy's shadow economy at around 26 per cent of GDP, the highest in Europe after Greece. Using 2009 figures, that works out as nearly €360 billion in untaxed, unregulated exchange, of which about half is attributable to revenues from organized crime. The rest is made up of 'grey market' activities – practices that aren't technically illegal but slip through the regulatory net, such as casual work and unrecorded trading. This spells significant trouble for state finances, but outside of the political class there is almost a universal distrust of the state as an effective mechanism for managing the economy. Since the unification of Italy in the mid-nineteenth century, faith placed in the national government has been abused and degraded in a wearisome cycle, with Italians consequently investing more energy in local political projects than sending bureaucrats to Rome. The grey economy is widely tolerated and often regarded as a positive result of creative autonomy rather than theft from the public purse. The *mercatini clandestini*, or secret markets, are conceived as a direct response to the state's failures to support small-scale agriculture and protect fragile rural economies. The intended result is a sustainable form of trade that plugs the leakages of money out of small communities, encourages social interaction and a closer producer-consumer connection, defies heavy-handed bureaucratic impositions and distributes food of exceptional quality at fair and negotiable prices.

'It started after Genova,' remembers Simone, a farmer and founder of a monthly secret market near Perugia in the central region of Umbria. His measured narration is punctuated by flashes of anger as he recalls the G8 Summit protests in 2001 which saw a young Italian demonstrator, Carlo Giuliani, shot and then run over twice by a police Land Rover. The police officer who shot and killed Giuliani was later cleared of any wrongdoing. 'When everybody was back we thought: Everybody's driven up to Genova and spent loads of money, given money to the multinationals again – for cars, trains, buying petrol and all the rest … So what are we gonna do? Are we going to carry on going to these demonstrations with them beating us over the head, carrying on just the same? Let's try and do something positive. It's very easy to say, "Oh we don't want this …" But is the alternative there? Or is it always "We don't want this"? And so we said that one of the things that would really change things here would be to take the money away from the multinationals … And how do you do that? Well, for a start, you recreate the local economy, the very local economy.'

Striking a blow against multinational corporations is more than just ideological. As in other European countries, small farmers in Italy have been particularly hard hit by the brutal corporate rationalization of agriculture. They have been mercilessly squeezed out of a market that favours capital-intensive monocultures and economies of scale, processes that keep prices depressed and militate against mixed farming and sustainable land use. The policy response to the crisis in agriculture has been to offer subsidies to farmers but – in a further insult to small producers – it's large agribusiness concerns that reap the lion's share of these subsidies. In response to being locked out of an existing market, farmers like Simone and his wife Mara have invented an alternative.

'We were just making it up as we went along,' explains Mara. As relative newcomers to the countryside (they've been farming in Umbria since the early 1980s), they lacked the extensive familial and social networks that had traditionally provided the basis of food exchange in rural Italy before the widespread adoption of industrial agriculture (and related rural depopulation). Friends, neighbours and fellow farmers were marshalled for the first market, which drew only eight vendors and a small number of invited customers. Mara says that this first result was dispiriting, but they felt determined to press ahead with a process of expansion that she describes as 'very, very, very slow.' They recently celebrated their 100th market, an event that marked the solidity of what is now an established network of dozens of famers and regular customers who see themselves as equal participants in a collaborative experiment.

Who can participate in the markets is ultimately up to the organizers, but the criteria for inclusion is flexible. Most of the vendors represent organic family farms or artisanal producers of meat, cheese, bread, oil and wine. Sellers pay 15 euros a year to cover running costs (photocopying and postage, mostly) and the location rotates each month. Efforts are made to ensure that a good balance of products is offered and that the markets don't have an excessive supply of one particular foodstuff, which would put the vendors in awkward competition with one another. Producers barter amongst themselves, trading their own surplus with other vendors and reducing the flow of money out of the community and into the hands of national or multinational chains. Many suppliers come to the markets with fixed prices in mind but negotiate with their customers on a face-to-face basis, both parties

articulating a case for what is fair and reasonable. The success of a
market trader ultimately comes down to establishing trust, an objective that corporations must employ armies of PR agents to sustain.

'That's the guarantee you have in a market like this,' says Simone,
'the fact that we all know each other and we're friends. So there's no
piece of paper saying that [a vendor] sells good cheese, but he's a friend
of yours. Not only that, but it's also part of a whole social network,
and if you sold them something that was really rubbish you'd really
ruin your reputation. That doesn't happen if you go to the supermarket. They get something wrong, you can bring it back but nobody
gives a damn ...'

Trust, of course, is fundamental to any market transaction and
works as an essential but often unacknowledged mediator between
supply and demand. It is a simple point but one worth emphasizing,
especially with consideration to how that trust is established and maintained. For most people in wealthy countries, economic exchange has
little to do with intimate knowledge of provenance and supply chains.
Economists would argue, however, that without some implicit sense
of quality guarantee (communicated through all manner of assurances
including verbal promotion, refund offers, labelling standards and
brand identity) consumers generally reject transactions with too many
unknown variables. Signifiers of trust are therefore embedded at all
stages of exchange, some delicately nuanced and others far more overt.
The complexity of highly developed economies, however, encourages
an uncritical internalization of these guarantees, dissuading consumers
from prying too deeply into the evolution of a product prior to resale.
This suits big business perfectly. Obfuscating a product's origins
helps to devolve accountability to a complex network of actors and by
extension disempowers consumers to make directly informed choices.
In modern economies, the expectations and guarantees that underpin
market performance are managed by corporations, quangos and
governments. A supermarket shopper doesn't expect to get sick from
food bought there because the scale of the supermarket's supply chain
suggests an equally baroque network of regulation. For many people,
food passed direct from farm to fork suggests risk, especially in this age
of BSE, salmonella, *e. coli* and other food-borne pathogens. As the

food writer Joanna Blythman sardonically notes, 'We find it reassuring to think that our food comes from large, modern industrial factories, kitted out with cutting-edge technology, staffed with men in white coats and policed by earnest inspectors with clipboards and lengthy checklists.' A factory-reared supermarket chicken is 'good' because it probably won't kill you and tastes more or less as you'd expect (since few other varieties are commonly available). When sanctimonious killjoys argue that flavour, nutritional quality and rural economies suffer as a result of this preference for the predictable and homogenous, PR experts are on hand to counter public concerns.

To be fair, there is some sense in a detailed regulatory scheme, at least when monitoring industrial-scale food production. It would be dishonest to cast all food safety programmes as needlessly intrusive and counter-productive, especially given the dangers imparted by high-density livestock rearing, globalized distribution networks and the arcane chemistry of extended shelf-lives, artificial colouring and flavour enhancement. This need for a vast regulatory framework communicates just how severely knowledge has broken down between consumers and producers as the interfaces between nature and plate have grown more complex. Sadly, it also demonstrates how little trust in nature is held by the food industry and encouraged in consumers. An obvious discrepancy exists, though, between industrial food webs and artisanal production. In Italy, as elsewhere, the laws that govern the former are nonetheless clumsily applied to the latter so that small producers are subject to the same crippling bureaucracy that large-scale firms can employ entire departments to handle. As much as large companies love to complain about costly adherence to regulations, their collective leverage largely enables them to determine what is permissible. Terms such as 'food standards' and 'quality assurance' assume that standardization is desirable (or at least inevitable) and that 'quality' is best determined by experts working to a highly rationalized set of values. However well-intentioned they may be, regulatory schemes militate against producers of artisanal goods by demanding adherence to standards that have been designed for growers and processors operating on entirely different scales, whose target consumers are more likely to passively accept the quality judgments of distant intermediaries. Consumer responsibility is abdicated to the relevant authorities, and the long-term result is the increasing homogenization of the food supply. Small producers are therefore caught in a double bind, trying to meet the subjective standards of those who appreciate artisan foods and the ill-fitting regulations of national bureaucracy.

Casa Lanzarotti is a tiny farm tucked in the Apennine hills of Emilia–Romagna, in the province of Parma near its western border with Liguria. Iris, a Swiss-German who has been farming here with her husband since the mid-90s, claims that the farm's annual hygiene and organic certification bills run to nearly €900, basically securing her the right to use a certifying body logo. There are more than 20 authorized organic certifiers in Italy, a confusing jumble of varying prices and services. Iris has remained with the same certifier for years but feels exasperated by the annual ritual it imposes: 'They calculate that you have a certain amount of land, that you have a lab for processing food so of course this is extra ... We decided not to certify our honey because that would have cost about €200 and that's just about the profit we can make in a year from 10 beehives.'

Complaints about the cost of organic certification are rife, but artisan food producers feel particularly persecuted by the absurdly nitpicky strictures of food hygiene laws. The campaign Genuino Clandestino, which has made a public declaration of the fact that many small farmers are given no choice but to operate in the grey economy, has focussed most of its ire on food safety regulations. Affiliated to the Campi Aperti (Open Fields) organization in Bologna, Genuino Clandestino – through markets, public meetings and campaign literature – has tried to illustrate the ridiculous contrast between the high-quality food produced by small farmers and the wearying compliance regimes to which they're subjected. At Casa Lanzarotti, for example, Iris makes bread, jam and apple juice for sale at the weekly Parma farmers' market. Her workshop, or *laborotorio*, meets all the standard regulations but this has again come at considerable cost, more than many farmers can manage. 'In Italy they wanted to dictate from the beginning exactly how you have to do things. The lab we have over there for the jam is a multi-functional lab. It has to be three metres high, there has to be a certain proportion between light and window and volume of the room ... There has to be a bathroom, the bathroom can be without a window but the room in front of the bathroom where you change yourself needs a window. You need a cupboard for changing clothes ... Of course it makes sense if your logic is not to check the product at the *end*.'

The implication here is that these regulations embody the interests of big agribusiness. Emilia–Romagna is the home of the multinational Parmalat and Barilla corporations, to name just two of the region's major food processors. It can also boast an exclusive claim to *parmigiano-reggiano* cheese, balsamic vinegar of Modena, Parma ham and several protected varieties of wine and olive oil. The food industry is a major player in local politics and small farmers like Iris think that this gives them a license to write the rules. 'They can afford stainless steel machinery, other kinds of big tools to process food ... And they have to have means to protect themselves. So if you want to compete with them and set up the same kind of thing, you have to have what they have ... It's costly but that's not even the worst part. The worst is the paperwork. Hours and hours we spend on this stuff ...'

The production facilities at Casa Lanzarotti were designed to satisfy regulators, and built more or less from scratch in the shell of an old farmhouse. Farmers who retrofit or adapt an existing *laborotorio* will generally fail to meet these standards simply because the rules are realistically applicable only to new facilities. This means that their retail possibilities are restricted, at least if they want to market their products as organic. This is precisely what has happened to Luigi and Francesca, who produce honey, *pecorino* cheese, fruit preserves, olive oil and wine from their small organic farm in Umbria. Their lab has been adapted from an older workshop, with less efficient technologies replaced by modern equipment. Despite the age of the farmhouse, everything about the lab expresses a craftsman's attention to detail and the utmost care for quality. It is consummately clean, with gleaming tile floors, spotless work surfaces and a systematic ordering of materials. The food produced there, claims Luigi, could never make it to a mainstream market. Despite the appearance of care and professionalism, the room is just too small, the ventilation not quite right, the fire exit too narrow. Inspired by Simone and Mara's *mercatino clandestino*, about 50 km away on the other side of the region, Francesca and Luigi have initiated their own market near the town of Città della Pieve. Like their forebears, they have started modestly and cautiously, sending out a small number of invitations to friends and family and assembling about half a dozen farmers to sell their produce. They recognize that growing the market will be long-term project, particularly if it is to provide a genuine lifeline to struggling farmers. According to Simone and Mara, some producers who sell at every *mercatino clandestino* rely on the money earned there as a fundamental component of their income. In less established markets, vendors inevitably regard participation as a supplemental experiment to begin with, potentially morphing into something more substantial. The significance of the markets' financial impact on farmers is perhaps secondary to the networks of solidarity engendered by the events. For both buyers and sellers, the markets represent a way to revive community through food and ensure that money is prevented from bleeding out of rural areas and into distant city coffers. The goal, then, isn't several large secret markets but hundreds of small ones, acting as multiple sutures over the massive wound of the depopulated, industrialized countryside rather than an inadequate few.

The *mercatini clandestini* operate in a novel format, eliciting excitement and a sense of empowerment. Their newness and growing popularity shouldn't exaggerate their standing in Italy's unofficial trade in gastronomic goods, however. Enterprising Italians have been running underground food economies since the end of feudalism, many of which are officially tolerated. Mara and Simone point out that local Green Party politicians are regular attendees at their secret market and proved useful allies when the police came to confiscate the raw (unpasteurised) cheese being sold by a vendor in the market's early days. After a period of considerable worry about the market's future and the livelihood of the raw cheese producer, some benevolent intervention allowed them to continue as before, with one slight alteration – the raw milk cheese, according to a prominently displayed notice, was now sold 'for decorative purposes only.' Generally speaking, an autonomous underground food economy can thrive in Italy if it is not working in direct competition with another (read: Mafia-related) secret economy, if the region in question hasn't been fully transformed by corporate industrial agriculture and its political disposition tends to

favour the small and slow over the fast and faceless. These conditions
coalesce in several areas of Italy's traditionally left-leaning central
region, Tuscany, Umbria, Emilia–Romagna and Le Marche.

A few miles from Assisi, Spello is perhaps the quintessential
Umbrian hill town. Narrow streets and tightly adjoined houses of
local stone cut complicated patterns over its peak, twisting into tiny
alleys that coil around the city's topography into shadowy darkness.
A Franciscan monastery, encircled by high stone walls, occupies
the town's highest ground and claims its most panoramic vistas. The
view from up high takes in large industrial farms in the valley below,
terraced olive groves constricting the hills, and the green forested
peaks of the Appenines beyond. Potted plants, fruit trees and horticul-
tural gardens are visible everywhere, in large multi-generational family
homes, small plots jutting out from the city's stone foundations and
cluttering the balconies of apartment blocks. Food is the focus of
Spello's cultural and economic life. Evidence of this is everywhere,
from the glowing greenery of the surrounding countryside to the
densely concentrated restaurants, wine bars and independent food
retailers that line the smooth cobbled streets, many named after prominent Leftist intellectuals and revolutionaries.

'Did you see that little empty shopfront between the hotel and *tabac-
cheria*?' asks Karen, an American who migrated to Spello four years ago
to set up a city farm, an experiment in urban self-sufficiency. 'A
woman comes along twice a week with fruit and vegetables she's
grown. Her family owns the building, and she just sets up a stool and a
little cashbox and waits for the cooks from all the local restaurants to
buy her produce. All completely off the books, of course.'

Chugging up the cobbled hills in an APE, or three-wheeled farm
vehicle manoeuvred by motorcycle handlebars, she sketches the city's
shadow food economy. Mini-orchards in families' back gardens, a city
farm, herbs, flowers and fruit growing down alleyways and in public
squares ... To make her own project viable Karen has had to locate the
often spontaneous byways of informal trade that sustain small producers. She barters home-grown herbs and vegetables with a neighbourhood restaurant in exchange for meals, sells produce to locals from her
front door and swaps medicinal plants collected from the surrounding
hills for other goods. Apart from one tiny branch of a supermarket

chain in the centre of town, almost all of the food retailers are small and locally owned. Independent shops deal directly with producers and often buy in small quantities, a fact that accounts for the great number of olive oil and wine varieties that weigh on the store shelves. 'If it's good enough it will get sold,' says Karen.

A city like Spello offers a glimpse of creative and relatively autonomous economics, bound though they are by the impositions of capitalist hegemony at large: formal currency, swelling rents and land values, commodity prices determined by external markets and bank credit supporting many of the businesses that appear cosily 'independent'. These realities mitigate any temptation to see the grey economy as stimulating widespread revolutionary alternatives in the near future. The network-building potential of the secret markets holds greater transformative potential than their current economic effects, at least measured in the crude terms of gross productivity. In other words, the underground artisanal food market makes a miniscule dent in the national economy, but it nonetheless promotes creative resistance to capital's most oppressive processes. The model of the *mercatino clandestino* is useful precisely as that – a flexible platform on which to socially organize, conceive alternatives and experiment with novel forms of exchange. Food provides an ideal focus for such experiments because it is absolutely fundamental – to physical survival, obviously, but also to culture, so that its meaning, form and value are permanently subject to critical consideration. Participants in the *mercatini clandestini* should, at the very least, be inspired to question why buying good produce from local farmers is such a novelty – and only a quasi-legal one at that. Corporate propaganda, blandly wrapped in the rhetoric of 'choice', 'quality' and 'service', is easily resisted when real alternatives exist. Once again, food acts as a superior test case for this: a multi-sensory, culturally contingent experience, a node that joins social, ecological and economic consequences. Currently alternative economies must cohabit society with their parent structures, for better or worse. Some will be theoretically precise and full of revolutionary ambition, others more spontaneous and dependent on existing formalities of exchange. Practical experimentation is necessary in any case, and the guiding philosophy of many *mercatini clandestini* founders holds that 'If we don't do it, nobody else will.' 🐌

THORSTEIN VEBLEN AND THE

VIOLENCE OF LEISURE

Bernard Manzo

OTIUM CUM DIGNITATE – 'LEISURE WITH DIGNITY'. YOU
could take this to mean not just that leisure time should be
devoted to dignified and ennobling pursuits, but that leisure is
dignified in itself. As Herman Melville said, 'They talk of the dignity
of work. Bosh. The dignity is in leisure.' But what does this mean
exactly? Being dignified sounds a little bit too much like hard work.
Thorstein Veblen believed that the essence of dignity consisted in
being exempted from having to work. But, for Veblen, this was not an
ennobling thing. For Veblen, leisure was something bound up with a
system of status that was, in essence, cruel, its seeming innocence an
illusion.

The most famous work of Veblen – *The Theory of the Leisure Class* –
is a skewering of the pretensions of those inclined to associate wealth
with virtue. For Veblen, it is not that leisure is wasted on the rich: it is
itself the wastefulness of the rich. He directs his efforts, in *The Theory
of the Leisure Class*, towards a disdainful, artfully needling critique of
a regime of status that he considered exploitative and, ultimately,
violent. America in the late nineteenth and early twentieth century,
the Gilded Age, having emerged from the turmoil of the Civil War,
was a place in which vast fortunes could be made. It was a society, like
our own, in which status attached to wealth and the rich formed a class
with its own self-justifying mythologies; Veblen did not have much
time for those mythologies. His ideas call into question areas of life
that had not seemed to require explanation, and they centre around a

paradox: not only does he claim that many of the activities belonging to a certain form of life are a waste of time, but he goes on to say that their very pointlessness is their point.

For Veblen, wastefulness is honourable because it shows how much one can afford to waste. Vanity, vanity, all is vanity: the more futile the activity one engages in, the more it is a form of showing off, because it shows how little one needs to engage in anything useful. The idea is simple, but contrary to the way in which the activities that Veblen describes as 'waste' – ranging from playing sport to reading Virgil to going to church – are actually experienced. Veblen needs to establish whether these things really are 'waste', and why it is that waste might become honourable.

So why is wastefulness valued? Veblen begins *The Theory of the Leisure Class* with a quasi-mythic account of the evolution of society, a genealogy of morals. His story begins with society in a 'peaceable' condition, without much in the way of technology, without definite notions of property, and with much of daily life having a strongly communal character. What propels society from this stage is an increasing appreciation of the value of violent exploit: an increasing tendency to judge everything from the point of view of the fight. Several factors produce this mentality. Veblen claims that all human beings possess an 'instinct of workmanship', a sense of effectiveness. The expression of this instinct increases the productivity of society, as more effective ways of acting on the world are discovered, and it gives rise to an appreciation of effective action so that individuals are compared in terms of their personal effectiveness (Veblen terms this 'invidious comparison'). This instinct therefore produces a state of affairs in which society has a surplus of goods – a surplus that may be fought over – and in which the members of society are in the habit of comparing individuals with respect to their personal effectiveness and force. In addition to this, primitive societies tend, Veblen claims, to distinguish between two kinds of effective action: action on inanimate or inert matter, and action on animate entities – or, 'drudgery' and 'exploit'. The violent compulsion of 'animate' entities – exploit – is more honourable than the manipulation of inert matter – 'drudgery'.

Where there are surplus goods that may be obtained by conquest, and where there is a tendency to appreciate the capacity for exploit as a form of personal worth, successful predatory action becomes honourable, and signs of successful violence – trophies – become tokens of personal worth.

> With the primitive barbarian ... 'honourable' seems to connote nothing else than the assertion of superior force ... A honorific act is in the last analysis little if anything else than assertion of superior force ... The taking of life – the killing of formidable competitors – whether brute or human – is honourable in the highest degree. And this high office of slaughter, as an expression of the slayer's prepotence, casts a glamour of worth over every act of slaughter and over all the tools and accessories of the act.

Veblen maintains that ownership occurs once this mentality has arisen, and he claims that the primary form of ownership is an ownership of persons rather than things.

> The ownership of women begins in the lower barbarian stages of culture, apparently with the seizure of female captives. The original reason for the seizure and appropriation of women seems to have been their usefulness as trophics ... [The institution of ownership-marriage was then applied to other captives, producing the institution of slavery] From the ownership of women the concept of ownership extends itself to include the products of their industry, and so there arises the ownership of things as well as of persons.

This startling claim is presented by Veblen without any prelude (or, it must be said, any supporting evidence). It is a claim that involves some tortuousness of logic, for how can the 'products' of the 'industry' of slaves become the property of their owners if they are not seen as, in some sense, the property of those who made them? The willingness of Veblen to make this claim, however, is an indication of how much he

sees the basic institutions of society as essentially violent. He sees the
possibility of having something that is 'one's own' as depending on the
suppression of someone else.

As property, then, originates in a desire for honour, so the desire for
property is insatiable. Whatever others have, one desires to have more
than them, because this was the point of having anything in the first
place.

> The motive that lies at the root of ownership is emulation; and
> the same motive of emulation continues active in the further
> development of the institution to which it has given rise and in
> the development of all those features of the social structure which
> this institution of ownership touches. The possession of wealth
> confers honour; it is an invidious distinction.

The perception of what it is 'decent' to own, or 'demeaning' to lack,
therefore continually changes, as the members of a society concerned
with honourable ownership seek ever greater wealth and the 'base' or
'average' level of wealth moves steadily upwards. To stand out from
others one must continually seek to have more.

It is in this context that leisure, Veblen maintains, acquires a special
value. Since useful work has come to be associated with working for a
master and is therefore degrading, exemption from work has become
honourable. The 'leisure class' proper comes into being when the
'predatory' segment of society – those who engage only in the kind of
work deemed 'exploit' – no longer contribute through their activities
(hunting, looting and so on) to the sustenance of society (who needs
hunters when you have shepherds?). The 'leisure class' is perfected
when it becomes perfectly useless.

As it becomes important to provide evidence of leisure – of time
spent unproductively – a greater value is accorded to acquirements that
are time-consuming and useless: like a knowledge of obscure things
that are of no benefit to anyone, or a mastery of 'all that class of ceremonial observances which are classed under the general head of
manners'. The codes of decorum become extremely rigid. As wasting
time becomes a matter of status, so these codes are elaborated in such a
way that to acquire them takes time. As more and more activities are

prohibited because of their resemblance to useful work, so the rules concerning which activities are honourable and dishonourable become more subtle and complex.

> In persons of a delicate sensibility who have long been habituated to gentle manners, the sense of the shamefulness of manual labour may become so strong that, at a critical juncture, it will even set aside the instinct of self-preservation ... [A good illustration] is afforded by a certain king of France, who is said to have lost his life through an excess of moral stamina in the observance of good form. In the absence of the functionary whose office it was to shift his master's seat, the king sat uncomplaining before the fire and suffered his royal person to be toasted beyond recovery. But in so doing he saved his Most Christian Majesty from menial contamination.

Some might admire a king who would rather be toasted than move his chair. Not Veblen.

Veblen goes on to claim that, from the leisure of the masters, a kind of leisure for the servants develops. When the members of the leisure class acquire a larger number of slaves in their households, the servant classes come to be divided up into those who produce the things the household needs, and those who simply wait on the master of the household. The unprofitable servants make an elaborate show of attending to their master – performing the function of symbolizing his dominance – but much of what they do is merely ceremonial, and their uselessness shows that their master can waste his resources with impunity. They exist in a state of 'vicarious leisure'. It is all the better if they show evidence of a special training in ceremonial niceties, because this training must itself have taken up time, uselessly.

Leisure itself, as a token of status, comes to be superseded, to some extent, by conspicuous consumption – a consumption of the best goods as an indication of wealth – which gives rise to various forms of honourable wastefulness that show how much those who make these displays can afford to waste. Conspicuous consumption, as a way of showing that one has no need to work, has, in a sense, more scope for development than ostentatious leisure, because more stuff can be wasted quickly and dramatically. It is a more efficient form of waste.

Vanity, vanity, all is vanity. There is something irresistibly comic in the claim that Veblen makes: that certain highly valued aspects of human life are pointless and that their pointlessness is their point. His vision is essentially ironic. Human instincts are seen to work against themselves: the 'instinct of workmanship' creates a competitiveness that creates a competition in uselessness. Veblen presents his ideas in a style that is a powerful mixture of different registers – a language of scholarly detachment combining with a language of denunciation. Everyday vices appear all the more absurd for being described in a language of quasi-scientific detachment ('pecuniary emulation' refers to competition over how much you have, 'conspicuous consumption' to wasteful showing off). Veblen, moreover, makes use of terms – while insisting always that he is using them in a neutral, technical sense – that cannot but seem condemnatory: 'invidious', 'predatory', 'barbarian' and so on. He draws startling parallels – developing a comparison, in an entirely po-faced manner, between the successful businessman (or 'ideal pecuniary man') and the criminal, the 'delinquent'. The effect is a kind of morose comedy, a prophecy that is without engagement, because the ironic distancing makes all pretensions – even those towards the betterment of human life – seem absurd. He envisages a process of social evolution that does not make for human welfare and happiness, and, in his scheme of things, the efforts of individuals do not appear to matter very much, because the development of human society determines, rather than is determined by, their efforts.

So peculiar, in many ways, are the vision and style of Veblen that the quasi-scientific language can sometimes appear not so much a feature of a scientific method as a stylistic device adopted to intensify the pervading sense of the absurd, to mortify ordinary human concerns and pretensions. Veblen insists that he is strictly confining himself to the 'economic point of view', that other perspectives, informed by other values, are possible, and might even take precedence over this point of view. He also remarks here and there that the various activities that he describes as being pursued under the pressure of the rules of status do not necessarily have their origins in the regime of status. (Manners, for instance, might arise out of a desire to show good will, but it so happens that they are cultivated more and more as proficiency in the rituals of decorum becomes a matter of status.) But does his argument really allow for other perspectives? If a particular activity cannot be assigned to the processes of material production, Veblen describes it as 'waste', and having provided an account of why wastefulness might be valued, he can therefore suggest that he has explained why this wasteful activity might exist. All the positive values that cannot be absorbed within the life of the industrial process – values associated with individuality, with artistic expression, with the religious life – can be dismissed; indeed, they come under suspicion, because they appear to be complicit in violence.

This vision itself appears to proceed from a sense that relations between persons are set within a zero-sum game, in which all that enhances the life of one person is obtained at the expense of someone else. Zero-sum situations evidently do arise, and one can see how the institution of private property might generate them, particularly if the right to possession is treated as unqualified and absolute; but then, this right can be (and often is) treated as conditional, holding only where possession does not infringe the basic needs of others (the right to life trumping the right of ownership). To account for the existence of private property, one need not see it as the result of sheer self-assertion, sheer force. But Veblen does not simply maintain that property rights *can* produce exploitation and injustice but that property is created through violent dispossession and that it develops as a form of self-assertion against others, so that ownership is itself a show of force. The realm of industry seems to be, in his view, exempt from this, because it involves an engagement with, and exploitation of, non-human nature, and the products of industry are not, by virtue of the process of production, arrogated to anyone in particular. Industry overcomes conflict, Veblen suggests, not by producing an abundance of things (a surplus may occasion competition or unjust appropriation) but because those involved in the process of production are not in relationships of violent competition (or 'emulation', as Veblen would say) but in relationships of co-operation. But one notices here that the dynamic of exploitation or appropriation is not transcended; rather, it is simply re-directed to the non-human world of nature. What seems to be missing from this picture of things is a sense of the possibility of 'the gift', of what might be simply given, beyond relationships of dominance and aggression: a sense that there might be goods that are not acquired through dispossession or through work.

It is possible that some societies might consider exploitation honourable, and might value leisure as an index of exploitation. But then one can say that this is not all that leisure is, or all that it could be. To define leisure in reference to the leisure of the wealthy – as Veblen does – might be to reinforce the illusion of the omnipotence of money. Another approach would be to distinguish between true leisure and a simulacrum of it that exists primarily as a form of showing off: between true leisure and the 'leisure' that belongs to, or is appropriated by, a regime of status. Leisure is, in fact, simply a sphere of life in which things are done for themselves, not, as in the workaday sphere, in order to accomplish something else. By assigning a purpose of 'invidious comparison' to leisure, Veblen makes it into something that exists for the sake of something else: a tool in an ongoing competition for status. By envisaging leisure as an indirect expression of how much one has, he sees it as merely a sign of a power one might exert in the realm of utility rather than something distinct from that realm: he absorbs it into the workaday sphere of exchangeable commodities. Against this, by seeing leisure as a sphere of life where things are done for themselves, one envisages a realm where things are not exchangeable in this way; one sets a limit. True leisure – and the notions of inherent human value associated with it – could therefore become a basis for a critique of exploitative social relations; and one could condemn exploitative social conditions because they deprive the exploited (and, indeed, the exploiters) of the opportunity of experiencing genuine leisure.

Veblen seeks to expose a situation of violence but he does not reveal an alternative to violence. Another approach to unmasking the violence of society would be to discover ways of associating with others free from violence; and part of the ideal, or dream, of true leisure is that the forms of conflict that arise where finite, limited goods occasion competition can be overcome: that innocent forms of association – characterized by something like friendship rather than something like dominion – might be discovered. The question is ultimately whether one can hope, or trust, in such a possibility. 🐌

THE RETURN OF THE
ETON MOB

Toby Young

'WHAT SCHOOL DID YOU GO TO?'
I must have been asked that question a hundred times
during my first week at Oxford. This was in the autumn of
1983 and I was 19 at the time. I would always respond in the same way
– 'I went to a school called …' – until another fresher pointed out that
prefacing your answer with these words made it sound like you were
slightly embarrassed by your *alma mater*. You were telling the person
that the school you went to was so insignificant they wouldn't have
heard of it.

The boy who pointed this out had been to Lancing and had been
told how to answer this question by his headmaster. 'When people ask
you where you went to school, don't say, "I went to a school called
Lancing." Just say, "Lancing".'

I was surprised to learn that the headmaster of such a famous public
school suffered from an inferiority complex. Hadn't Evelyn Waugh
been to Lancing? But I was an innocent in such matters. I didn't know
that public schools divide themselves into four different categories:
'major', 'minor major', 'major minor' and 'minor'. Lancing was a
'major minor', apparently. William Ellis, where I'd done my A-levels,
was a state school in North London. Before that, I'd been to King
Edward VI Comprehensive in South Devon and, before that,
Creighton Comprehensive in Muswell Hill. The only time I'd been
asked what school I went to was at the back of a bus on the Seven
Sisters Road.

At Oxford, the penalty of giving the wrong answer was more severe than having your dinner money stolen. When I told people I'd been to William Ellis – or, rather, a school called William Ellis, since I could never bring myself to follow my friend's advice – they would always follow up with, 'And what sort of school is that?' I would explain that it was now a comprehensive, but that it had been a grammar school and that I was in the last grammar school year. Too much information, obviously, and guaranteed to make it sound as if I was embarrassed about having been to a comprehensive.

As the person took in this information – and they had invariably been to a major public school – I always had a sense of a door closing. The point of the question, of course, was to establish what class I was and my answer branded me as a bit *infra dig* – or, rather, I thought it did and it was that, rather than the school I'd been to, that led to my being ruled out. (According to Evelyn Waugh: 'It is essentially a process of ruling out. If you examine the accumulated code of precepts which define "the gentleman" you will find that almost all are negative.') When it comes to such questions, it is the manner in which you answer them that counts – how self-conscious you are, your body language – rather than the facts themselves. Being 'class conscious' is more *infra dig* than being middle class – though, to complicate matters, that is partly because being embarrassed by such questions is a hallmark of being middle class.

But why was I embarrassed about having been to a comprehensive? Surely, the less distinguished my *alma mater*, the more pride I should have felt about getting into Oxford? That was certainly my father's attitude. He liked to brag about my academic success to friends who'd lavished tens of thousands on their children's education only to see them end up at some red brick university. As far as he was concerned, it was proof of my intellectual merit.

Part of the reason I didn't feel more pride about having been to a comprehensive is that the atmosphere in Oxford at the time wasn't particularly meritocratic. Margaret Thatcher may have been an Alderman's daughter, but her election victories in 1979 and 1983 weren't perceived as a blow against privilege. On the contrary, it was as if the tide of egalitarianism that had swept Britain in the Sixties and Seventies had finally been turned. At Oxford, the Sloane Rangers and

the Hooray Henries were out in force. The Bullingdon Club, which
had been more or less dormant a few years earlier, sprang back to life.
The most popular parties were the ones thrown by Chapsoc – the
Cheese and Wine Appreciation Society.

Which isn't to say there weren't plenty of state-educated people
around – and some of them part of the university's social elite. Hugh
Grant, one of the most prominent 'Bright Young Things' of his generation, had attended a grammar school in West London. I missed him by
a couple of years, but the Big Man on Campus when I arrived was
Andrew Sullivan, who was then in his third year at Magdalen. He had
become President of the Union in spite of having been to a grammar
school in East Grinstead.

The reason Hugh and Andrew thrived where I stumbled is that they
were able to take on the plumage of Oxford's gilded youth. Any trace
of middle-class ordinariness was expunged and, to all intents and
purposes, they were indistinguishable from the sons and daughters of
England's grandest aristocratic families. When Hugh Grant later found
fame playing a succession of public schoolboys he liked to joke that he
was pretending to be the kind of person who used to call him 'oik' at
university. In fact, he had already perfected this act at Oxford where
he was known as 'Hughie'. (Point of information: No public school-
boy at Oxford would ever call a grammar school boy an 'oik' because
to be so crudely snobbish is a low status indicator – they were too
snobbish to be snobbish. Rather, the term 'oik' was reserved for those
who'd attended less distinguished public schools. George Osborne's
nickname in the Bullingdon was 'oik' because he'd been to St Paul's.)

Since leaving Oxford, Andrew Sullivan has carved out a career in
America as a 'log cabin Republican', championing a number of unfashionable causes. As an undergraduate, he was 'out and proud', making
no effort to conceal his homosexuality, but his social origins were
another matter. Before arriving, he reportedly taught himself
'Received Pronunciation' by listening to the World Service and in his
first year he started an organization called the Pooh Sticks Society,
inspired by the television adaptation of *Brideshead Revisited*. As a gay
Catholic conservative, he was the nearest thing we had to Sebastian
Flyte and he was happy to play up to that role. In retrospect, it seems

extraordinary that, for all his courage, the only thing he wasn't prepared to come clean about was his lower-middle-class background. Snobbery was the one aspect of English life he wasn't brave enough to challenge.

Or perhaps that isn't so extraordinary. The tendency of talented and energetic members of the lower middle class to abandon their origins and join the ranks of the upper middle class is hardly unique to Oxford. The 'aristocratic embrace' helps to explain why Britain's Industrial Revolution didn't produce a corresponding degree of political upheaval. As George Orwell puts it in *The Lion and the Unicorn*:

> After 1832 the old land-owning aristocracy steadily lost power, but instead of disappearing or becoming a fossil they simply inter-married with the merchants, manufacturers and financiers who had replaced them, and soon turned them into accurate copies of themselves. The wealthy ship-owner or cotton-miller set up for himself an alibi as a country gentleman, while his sons learned the right mannerisms at public schools which had been designed for just that purpose. England was ruled by an aristocracy constantly recruited from parvenus.

In a sense, the porousness of England's social elite meant that Britain wasn't as rigidly stratified as it seemed. Someone born on the wrong side of the tracks could gain admittance into the charmed circle. It wasn't the lack of social mobility that accounted for the peculiar character of the English class system, but the transformation undergone by those on their way up. With few exceptions, only those willing to ape the manners and habits of their superiors were able to win acceptance. They had to pretend they were to-the-manor-born and even though no one was fooled their willingness to engage in this charade was good enough. It was almost as if the privileged class demanded that anyone who wanted to be admitted to their ranks pay them the tribute of impersonating them. The essential thing was not to fool your superiors, but to flatter them.

It was my inability to do this that rendered Oxford inaccessible. I imagined I was being excluded because I'd been to a comprehensive, but that wasn't it. The Union elected its first ever comprehensive-educated President in 1986 in the form of Anthony Goodman. I can't even claim I disapproved of people like Anthony – or Hugh or Andrew – who did manage to penetrate the higher reaches of Oxford society. It wasn't that I was unwilling to engage in the necessary play-acting; I just wasn't very good at it. Like Philip Larkin, I was handicapped by self-consciousness.

In retrospect, I might have been better off trying to pass myself off as working class. If this was the era in which Oxford's public school elite were emboldened by the triumphs of the Conservative Party it was also the era of the 'mockney' accent whereby a significant minority of them – those that sympathized with the Labour Party – began to talk like stage cockneys. This was partly just the fashion at the time – their 'street cred' accents were accompanied by Levi 501s and MA-1 Air Force jackets – but it was also a way of signalling their political radicalism. During the Miners' Strike, it was not uncommon to see the son of a hereditary peer rattling a tin outside MacDonald's and asking passers-by to 'spare a few coppers' in the voice of a Dickensian pick-pocket.

In my chippy, state-school way, I loathed these characters even more than I did the 'rahs'. They were the beneficiaries of inherited privilege, yet they didn't want any part of defending the system that had conferred these benefits upon them. Not only were their manners perfect, but their consciences were clean. 'I'm with you, comrade,' was the message they wanted to convey – which was like having your cake and eating it as far as I was concerned. There was also plenty of evidence that their commitment to egalitarianism was only skin-deep. For instance, there was more than a trace of snobbery in their contempt for the Oxford University Conservative Association, which was dominated by boys from minor public schools. (It was the same snobbery that was detectable in the hatred of Margaret Thatcher by Antonia Fraser and John Mortimer.) They tended to win the glittering prizes of Oxford undergraduate life, such as the Presidency of the Oxford University Dramatic Society and the editorship of *Isis*, and they invariably passed them on to likeminded souls from the same background as themselves. Politically, they challenged the status quo at every opportunity – and they enjoyed the cachet of being high-minded socialists – but they did very little to upset the apple cart, socially.

What was so striking about my Oxford generation is that the identities they plucked off the shelf – the masks they wore – were located at either end of the class spectrum. Whether it was the 'swells' of the Bullingdon or the mockneys of the Labour Club, they all seemed to belong in an eighteenth-century comedy of manners. None of these stereotypes were in any sense 'real'; but everyone was following the same playscript in their heads. It was as if the class system existed, first and foremost, in people's imaginations and they then struggled to reproduce it without quite realizing what they were doing.

As the American sociologist Stein Ringen writes: 'What is peculiar in Britain is not the reality of the class system and its continuing existence, but class psychology: the preoccupation with class, the belief in class, and the symbols of class in manners, dress and language.'

Looking back, my hatred of Oxford's 'champagne socialists' strikes me as a bit uncharitable. Their social elitism, while certainly hypocritical, wasn't deliberate. On the contrary, like most of the behaviour I witnessed at Oxford that preserved the ancient hierarchies of English life it seemed almost involuntary. It was as though the class system was a sinister organism that had enslaved everyone within the city's walls, whether they'd been born in East Grinstead or a Scottish castle. No matter what our political beliefs, we were all press-ganged into keeping it alive. It was what Karl Marx refers to as an 'unconscious conspiracy'.

I left in 1986 with a good degree, thankful to have salvaged something from a pretty miserable three years. I had failed to secure the editorship of the magazine I set my heart on – it was given to an Old Etonian – and failed to win any elections at the Oxford Union. The one bit of extra-curricular activity I enjoyed was being involved in a society that campaigned to get more state-educated students into the university. I visited several comprehensives in different parts of the country, urging the best and the brightest to apply. I took some comfort from the thought that, in the long run, Britain's public school elite were on their way out – and as they began to fade, so too would the cult of the gentleman that had mesmerized the upwardly mobile for at least 200 years. Oxford might not be a meritocratic institution at present, but at least the colleges' admissions policies were trending in the right direction. Eventually, a meritocratic culture would emerge to compliment the new social composition of Britain's elites. Like George Orwell, I eagerly anticipated 'the disappearance of that horrible plummy voice', as well as its absurd mockney counterpart. The English class system couldn't survive, could it? Not in a modern social democracy like ours?

Fast-forward 24 years and at first glance this hope seems almost comic in its naivety. I had regarded Oxford University as an antediluvian relic – a throwback to an era in which social relations were still circumscribed by class. Now, the whole of the Westminster Village is beginning to resemble Oxford in the Eighties, with the same public schoolboys in charge. By 'the same' I don't mean people of a similar type, I mean exactly the same ones. Boris Johnson, who was President of the Union in 1985, is now the Mayor of London. George Osborne is the Chancellor of the Exchequer. David Cameron, who was two years beneath me at Brasenose, is the Prime Minister.

How did this happen? To a great extent, the elimination of the English class system was the post-war project. Even the Tories were committed to equality of opportunity. After Sir Alec Douglas-Home was trounced by Harold Wilson in 1964, a consensus quickly emerged that the party should never again be led by someone who had a 'grouse moor image'. From now on, only politicians from middle-class or lower-middle-class backgrounds would be eligible for the top job. Indeed, it was this consensus that killed off Douglas Hurd's leadership bid in 1990. He was ruled out on the grounds that he was the son of a peer and had been to Eton. 'This is inverted snobbery,' he complained. 'I thought I was running for the leadership of the Conservative Party, not some demented Marxist sect.'

Yet 20 years later, the Etonians are back on top. Among Cameron's close circle of political advisors, his stepfather Viscount Astor, his speechwriter Danny Kruger and his chief of staff Ed Llewellyn are all Old Etonians, as is Hugo Swire, the Minister of State for Northern

Ireland, and Oliver Letwin, the Minister of State at the Cabinet Office.

True, Nick Clegg went to Westminster, but few people would regard that as evidence of social diversity. The difference between Old Wets and Old Etonians is that the Old Wet thinks Westminster's the centre of the world, whereas the Old Etonian thinks the world ends three miles outside Eton.

So was John Prescott right to say that the Eton mob is back? Is the country once again being run by what Alan Clarke referred to as 'the Old Etonian cabal'?

It would be a mistake to see a Cameron victory as signalling the resurgence of the Old Establishment. That network of socially inter-woven men and women who wielded such power in the Fifties and Sixties, many of them connected to England's great aristocratic fami-lies, won't be returning to the forefront of British politics. The 'ruling class' no longer exists, not in the old-fashioned sense of a land-owning elite with a shared political outlook.

With the exception of Boris Johnson, the New Tories don't give the impression of being posh. They may not speak in mockney accents like the St Paul's educated Harriet Harman, but the plummy voice that was the hallmark of the ruling class for so long has been discarded in favour of something more 'classless'. David Cameron lives in a terraced house in North Kensington and is a fan of The Smiths. In the words of Matthew d'Ancona, he looks good in trainers. By some extraordinary sleight of hand, the Boys from the Bullingdon, who used to dress up like pantomime toffs, have re-branded themselves as meritocrats.

In a sense, they are meritocrats. By and large, the New Tories hail from the class Keynes referred to as 'the educated bourgeoisie' – a class that has proved very good at adapting to the 'meritocratic' culture of modern Britain. Among the families of the professional upper middle class, there has been an impressive focus on getting their children to leap the various hurdles that Britain's major public schools and ancient universities have placed in their path, such as competitive entrance examinations. Indeed, by the time the current generation of Conservative leaders arrived in Parliament, having worked their way up the greasy poll of the Party's Research Department, they could legitimately claim to have 'earned' their place at the top. It wasn't handed to them on a silver platter.

Of course, this doesn't mean that Britain really is a meritocracy. Schools like Eton are selective, but the pool of boys they select from is drawn from the most privileged strata of our society. And those boys that don't pass the entrance exam don't sink to the bottom as they would in a genuine meritocracy. As David Goodheart pointed out in a recent article in *Prospect*: 'Social mobility has always been "sticky" downwards – once people reach a certain level of wealth or position their children tend not to fall back too far ... When, for example, Big Bang swept out some of the dull but well-connected stockbrokers from the City they did not become binmen, rather upmarket estate agents.'

What's fascinating about our new lords and masters is that the electorate appear to have more or less accepted their claim to be meritocrats. They have taken them at their word. The reason being an Old Etonian is no longer an electoral handicap is that ordinary people don't think of an Eton education as giving someone a particular advantage in life. On the contrary, they think of 'class' as a thing of the past – an irrelevance. In this light, the Conservative Party's hostility to 'toffs' like Douglas Hurd has actually helped David Cameron. Far from being to-the-manor-born, he is seen as a striver who should be rewarded for having overcome the handicap of having been to Eton.

Cameron famously described himself as the 'heir to Blair' and he does seem much more like Blair's natural successor than Gordon Brown. Like Cameron, Blair is the product of an elite public school who successfully re-invented himself as a meritocrat to neutralize the charge that he was born with a silver spoon in his mouth. In order to maintain this façade, he was obliged to talk about Britain as a 'classless society' – yet it was also something the electorate wanted to hear – and still do. To a large extent, it was Blair's success in re-branding Labour as the 'party of opportunity' that explains his three election victories. As Mandelson says, it's not your backstory that counts in politics, but constructing a compelling narrative in the present. Whatever the shortcomings of Tony Blair and Gordon Brown, they have left Britain more at ease with itself on the class issue.

What's so extraordinary about this is that Britain is in many respects more class-bound than ever. In the mid-Eighties, the country seemed in the process of becoming a genuine meritocracy – all the social barometers were pointing in the same direction. Twenty-five years later, this trend has been reversed. According to Alan Milburn, Gordon Brown's 'mobility tsar': 'Children born – as I was – in 1958 were far less dependent on the economic status of their parents than those born in later years. Birth not worth has become more key to life chances.' Only 7 per cent of the population attended independent schools up to GCSE level, yet 75 per cent of judges, 70 per cent of finance directors and 45 per cent of top civil servants. Of the present government, 65 per cent of were privately educated. A staggering 75 per cent went to either Oxford or Cambridge.

The political triumph of the Notting Hill Tories is a vivid illustration of just what's gone wrong. There is no longer any room at the top. The ladder has been kicked away and, with one or two exceptions, those at the pinnacle of our society were born to a life of privilege. The joint project of successive post-war governments – the effort to dismantle the English class system – has proved a failure.

Ironically, the survival of the class system hasn't happened in spite of this effort but partly as a result of it. I'm thinking, obviously, of the dismantling of England's grammar schools. And I regret to say that my father, Michael Young, was partly to blame. As one of the Labour Party's in-house intellectuals in the Forties, Fifties and Sixties, he was a passionate critic of selective education. He was also the author of *The Rise of the Meritocracy*, a scathing attack on grammar schools. Indeed, he invented the word 'meritocracy' to describe a dystopian society of the future in which status was based on merit.

He regarded the 11-plus exam as an instrument of social exclusion, creaming off the brightest offspring of working class families and condemning the rest to secondary moderns. Not only did this deprive working class communities of their natural leaders, making them less capable of organizing themselves into a politically effective lobby, but it made those who weren't lucky enough to attend grammar schools feel like second-class citizens.

Along with Anthony Crosland, the architect of Labour's comprehensivization policy, he regarded equality of opportunity as ideologically suspect – a way of harnessing the widespread desire for equality and using it to legitimize social and economic inequality. Those at the very pinnacle of a meritocratic society might not inherit their privileged position, as their forebears had done, but its pyramid-like shape would be preserved. After all, if everyone starts out with the same chance then the resulting distribution of wealth seems fair, regardless of how unequal it is. In this way, greater equality of opportunity inevitably led to greater inequality of outcome.

Yet the effect of eliminating selection in the state education sector while preserving it in the private sector has had no impact on the pyramid-like structure of our society; it's just made it harder for anyone born at the bottom to climb to the top. A 2005 survey carried out by the Centre for Economic Performance at the LSE discovered that children born in 1958 had a greater chance of moving up through society's ranks than those born in 1970, largely due to the disappearance of grammar schools. 'The harsh reality is that in the bad old days of the 11-plus there was more social mobility than there is now,' says David Byrne, a Professor of Sociology at Durham University.

Not all comprehensives are failures. As most parents of children of secondary-school age know, there are some good ones. The problem is, you have to live within the catchment area for your son or daughter to qualify for a place. There is still a selection mechanism at work within the state system, only instead of being based on the 11-plus it is based on your postcode. In effect, the grammar school/secondary modern divide has been preserved, but middle-class parents can now buy their way into the better schools by moving into the right catchment areas.

The effect of the education policies pursued by both parties over the past 45 years has been to accentuate the advantages of being born to well-off parents rather than eliminate them. According to research published by the Cabinet Office in 2009, in 9 out of 12 professions there has been an increase in the proportion of people coming from better-off families over the last 20 years.

Oxford in the Eighties certainly didn't seem like a harbinger of Britain's future. If you look at that famous photograph of David Cameron and Boris Johnson in their Bullingdon tails, it looks like a self-conscious attempt to recreate our imperial past rather than a portrait of our future leaders. I thought that Britain was bound to become more meritocratic – the arrow of history was pointing in that direction – and that, when it did, the aristocratic tenor of the ruling class would be replaced by something more 'classless'. What I didn't anticipate is that the public school elite would abandon the culture of privilege and camouflage themselves as meritocrats in order to preserve their influence. The idea that Britain would take on the appearance of 'classlessness', while social mobility actually declined, didn't occur to me.

In many ways, this is the worst of all possible worlds. The society I encountered at Oxford, which gave the impression of being rigidly stratified while accommodating a high level of social mobility, begins to look quite attractive. Those who had sufficient energy and talent rose to the top – Hugh Grant, Andrew Sullivan – while those that didn't – me – could tell themselves it was because they weren't members of the lucky sperm club.

Contrast that with the society we have at present, which appears to be open and fluid – classless – but which is relatively stagnant. Those lumpen proles who are euphemistically referred to as Neets – Not in Employment, Education or Training – can no longer point to the class system to excuse their failure to rise. At the other end of the spectrum, the so-called meritocrats who now make up the ruling class lack some the redeeming qualities of the old-fashioned Tory toffs. The fact that Anthony Eden, Harold Macmillan and Alec Douglas-Home started life with such an obviously unfair advantage – and couldn't disguise that from themselves – meant that they were burdened with a guilty conscience. They felt under a moral obligation to justify their privileged status, hence their commitment to public service, their incorruptibility and their sense of *noblesse oblige*. In the words of Goethe, 'Really to own what you inherit/You must first earn it by your merit.' No such patrician sense of honour seems to encumber the New Tories.

Contemporary Britain isn't a meritocracy, but a chimeritocracy. The 'classless' style of the new ruling elite creates the impression that we've moved forward – that the ancient hierarchies have been broken up – but in fact we've gone backwards. When I went up to Oxford in

1983, people like me, who'd been educated in the state sector, comprised approximately 65 per cent of the student body. In 2006, the percentage of people admitted to Oxford from state schools was 53.5 per cent.

Of course, I could be wrong about the New Tories. David Cameron may prove to be the heir to Benjamin Disraeli rather than Tony Blair. His pledge to fix the 'broken society', and the speed with which he jettisoned the inheritance tax cut and accepted the need for a referendum on AV in negotiations with the Lib Dems, may be the modern equivalent of Disraeli's extension of the franchise. Perhaps he doesn't think of himself as a meritocrat, but has simply pulled off a cunning, Old Etonian trick whereby he is pretending to be less grand in order to defuse any potential hostility. Perhaps beneath the shiny façade he is a tweedy, old-fashioned gent.

I'll leave you with a quote from Nancy Mitford, writing in 1954 in response to Alan Ross's famous essay on U and Non-U:

> The English lord has been nurtured on the land and is conversant with the cunning ways of the animal kingdom. He has often seen the grouse settle into the heather to rise and be shot at no more. He has noticed that enormous riches are not well looked on in the modern world and that in most countries his genus is extinct. It may be that he who for a thousand years has weathered so many a storm, religious, dynastic, and political, is taking cover to weather yet one more. It may be that he will succeed.

Pete Willis

HUNTER, FISHERMAN, SHEPHERD, CRITIC:

KARL MARX'S VISION OF THE FREE INDIVIDUAL

Lee Rowland

WHEN THE HISTORIAN TRISTRAM HUNT REVEALED IN his recent biography of Engels that the famed communist was also in many ways a typical Victorian gentleman who liked to go fox-hunting and drink champagne, there was much amusement among the commentariat of the mainstream press. Hacks raised a knowing eyebrow at the hypocrisy of 'champagne socialism', fancying themselves penetrating iconoclasts by pointing out that this self-appointed champion of the working class was actually a hated bourgeois – a factory owner and *bon viveur* who was fond of eating lobster salad while lecturing on the evils of capitalism. After fairly and accurately summarizing Marx's *Capital*, and acknowledging Engels's vital contribution to this work, Hunt himself turns to a moral judgement:

> And yet one always had to remember that the funds which kept Marx afloat through *Das Kapital*'s long literary gestation, the money that powered the excoriating prose, came ultimately from the very same exploited labour power – the mill hands of Ermen & Engels [Engels's father's Manchester cotton business] ... [1]

The charge is clear – Marx and Engels were hypocrites, and their socialism fraudulent. They are given the treatment Western culture metes out to its wise prophets and visionaries and dissidents: they are ignored or misrepresented when possible, drowned out with gales of scoffing laughter when not – a reaction that will be familiar to all socialists who inexplicably do not live in North Korea, and to all self-proclaimed idlers who set up in business or have jobs. Hunt, to be fair, is not quite that bad. Nor is Marx's most recent biographer Francis Wheen,[2] who wrote in a similarly light-hearted and entertaining vein. But the general effect of their books is nevertheless trivializing. They have great fun telling us about Marx and Engels's booze-ups and fights and affairs and political scraps. They recount with glee that, for all the talk about production and the working class, Marx and Engels spent most of their lives bunking off, getting by whenever possible on their inheritances and by scrounging and begging, by embezzling funds from Engels's father's business, by playing the stock exchange, and only occasionally, and only if desperation drove them to it, by doing a fair day's work. While penning polemics on behalf of the downtrodden and dispossessed, the authors themselves lived carefree lives of great joy, seeming more fond of marathon drinking sessions, good food and cheap cigars than of political organisation or charitable work. It's amusing stuff, and makes for page-turning biographies. But is there, as implied, anything *hypocritical* about any of this? To prove that there is, you would have to show that Marx and Engels's actions and the way they lived their lives were in some contradiction or conflict with their stated beliefs, or with the content of their theories. Well, just what *did* they believe?

MARX AND ENGELS: PHILOSOPHERS OF ANARCHISM

This essay will focus mostly on the work of Marx – Marx and Engels worked closely together and were in more or less complete agreement anyway. Marx's writing ranges over 50 volumes, and over every subject imaginable, from art and poetry to economics and anthropology, from polemics against now-obscure and forgotten philosophers to seemingly ephemeral political pamphlets that are still in print and read by millions today. But there is a consistent, unchanging thread that runs through all of this work, and if you grab hold of it, and follow it, you can take a shortcut through the massive Marxist maze and cut to what's important. The thread is Marx's vision of the free individual. It is, in the words of Maximilien Rubel,[3] Marx as a theorist of anarchism.

It may seem strange to insist on the importance of the individual in Marx's thought. It seems strange because we are so used to hearing about the conflict between the demands of a free, essentially selfish individual on the one hand, and those of society on the other; between the 'free' market and state tyranny, between the wise individual and the unthinking mob. The first term of the contradiction is supposedly represented by capitalism, liberalism, the free market – in its extreme form, anarchism. The second term by socialism, authoritarianism, the state – in its extreme form, communism. Such ideas are part of our cultural inheritance. But although an inheritance may set us on the path to prosperity, it may also alienate us from life – and ultimately poison our efforts to become who we are, betray our true inheritance as human beings. And the latter is the case here, because the manufactured contradiction is a false one.

Marx's starting point was the individual. He was not opposed to the liberal-capitalist ideas we still hear so much about today; for who could be opposed to choice, liberty and freedom? He liked the ideas, but opposed the social arrangements that prevented them becoming a reality. For there is indeed a great obstacle that stands in the way of individual freedom. But that obstacle is not society, or the collective, or 'socialism', or other human beings as such. It's work. Here's Marshall Berman:

> The thing I found so striking in Marx's 1844 essays, and which I did not expect to find at all, was his feeling for the individual. Those early essays articulate the conflict between *Bildung* and alienated labour. *Bildung* is the core human value in liberal romanticism. It is a hard word to put in English, but it embraces a family of ideas like 'subjectivity', 'finding yourself', 'growing up', 'identity', 'self-development', and 'becoming who you are'. Marx ... asserts the universal right of men to be 'freely active', to 'affirm himself', 'to enjoy spontaneous activity', to pursue 'the free development of his physical and mental energy'.[4]

But why should there be a conflict between *Bildung* and work?

MARX'S FAIRY TALE

The argument is made best in Marx's masterpiece, *Capital*[5] – a book wrongly taken by most to be a dry economics textbook, but which is actually, as Francis Wheen rightly says, an ingenious satirical utopia in the mode of Swift. There is a key turning point in the book, at the end of chapter six, a moment of high drama, one of the most enjoyable in all of Marx's writings. In the build up to this moment, Marx has told us a fairy tale. It is the tale of freedom and equality, as told by the leading economists of his day, people like Adam Smith and David Ricardo. Marx accepts the basic truth of their story. The story he tells is in all essentials theirs. In outline, it goes something like this.

Once upon a time, there was an article of commerce, the product of an individual's labour, something made in order to be sold, a *commodity*. It matters not what this article is. It could be a yard of linen, a coat, a bottle of whiskey, a Bible, a watch. But this thing, as a commodity, has strange powers. Although as inert as a table, it develops in its wooden head a need for a social life and a change of scene, and its magic therefore brings together two creatures – two human beings who may or may not know each other, but who are summoned nonetheless by their own products to meet in the marketplace. In the hands of one of our ensorcelled creatures is the commodity. But he wishes to be rid of it. It is of no use to him, except in that he hopes it might bring him something that his heart – or stomach – desires. In the hands of the other is a commodity of equal value (or a quantity of money of equal value). The same considerations apply. The other creature too wants rid of his commodity. Our two creatures find, in each other's hands, the object of their individual desires. Their eyes gleam at the sight of them. All that now needs to happen is for the commodities to change hands.

Not all stories have happy endings – it might be that such meetings lead not to exchange but to nothing more than a parting of the ways. (Magic does not always work, and the story of crisis starts here.) But in our story, the magic happens, the deal is done. Each human creature, seemingly of his own free will, and according to law, decides to dispose of what is his, on condition that he receives in return the commodity in the other's hands. The contract agreed, both exchange commodities, then walk away as free men, both the richer for the encounter, both blissfully unaware and unconcerned with the other except in as far as it affects his own gain, his own interests. In this happy tale, an equal exchange has been made – neither man is better off than the other in terms of value. But both are richer nonetheless as they have disposed of the thing of no use to them and won instead just whatever it was their hearts yearned for. Meanwhile, our wooden-headed protagonist, the commodity, its desire for social life satiated, settles down in the world for which it was destined: the realm of consumption.

The setting of this story, what Marx calls the sphere of exchange, is an Eden of the innate rights of man, a world of freedom and equality. So far, so good. Unfortunately, the tale needs some modification before it can tell capitalism's story quite accurately. In the real world, the world in which we live, in which Marx lived, two people do again meet in the market. And, as before, one of them has in his hands a thing – a quantity of money – that the other desires. The other creature, though, comes to market in an unusual position – she comes empty-handed, she has nothing to sell – or *no thing* to sell, at any rate. (The story of how it came about that this poor soul should have nothing to bring to market is written in blood – you can find a version of it in the final part of volume 1 of *Capital*.) The two meet in this Eden of freedom. Then, something horrific happens. The money-owner changes shape; his face changes expression. Marx writes:

> When we leave this sphere of simple circulation or the exchange of commodities, which provides the 'free-trader vulgaris' with his views, his concepts and the standard by which he judges the society of capital and wage labour, a certain change takes place, or so it appears, in the physiognomy of our dramatis personae. He who was previously the money-owner now strides out in front as a capitalist; the possessor of labour-power follows as his worker. The one smirks self-importantly and is intent on business; the

other is timid and holds back, like someone who has brought his own hide to market and now has nothing else to expect but – a tanning.

Off they go, but where are they going? They head for a dark underworld – the hidden abode of production. They reach the entrance, which is barred with a door, and on the threshold there hangs the notice 'No admittance except on business'. At this door, you hang your coat for the day – along with your independence, your freedom, any notion of democratic participation, your self-confidence, your ability to make free decisions about what to do with your god-given energies, your self-respect. You hang your coat, and the door slams behind you.

In this story, then, as opposed to our first fairy tale, nothing at first changes hands when our two creatures meet in the market, but both first enter the workplace. But when we next see them both, emerging blinking into the daylight, and the two go their separate ways, we find that the capitalist still has in his hands his money, but it has magically increased in size. This he calls his profit. Our worker, however, leaves with nothing but an invoice for expenses. On cashing this in, then using the money to renew the energy and spirit drained in the dark abode, she finds that the prize she held has mysteriously vanished.

And so she sets off, once again, with nothing but her own hide, to market. And eventually, after a brief period of youthful illusion and optimism, she abandons all hope, all *Bildung*, at the door of the dark abode, along with her coat, and settles down for a lifetime of wage slavery.

FROM FAERIE TO REALITY

Surely most of us will recognize this story, and identify at once with the timid creature straggling along behind the smirking businessman. Anyone, at least, who has ever been for a job interview, and experienced the first day on the job for an employer, will see in this story a mirror for their own experience. When Marx in later chapters give us a peek into this dark abode of production, it is a Dickensian workhouse we see – the world of the Victorian factory, of 12-hour days,

overtime with shifts sometimes dragging on for 40 hours or more,
'accidents' and loss of limbs and mutilation due to the pace of work
and physical exhaustion, suffocating heat and toxic atmospheres, gaps
in the day filled up with the ever increasing demands of work, wages
insufficient to cover the cost of living, the wearing out and crippling
of the human body and mind as a sacrifice to the altar of profit-
making. To present the workplace as a hellish, dark underworld could
therefore hardly be held an exaggeration in Marx's day. Novelists,
journalists, factory inspectors, parliamentarians – all testified to the
horrors of the factory system. It was no fanciful invention of a socialist
with a grudge. But anyone who has sold his or her hide on the wage
market will recognize the story told in *Capital*, even today. The fact
that, in some parts of the world at least, the dark abode now has strip
lighting, new carpets, perhaps computers and printers and phones instead of spinning machines, contracts less devilish, wages less likely to
leave you hungry at the end of the month, is but a small weight in the
scale balanced against the crushing of the human spirit, the frustration
of our human nature, the betrayal of our birthright.

NICE IDEA, WRONG SPECIES?

Because that's what you leave at the door of the dark abode, according
to Marx's writings: your human nature. When you sell your hide to an
employer, you exchange your birthright for a mess of pottage. But
what is your birthright? What is human nature? People will often say
that Marx is all very well, but he didn't understand human nature (nice
idea, wrong species, as the sociobiologist E. O. Wilson put it). The implication in this charge is generally that Marx thought we could shrug
off our natural instincts and urges and instead become saints, giving up
all our wealth to the poor, sharing all our belongings, and so on.
Needless to say, there is *no basis at all* for this view in Marx's writings.

There are two main aspects to Marx's view of human nature, as spelt
out in his essays in the *Economic and Philosophic Manuscripts of 1844*.[6] The
first is that we are only truly human when we are free to work at activities of our own choosing, guided and directed and motivated by our
own minds, our own decision-making. According to Marx, 'free con-

scious activity is man's species character'. When the capitalist buys this ability to work, then turns it to his own ends, he perverts our human nature, and turns our free activity into suffering (for us) and profit (for him). The second aspect is that humans, although obviously biological individuals, *are also naturally and inevitably social beings*. We must avoid, says Marx, thinking about society on the one hand, and the individual on the other. Literally from the moment of our birth as individuals, we are bound up with social life, we are born simultaneously into a natural world, of cold and warmth and milk and table legs, and into a social world, of mothers and brothers, of schools and churches, of expected behaviours and reliance on others. We are at our happiest, not when we struggle alone as individuals against nature, red in tooth and claw — indeed, human life has never been like that in its evolutionary history — but when we work and play for and with each other. Free individuals in a free society would not confront each other, like the creatures in our fairy tale, as indifferent individuals, each looking only to his own advantage, but as true human beings, creatively active, treating each other as an end rather than a means to an end.

This view of human nature can help us make sense of Marx's otherwise puzzling comments about morality. How could Marx on the one hand dismiss and reject what he called 'bourgeois morality', and yet, at the same time, in *Capital* and elsewhere, employ moral language to condemn capitalism and praise, say, the honesty of the British factory inspectors? As Paul Blackledge[7] points out, what Marx was rejecting was the modern, liberal and Darwinian assumption that moral behaviour involves 'the suppression of natural desires that are seen as selfish and individualistic'. Marx instead followed Aristotle and the classical Greek conception of ethics and saw that being 'good' meant fulfilling human needs and desires — giving free rein to human nature, not suppressing it. The virtues, according to Aristotle, are those qualities that would enable individuals to flourish within a community. And because humans are only able to flourish within communities, Aristotle made a direct link between ethics and politics. Marx's ideas about human nature and morality start to make sense in this context.

They become clearer still if we consider the poetry of Lao Tzu, who may have lived about 2,500 years ago in China. This is an extract from the classic *Tao Te Ching*:

In the degradation of the great way
comes benevolence and righteousness.
With the exaltation of learning and prudence
comes immense hypocrisy.
The disordered family
is full of dutiful children and parents.
The disordered society
is full of loyal patriots.

. . .

Stop being holy, forget being prudent,
it'll be a hundred times better for everyone.
Stop being altruistic, forget being righteous,
people will remember what family feeling is.[8]

For Lao Tzu, benevolence, righteousness, duty and so on – 'bourgeois morality' – are second-bests. He's saying, if you don't have a genuinely free and ordered society ('anarchy is order', as the classic anarchist slogan has it), if you don't have a genuinely loving family, then you need to impose some kind of morality to keep it all together, keep it all working. If, on the other hand, you have a society where people live naturally – follow what Lao Tzu calls the Way, the Tao – if people are left alone to order their lives, then there will be no need for morality because 'people will remember what family feeling is'.

Our birthright, then, is the uncut wood of our human nature – and that nature rebels against enforced morality, forced labour and submission to usurped power. What we should do, as Lao Tzu insists throughout the book, is *not do*. 'Doing not doing.' Unforced, effortless, trustful accomplishment.

'COMMUNISM': REVERSING THE SPELL

At this point we have to start wondering about the contradiction we have set up between 'free conscious activity' – doing not doing – and the inevitably social character of our existence on the one hand, and on the other the fact that we and the vast majority of our fellow creatures spend most of our lives locked up in the dark and lonely abode of production. How can these contradictions be reconciled? By extending democracy. The democracy and choice and liberty and individual freedom that capitalism promises us in the sphere of exchange needs to set up home in the sphere of production. That door with the forbidding sign upon it needs flinging open. We need to let light and fresh air in. To return to our fairy story, and the commodities with strange and magical powers, this would mean reversing the spell – it would mean not handing over our creative and magical powers to things and bosses and money and markets; it would mean keeping those powers instead in our own hands, under our own control, mastering them, producing collectively and directly for our own needs as a community, rather than as isolated individuals for the alien needs of the market. This is what Marx meant by communism.

In fact, as Berman points out, Marx envisioned two very different kinds of communism. One, which he wanted and approved of, was a 'genuine resolution of the conflict between man and nature, and between man and man'; the other, which he dreaded, 'has not only failed to go beyond private property, it hasn't yet attained to it'. What this means is that, for Marx, genuine communism was only possible on the basis of the legacy of a mature and fully developed capitalism. The communism we have seen in the twentieth century, and which most people rightly dread and condemn, is more a kind of state-capitalism, brutally managing poverty and imposing industrial development. The years since Marx's death have seen very many examples of the second kind of communism; but none yet, unfortunately, of the first.

And what would this genuine communism look like? As many commentators have noted, Marx did not have very much to say about this. This is sometimes levelled at him as a criticism. But it's very much a logical consequence of his ideas about individual freedom, as outlined here. Marx could hardly say on the one hand that he was in favour of the free development of individuals, and then lay down a universal plan, for everyone to follow and obey. Of the little that he did say about communism, perhaps the most famous statement, alluded to in the title to this essay, is the following, taken from *The German Ideology*:

... as soon as the distribution of labour comes into being, each man has a particular, exclusive sphere of activity, which is forced upon him and from which he cannot escape. He is a hunter, a fisherman, a herdsman, or a critical critic, and must remain so if he does not want to lose his means of livelihood; while in communist society, where nobody has one exclusive sphere of activity but each can become accomplished in any branch he wishes, society regulates the general production and thus makes it possible for me to do one thing today and another tomorrow, to hunt in the morning, fish in the afternoon, rear cattle in the evening, criticise after dinner, just as I have a mind, without ever becoming hunter, fisherman, herdsman or critic. [9]

Francis Wheen wonders at the rural examples Marx and Engels chose in this passage, given Marx's famous hostility to 'the idiocy of rural life'. But it seems clear that they needed examples, not so much of exactly what would go on in communist society, but of activities in their own society which everybody would readily grasp as 'free, conscious activity', not forced labour. I presume that 'fisherman' conjures up for us, as for Marx and Engels, a happy fellow, sitting on a river bank, doing just as he pleases, not a poor soul driven from his bed on an icy winter morning to trawl the sea bed to provide fodder for the city's wage slaves.

No one can know what a future communist society will look like. But what we do know is that, until we are as happy as a fisherman at our work, then we have some way to go before we come into our inheritance as human beings.

THE LAUGHTER OF FOOLS

We should now be in a position to answer the charge of hypocrisy with which we began this essay. Is there, in any of the writings of Marx and Engels, any moralizing commentary on what individuals living within capitalist society should do with their lives? Do they have anything to say, for example, about what kind of jobs workers should take? What the rich should do with their money? What capitalists should do with their capital? Whether or not it's acceptable for individuals to set up in business, for workers to join communes? What the state should do about the problems capitalism throws up? Do they tell us what kind of relationships we can enter into and with whom, what kind of food to eat, what it is acceptable to drink? Should socialists renounce all worldly goods and live a monkish existence of poverty, charity, duty and brotherhood? No. Not a word. The laughter of the scoffers stands revealed as the laughter of fools who cannot distinguish between Marx's social theory and Christianity.

Marx, in the Victorian parlour game of 'Confessions', once gave his idea of happiness as 'to fight', the vice he most detested as 'servility', and his motto as 'doubt everything'. The scoffers looking for some moral code in Marx would be better to start with his 'Confession' and his own words than with their preconceptions and ignorance.

Notes

1. Hunt, T. 2010. *The Frock-Coated Communist: The Life And Times Of The Original Champagne Socialist.* London: Penguin.

2. Wheen, F. 1999. *Karl Marx.* London: Fourth Estate.

3. Rubel, M. 1973. *Marx, theoretician of anarchism.* L'Europe en formation, No. 163–164, Octobre–Novembre, 1973. Available in translation at: http://www.marxists.org/archive/rubel/1973/marx-anarchism.htm

4. Berman, M. 1999. *Adventures in Marxism.* London: Verso.

5. Marx, K. *Capital.* 1990 (first published 1867). Translated by Ben Fowkes. London: Penguin.

6. Marx, K. 1973. *Economic and Philosophic Manuscripts of 1844.* London: Lawrence and Wishart.

7. Blackledge, P. 2008. 'Marxism and Ethics.' In: *International Socialism.* Avaiblable at: http://www.isj.org.uk/?id=486.

8. Lao Tzu. *Tao Te Ching: A Book About The Way And The Power Of The Way. A New English Version by Ursula K. Le Guin.* 1999. Boston and London: Shambhala.

9. Marx, K., and Engels, F. Edited by Arthur, C.J. 1970. *The German Ideology.* London: Lawrence and Wishart.

CONDUCT DURING
DEBATES AND ARGUMENTS

OR

ARGUING:
A SCIENCE AND AN ART —
Perfected

N. M. Gwynne

A debate is conducted through argument.
Now argument is reasoning to settle a matter of doubt.

Saint Thomas Aquinas: *Summa Theologiae*, 2a 2æ:10, 7

PREFACE

IT IS DIFFICULT TO OVERESTIMATE THE IMPORTANCE OF this subject; it really is. It is possible to be right on a matter, and to have all the evidence and logical arguments one needs in order to be able to prove that one is right, and yet ... It is possible, in short, to be in a position to win an argument decisively, perhaps for the great benefit of one's 'opponent', or for the great benefit of oneself, or for the great benefit of both, and yet ...

That is to say, it is possible to have all these advantages and incentives and yet to lose the argument, to lose it completely, disastrously and irreversibly.

All this is possible, and it happens all too often. The fact is that debating and arguing are not simply a science, though they certainly are that. They are also an art, and a very important art and a very demanding art, and for many people an art which is exceedingly difficult to acquire. It is an art which requires self-knowledge, a constant appreciation of the needs of one's 'opponent', and, perhaps for most people, very considerable self-discipline. In fact, it often requires going massively against one's nature. (As always in these notes, I am using the word 'opponent' simply in the technical sense of referring to the party opposing your position, not with any implication of hostility between you and him. The aim and hope is that you and your 'opponent' should both be at one in the pursuit of truth, and in agreement that you are engaged in the best means of doing this.)

'Not simply a science' but 'also an art'? What, then, is the difference between science and art? That is important in all areas of philosophy, even in the matter of how I am writing this piece! And it is certainly important in the arena of debating and arguing. It is worth, therefore, spelling out the answer hallowed by tradition:

The fundamental difference between science and art is that *science* refers to *knowledge*; *art* refers to *practice*. From this it necessarily follows:

1. True science, based on universal laws, is valid for all men (including women, here and elsewhere in this essay!) always and everywhere. Art is more personal, and more changeable according to times and places.

2. Science is acquired by *study*; art is acquired chiefly by *practice*. Certainly science may have a practical purpose, and indeed certain sciences, e.g. logic, medicine, etc., may also be arts; but the formal difference remains. As *sciences* they deal with what *is*, with the truth, and with *the reasons of things*. As *arts* they deal with the *production of what does not yet exist*, with *the practice* and with *the action*. A man may have the complete science of medicine without ever applying it. He knows the causes and remedies of diseases without using this knowledge. On the other hand, a man may possess only the art of medicine. His own experience, or that of others, may have taught him the value of certain plants or remedies which he may use to good effect without knowing the reasons why they are beneficial.

As to the category of arts, a little further clarification is needed, for the sake of complete understanding. Arts are divided into (a) *useful* or *mechanical* arts, on the one hand, and (b) aesthetic or fine arts, on the other hand. The *useful* or *mechanical* arts tend to the production of something *useful*, obviously! The aesthetic or fine arts tend to the production of something *beautiful*. The artisan, or handicraftsman, will select materials such as wood, steel, or stone in order to make something useful, a table, a saw, or a house. This object itself is destined to serve a purpose; it is a means to something else, not an end in itself. The *artist* tries to produce something which is *an end in itself,* and not simply a means.

Yes, it is often difficult to draw the line between the two because the beautiful is also frequently useful, as perhaps most obviously in the case of a building; but, still, the two aspects must be distinguished.

And now, as to the ability to dispute competently and effectively...

From what we have seen and shall be seeing, disputing is clearly a science, the rules of which must be learned and adhered to. Equally, however, it is very much an art. Knowledge of the rules must be put into practice. And this can only come from study, watching others, practising, learning from one's mistakes, and so on.

A useful art or an aesthetic art? Basically, even at its most eloquent, it is not one of the fine arts, for it aims at persuading others, whereas fine arts tend primarily to the production of beautiful works without regard to any other purpose except the satisfaction of the mind's aspirations toward beauty. At least in theory, argumentation *can* also be a fine art – for instance, if the grace of the gestures, the harmony of vocal inflections, the charms of the style and composition, etc., are actually intended for an artistic purpose. But such considerations need not concern us here!

And now, at last, to the point.

* * *

I.
SOME ESSENTIAL BACKGROUND
TO THE ACTUAL RULES

1. Learn to love, respect and even venerate arguing, for at least these three reasons:

First, as Saint Thomas Aquinas implicitly pointed out in the quotation from his *Summa Theologiae* which I used as the introductory text, arguing in the context of debate is, according to the natural order of things, the *only* way of reaching the truth on a very large number of important subjects, some of them possibly even of life-and-death importance. And truth must always have priority for our devotion, before any other single factor, or combination of factors, in our lives.

Secondly, in cases of any complexity, even if we *are* right at the outset, we cannot necessarily be *certain* that we are right – sufficiently confident about it – until our position on a subject has been *tested*. And argument is the best means of testing, very often the *only* means of testing. Indeed, when we are forming a judgement on a position, especially a controversial position, and even more especially a position which has moral consequences, we should make it a matter of pride – in the best sense of that word – to look for the person most competent to refute our position if we are wrong, for the purpose of testing our position by debating it out with him.

This is such a crucially important point that I am not going simply to rely on its being self-evident as stated, though I hope it is that. Out of a multitude of confirmations by people in a position to know that I could offer, here is a fairly recent one, well-expressed by a Canadian judge on an important judicial occasion. Veteran Canadian judge of the Federal Court of Canada, Mr. Justice James Hugesson, to a security conference in 2002.

> The Justice Department lawyers strive to be fair at security certificate hearings, but there is no substitute for having two opposing parties reveal the shortcomings of the each other's arguments. It does not matter how good and how honest the lawyer is. If you have a case that is only being presented on one side, *you are not going to get a good case*. (Emphasis added.)

Thirdly, our skills in this discipline – the discipline of arguing – can crucially affect those whom we are in a position to influence, possibly for their enormous benefit.

2. Recognise that there are times when testing, as best we can, conclusions we have arrived at by the reasoning process is actually morally *obligatory*, a grave duty, and when the only really adequate test is to submit them for cross-examination; that is, to the ordeal of debate.

This applies *especially*, I am afraid, when recognising such a duty will seem most tiresome to us, or even worse than tiresome.

This necessity typically occurs when we are faced with a decision with moral consequences. In such situations, most people are going to be tempted to take the decision which suits their *preference*, if possible; and, in consequence, their reasoning is all too likely to be clouded by what they *want*. And anyway, it is notorious that even the wisest people are far more vulnerable to error when advising *themselves* than when advising *others*. Obviously a sense of proportion must be kept, and one should not feel obliged to debate out the smallest and least consequential decisions. But, for a decision of any importance, the appropriate measure is to find the person likely to be most competent to expose our reasoning, our conclusions and our intended decisions as incorrect, if this can be done, so as to give them all the best possible test.

This is an application of the natural-law principle, '*Audi alteram partem*' – 'Hear the other side'. That is a principle which is completely fundamental in philosophy, and has always been enshrined in the laws of every civilised nation, including the body of law which applies in almost every English-speaking country, the body of law known as the English Common Law. For confirmation, see again what Mr. Justice James Hugesson said (above).

3. We must always remember, too, that the purpose of any argument or debate is *to arrive at a conclusion*. Thus an argument's whole object is *to pin down* one side or the other. Don't be put off by an objection, on the part of the other party, that he is '*not* going to be told *by you* what to do.' That is a cheat on his part, if he uses it. It is not by *you* that he faces being tyrannised, nor you by him if it turns out that he wins the argument. It is *objective truth*, arrived at by logic, which is being 'domineering'; that is to say, truth – objective reality – which is external to both of the parties. And we are all of us *obliged* to be 'tyrannised' by *all*

reality, just as much as we are obliged to be 'tyrannised' into accepting that two-plus-two equals four, obviously, and that causes have effects, inevitably.

4. Further to the previous paragraph, remember too that a conclusion can *always* be arrived at in an argument. That is to say, if both parties to the argument are in good faith and argue fairly, *it is literally impossible that they will not reach agreement by the time the discussion is concluded*. Indeed, if this were not the case, arguing would be a pointless exercise, even a fatuous one.

In this regard, beware *especially* of the 'clever-clever' way of concluding an argument, much used nowadays and often self-righteously: 'We must agree to disagree'.

This warning is *not* at odds with the very important principle '*In dubiis libertas*' ('where there is doubt, liberty'), which should indeed be constantly born in mind and practised. Yes, it is indeed possible for an argument to end up without either one side or the other having been 'victorious', i.e. proved right. But ... *if* the debate is fairly and accurately conducted, this will be clear to *both* sides, and *not* a matter for the arbitrary decision of only one side. In other words, both parties will have seen and agreed that, in the light of evidence at present available, certainty is impossible, and both positions can legitimately be held *as opinions*. (There can, however, then still be room for useful debate as to which opinion is the better one.)

5. So important is this last point, and so utterly contrary to what is promoted by the 'deep thinkers' of the present day, that it is worth developing and emphasising it.

Arguing is *not* a game for us to play when we have the leisure and the fancy. As already made clear, it can be a *necessary activity*, sometimes a *gravely* necessary activity. And it is *purposeful* in its nature. Its objective, as already stated, is to *pin down* both sides, to leave no possible avenue of escape, sometimes in establishing facts, sometimes in establishing duties, sometimes both.

The *science* of arguing is to know the debating 'mechanics' by which the 'pinning down' can be achieved. The *art* of arguing is to do this in the most efficient and persuasive and acceptable manner.

Once again, the object of a discussion involving argument is to pin

down or to be pinned down in a position, and, in consequence, nor
mally in a duty or a set of duties. A right to our opinion? Freedom of
speech? To think simply as one *wishes* to think is a *capability*, not a right.

Our only *right*, as also our duty, is to think correctly and honestly.
Similarly, 'the right to say anything one wants' is at best a glib catch-
phrase reflecting a *physical capacity*, and *not a moral right*. To 'speak
wrong' is an evil that society may *tolerate* in most cases, but it is still an
evil, and there can be no possible *moral* entitlement to it. (And, it is
perhaps worth making the point that, in a teacher, teaching what is
false is a very great evil, and most certainly should *not* be tolerated.)

2.

THE RULES OF CONDUCT THEMSELVES

1. Before you engage in an argument on any subject, any subject whatever, *always* ensure that, *however* strongly you may believe that your
starting position is the correct one, and *however* strongly you may feel
about the importance of the subject under discussion, you are not –
absolutely not – *emotionally* attached to your position. Do not start
arguing until you have made sure of this.

If you break this rule, you will do no good to yourself or to the
person with whom you are arguing. The essence of good arguing is
coolness, calmness, quiet objectivity, and so on. And if you have not
got this *internally*, that fact – that deficiency – is going to show up
externally. And the exposure will be to your disadvantage, even to the
extent of making a fool of you. You will see the enormous importance
of all this if you recall people who have impressed you with their skill
at arguing – and also people whom you have clearly seen to be hopeless
at arguing, without any power to convince.

To put it another way, always remember that what matters is not
your victory or avoidance of defeat, but *the truth*. You must be *dominated* by truth, and that means dominated by *objectivity* – not by preju-
dice, habit of mind, dislike of changing your mind, fear of losing face,
and other things which have nothing to do with establishing the truth
in your mind or in the minds of others.

2. Elaborating further on the previous paragraph, always remember that *the truth* is what you are aiming at during the argument, *not* victory at any cost. It is *the truth* that must triumph, not necessarily you.

3. It follows, from what has been said so far, that the aim of an argument should always be to get to the bottom of the topic under debate.

4. Always argue against *exactly* what has been said, *exactly* as it has been worded, unless you yourself can genuinely word it better. Take the greatest care not in any way to misquote or misrepresent the other party when addressing yourself to what he has said.

5. Never, never 'fudge' if you look like being caught out. If you start finding yourself tempted in this direction, at once make whatever retraction is necessary, even if that means retracting your entire position and acknowledging to the other party that he is absolutely right.

6. Further to number 5 above, always be prepared to concede instantly to a valid point made by the other party.

7. Be prepared to stand by *exactly* what you say, and *only* by exactly what you say. From this it follows that, if it turns out to be necessary, you should withdraw what you have said and re-word it.

8. Developing that last point, speaking and writing come attached to obligations. It can often – perhaps very often – be legitimate for us not to open our mouths or pick up our pens, *but*, once we have done either, *we have responsibility for what we have said or written*. We have now incurred that responsibility. We are morally obliged, if challenged, either to defend what we have said or written or to withdraw it.

In other words, what is *not* open to us is to launch our words into existence, so to speak, and, if challenged, respond: 'I have said what I want to say and that is all there is to it', or 'I have told you what I have told you because I thought it worth saying, but I'm not going to indulge in pointless arguments', or 'I am simply too busy to go into the matter any further; I have too many other priorities.'

All those are failures to honour the responsibilities you have voluntary incurred, and are in effect cheats. If you are going to be governed by such considerations, you should have thought of them before incurring the responsibilities which come with utterance.

9. Further to number 8 above, take the greatest care about the *wording* of what you say and write. Word it exactly as you are prepared to

defend it, and, in deciding on your wording, anticipate all reasonable arguments that might be raised against it. In other words, try from the outset to make your argument, *as you have worded it*, assault-proof.

10. And further to numbers 8 and 9 above, watch the other party carefully, to make sure that he does not get away with rewording what you have said, and thus of bringing off a victory by 'proving' you 'wrong' on a position that you do not in fact hold; in other words, on a position which is subtly different from the one you are arguing. This tactic is often used, and all too often it creates sufficient muddle to leave you apparently having lost an argument that you should have won.

11. Developing number 10 above a little further, and also developing an earlier point about making sure you understand exactly your 'opponent's' point and/or that he understand yours:

   (a) In the case of yourself, do not hesitate to repeat his argument before answering it, so that both you and he can see that you have grasped it correctly (and also so that he cannot wriggle away by claiming that he had in fact put a slightly different argument which – he now claims – you are avoiding answering!).

   (b) In the case of your 'opponent', try, without appearing aggressive, to find a way of getting him to repeat your argument so that you both of you have confirmation of *exactly* what it is that he is about to address. These precautions may often be unnecessary, in which case there is no point wasting time by including them. Often, however, they are all too necessary, and virtually indispensable if you are to reach a useful conclusion.

12. As the debate proceeds, insist that the other party keeps at least as strictly to the rules of debating-logic as is necessary for the purpose. If, for instance, he asks a question which in fact amounts to several questions, and which therefore simply cannot be given a single answer, or if he repeatedly doesn't answer the exact point you have made, or, however unconsciously, falls into equivalent 'cheats', stop the discussion at once until the *principles* governing the conduct of such discussions have been established and agreed between you. Evidently, this must be done with the utmost tact, because, inescapably, you are implying a certain amount of arguing-incompetence (or worse) in your 'opponent'. But somehow it must be done, the only alternative

being to abandon completely the debate. There is simply no purpose in proceeding further if there is not agreement between you on 'first principles', and to do so would be very unwise as well as useless.

And do not be deflected by accusations by your 'opponent' that, when you broke off to introduce the subject of 'first principles' of debate, you were embarking on a digression, as a means of avoiding, rather than facing up to, what he had just said. First principles *always* take priority over anything else. They are the foundation on which the whole discussion must be built

13. Scrupulously avoid, to the maximum extent you can, all atmosphere of competitiveness between you and the other party. The *only* competitiveness should be in politeness, restraint, calmness, straightforwardness, etc. And, in respect of these, this is a competition that you should never, never, *never* lose.

14. Above all, never 'raise your voice', whether literally, or in the violence of the words you use, or in any form of denunciation of your opponent. There is no exception to this rule, as you will see from the examples of the great arguers/debaters of the past. Even if you are finding your opponent so hopeless in his consistent cheating, and so evidently in bad faith in his whole approach, that you decide to abandon the discussion, do not 'let him have it' in the manner in which you bring the discussion to an end. There are many reasons for this. For instance:

    1. It is undignified.
    2. It gives your opponent an excuse, however unreasonable, for blaming *you* for the termination of the discussion, on the grounds of your bad behaviour not his.
    3. There is even the reason that, however 'impossible' he may be, you never know what you might want of him in the future, perhaps in the form of information you need and which only he can supply; and it is simply quixotic and pointless – gaining you nothing except perhaps some internal gratification – to close down your options without objectively good reason.

Yes, you may very well in such circumstances be tempted to close the discussion down in the most scathing way you can think of, and you may be satisfied that he deserves everything you can throw at him and more. But I have already pointed out that the correct conduct in debate requires self-discipline.

15. This applies just as much, and indeed if anything more so, if your 'opponent' should raise the temperature. (To remind us, I am using the word 'opponent' simply in the technical sense of referring to the party opposing your position, not with any implication of hostility between you. The aim and hope is that you should both be 'at one' in the pursuit of truth, and in agreement that you are engaged in the best means of doing this.) If your 'opponent' should raise the temperature, *do not respond in kind.* If anything, become quieter and more deeply courteous.

This is not merely right conduct in itself. You will find that it gives you a very big advantage. The blunt fact is that the one who raises his voice has, by doing so, already lost the argument. And make sure that, if anyone puts himself in that position, it is your 'opponent' and not you who does it, no matter what – and however great – the provocation.

Note, though, that what has been said in the previous paragraph is not irreconcilable with the undoubted fact that some of the best and meekest debaters have been, to say the least, not only loud but even merciless in their denunciations of others, including people they have debated with. Such denunciations can certainly be permissible; they could even sometimes be obligatory. And indeed possibly the most terrifying denunciations of all were made by the ultimate in humility and meekness, Jesus Christ Himself – see Matthew 18 and shudder at the thought of being on the end of a public tirade such as that. But these are public matters when the public good demands it. And they bear no relation to one's conduct in private, which, as already emphasised, should invariably be scrupulously calm, dignified and so on.

16. If it should occur that, despite your best efforts, your 'opponent' has so far raised his own temperature that he is intellectually out of control, arguing loudly, passionately and illogically, temporarily close down the discussion if possible, with a view to reopening it as soon as possible in the future (preferably on the next day). However inconvenient this may be, it is normally preferable to continuing at the time. There is simply no realistic chance of getting anywhere if – and as long as – he is in this state.

17. Unfailingly avoid both lengthily worded arguments and multiple arguments (in other words, making points which require more than

one answer), and – politely – confine your opponent to doing the same.

18. On the subject of 'raising your voice', there is a form of doing this which must be steadfastly avoided, no matter how great the temptation. However certain you are that you have right on your side, in what you are putting forward and defending, be *tentative* in the *manner* in which you put your case. Remember unfailingly that it is not *forcefulness*, or any other rhetorical flourish, that must carry the day. This is for two reasons:

    1. Forcefulness generates resentment.

    2. The fact is that you don't *want* to convince by rhetoric which might leave the listener reluctantly defeated by not very convinced or only half-convinced. It is the *logic* of what you say which must win, not your personality or rhetorical powers.

       This is absolutely not to suggest that rhetoric has no place, and certainly you owe it to your 'opponent' to put your logic in the most convincing manner you can manage. All that is being asserted here is that it is not *primarily* rhetoric which must win, but rather eloquence-assisted logic.

19. Further to number 18 above, *never* include as part of your argument anything resembling '…which cannot be denied' or '…which stands to reason' or '…which is obviously true'. If anything in your case falls into that category, and you think it useful there to suggest this in order to save time, precede such qualifications with a question. For instance: 'Do we agree, as a starting point, that there is no disputing the fact that …?' And, if he *doesn't* agree, drop the question and prove the truth of that point before going any further. (And, if he is so obtuse that he refuses to accept what is *genuinely* obvious, and indeed what he himself would acknowledge as obvious if it weren't inconvenient to his case for him to admit it, there is no purpose to be gained by proceeding another inch in the discussion.)

20. And here is yet another form of 'raising your voice' which is not permissible, arguably the worst one of all. However obtuse your opponent appears to be in his responses to your arguments, never, never attack his supposed *motives* for saying whatever he says, for instance by alleging that he is refusing to concede your point because

he does not want to or it does not suit him to. Indeed, never attribute motives to him at all, in any circumstances, no matter how apparent it may be to you that he is not answering honestly and fairly because he does not want to lose the argument, or for some other reason not directed exclusively to arriving at truth. In other words, never accuse him of dishonesty in his answers, even by implication, let alone directly.

This is not to deny that your suppositions of unworthy motives, which, whatever they are, amount his being dishonest in his manner of answering, may perhaps be justified. (Not always though – he may have genuinely missed the point, or you may have misunderstood the point he is making.) But the crucial point is that the expression of those suppositions of yours is *not* an argument. It has no place in the course of a debate.

For a start, to ascribe thoughts and motives to someone is actually impossible to do with complete certainty (other than in the rare cases when the 'opponent' has previously admitted to his motives, whether to you or to somebody else from whom you have received the information). You are not an infallible thought-reader, any more than anybody else is.

And secondly, and more important, even if you happen to be right in what you ascribe, what then? You cannot possibly prove it, so what is the point of saying it, other than for the fatuous purpose of letting off steam?

The fact is that ascribing – whether validly or invalidly – motives in your opponent for saying what he says is simply irrelevant in the context, as well as ungentlemanly. The *only* relevant answers to what your 'opponent' says are answers addressed to whether what he has just said is factually true and logically coherent. If what he has just said is factually untrue, your obligation is to make the correction and to prove it. If it is logically incoherent, your obligation is to point out the fallacy (for instance, the fallacy commonly known as 'begging question'), so that he can avoid it in his next attempt.

And, if he doesn't avoid it, you must gently insist that he does, as often as is necessary. If you need to, you must continue to insist that he does until it becomes clear that the discussion can proceed no further

because he just won't. And even then, his *motives* must not be attacked
– other than, *possibly*, in the form of a question, very inoffensively put,
as to whether he is *certain* that his motives are pure?

Developing this important point, it must be remembered that your
obligation is to try to *persuade*, not to try to *convict*. What we are talking
about, as far as these rules are concerned, is private debates, not courts
of law or public disputations which are as much for the benefit of
others as of our 'opponent'. We are addressing ourselves to attempts
to persuade the person to whom we are talking, not to persuade *others*
in the course of arguing with him (as, for instance, in the case of
Parliamentary and other public debates).

And, incidentally, if your 'opponent' should, rather than directly
answering a point you have just made, attack *your* motives for saying
what you have just said, *stop there at once* – provided, of course, that
your motives are not what he alleges. Do not continue until he with-
draws the allegation.

There is a practical reason for this, as well as its being unseemly to
continue a discussion with someone who is accusing you of dishonesty. The practical reason is that the allegation is unfair in the sense
that it is impossible to answer it. One can prove *facts* and one can prove
logical validity. Other than it relatively exceptional cases, one *cannot*
prove the purity of one's motives. One cannot *prove* what is only in
one's mind.

Conversely, again other than in relatively exceptional cases, the
other party cannot prove the motive he is alleging. He too cannot
prove what is only in your mind. From this it follows that, as an argument, his allegation is an unfair tactic and must be stopped in its tracks.
(Incidentally, the Common Law assumes this fact about the frequent
impossibility of proving motives. That is the reason for the usual
Common Law principle that, if a definite criminal *action* – '*actus
reus*' – takes place, a criminal *motive* – '*mens rea*' – is to be assumed unless
the perpetrator of the criminal action can prove otherwise.)

This attribution of motives to your opponent falls under the heading of a form of argument technically known as '*ad hominem* argumentation', incidentally. I may as well quote a learned professor on
this rather than speak in my own name, because he says it about as well
as it can be said. Dr. Robert Faurisson, in an article 'Against the

Revisionists, Argumentation *ad hominem*' (The *Revisionist*, Castle Hill
Publishers, PO Box 257768, Chicago, Illinois 60605):

> At times, in a debate of ideas, an attack on the person of the
> adversary can be justified if, explicitly or implicitly, this type of
> attack is preceded or accompanied by an argumentation on the
> substance. On the other hand, a pure and simple *ad hominem*
> argument, without further ado, only betrays an inability to reply
> to the opponent's argument. If need be, this cowardly combat
> may draw its ammunition from rumours, stories and malicious
> gossip where a source is rarely given.

21. Never fall into the temptation of 'scoring' debating points for the sake
    of doing so, however open your opponent may leave himself to them.
    Debating points have an honourable and valuable place in public
    disputations, when both you and your opponent are trying to win
    others over to your respective standpoints. They have, however, no
    place whatever in private discussions and arguments, where you are
    not trying to persuade others, but trying to persuade *him* (or her!).
    And you are most unlikely to succeed in this endeavour by rhetorical
    techniques, which are the more likely to raises his hackles the more
    successful and devastating they are.

    The fact is that, to have the greatest chance of success, you must do
    your best to make him *like* losing the argument. It is a difficult task, but
    it can sometimes be done, and you are certainly not going to achieve
    this if you do not keep yourself always conscious of that goal.

22. This may be as difficult a rule as any to follow. Bend over backwards
    – turn backward somersaults if you can! – to be fair to your opponent
    and more than fair. For instance, do not take advantage of any slip he
    makes in his arguing. That is to say, do not win the argument on a
    technicality, by means of springing a trap, or whatever. Your entire
    conduct should show that what you are out to establish, to the satisfac-
    tion of both parties, is the truth, the right answer, the right decision, or
    whatever – that you are *not* out to establish victory-no-matter-what-
    the-cost.

23. Further to number 22 above, make absolutely sure you under-
    stand your 'opponent's' position exactly and also, equally exactly, the
    argument he is using at the particular time. More, *do your very best for his*

argument. Make it a matter of pride that you can express his argument *at least* as well and convincingly as he can.

24. It should be unnecessary to say this, but in fact it is all too necessary. *Never* back up your case with an untruth, or with any kind of falsehood, or with a piece of false logic, an invalid argument. Do not do so, however good your motive; not even if you think you might save someone's life by doing so. The ruling principle here is the natural law one, acknowledged by truly civilised people since the dawn of history: *a good end doesn't justify a bad means*, not ever. (This principle is sometimes 'short-handed' into 'the end doesn't justify the means'. As worded, that is completely invalid. On the contrary, the end certainly *can* justify the means, if the means is legitimate.)

   And, if ever you should find yourself using a falsehood or false logic, *either* by mistake, whether because of excusable ignorance, or because of carelessness, *or* – Heaven forbid! – on purpose (let us hope only because you got carried away in the heat of the moment), *retract what you have said*, at the earliest reasonable opportunity. Once again, the natural law operates here – you must act as you would want others to act towards you.

   This last point, incidentally, is not simply preaching. It is sound, even indispensable, *practical* advice – advice aimed at a long-term good, and a better good than the apparent short-term good of an immediate advantage, but an advantage secured as illegitimate cost.

   It is worth mentioning that many people would consider what has been said in this number to be controversial, at best. Please be assured that it can be sufficiently defended; but to do that here would take up more space than would be appropriate in a shortish exposition such as this one. It is an important task, but it must be for another occasion.

25. Normally it is preferable, and much more convenient and time-saving, to conduct arguments orally, face-to-face. If, however, your 'opponent' has a tendency to forget or deny what he has said or admitted previously, it can be necessary to conduct the argument in writing, or at least to note down important things which have been said.

26. Probably the most difficult advice of all to follow, yet probably the most important:

   Learn to relish *losing* arguments, provided that you have lost them fairly and justly.

Why? For this reason:

By losing, and in consequence changing your mind,

... you have gained more than your victorious opponent has;

... you have acquired a new truth or set of truths;

... you will have exchanged an incorrect/erroneous position for a correct one, possibly in a matter of the highest importance, possibly even in a matter of life-and-death;

... your opponent has given you a precious gift, and you have received a precious gift.

There is therefore *plenty* of good reason to relish losing arguments, and to be grateful that this occurs – which doesn't, however, make it easy to do until one has, with practice, learnt to make a habit of it.

A useful post script on the last two paragraphs. Here is one of the most famous arguers in the world today in action – best-selling atheist and 'partner' of Professor Richard Dawkins, Christopher Hitchens, as exposed in an article by Nigel Farndale, in the *Daily Telegraph*, 2nd June 2010:

'Another insecurity is that I never like to lose an argument, even a domestic one. Even when it might not matter.' Does that make him difficult to live with? 'It must do. In fact, I know it does. It's a vice.' What's wrong with losing an argument? 'What a question! I would feel it was a defeat.'... 'It doesn't take much to make me angry. Don't care about getting it back in return. There are all kinds of stupid people that annoy me but what annoys me most is a lazy argument ...

Readers with time to spare might enjoy identifying and counting the many illogicalities and absurdities in that paragraph.

27. Here I quote directly from a highly qualified authority, a notable American author on classical philosophy, the Rev. Charles Dubray (in his *Introductory Philosophy*, Longmans Green, New York and London, 1923):

(a) If victorious, practise modesty. Nothing is more cowardly than to abuse a defeated opponent. Arrogance is a sign of conceit, and indicates that a man loves his own satisfaction more than the truth.

(b) Be not depressed by defeat, and be honest enough to accept the truth. Always remember Cicero's maxim, *Cuiusvis hominis est errare, nullius nisi insipientis in errore perseverare* (Philipp. XII, c.2). 'Everyone is liable to error. It is the part only of a fool to *persevere* in error …'

3.
FINALE

One last point: By conducting ourselves in the manner described above, we are conducting ourselves as a gentleman or a lady. We are conducting ourselves in accordance with the highest principles of refined and civilised behaviour, and in the manner as far opposed as can be to savagery.

Moreover, we are not only defending, promoting and finding truth and goodness, and even sometimes beauty, as they best deserve. We are also acting *peaceably*. If *everyone* acted similarly, no disputes would ever need to be resolved by 'other means', whether litigation or violence. Everyone won't, of course, but the more who do, the better.

APPENDIX
but … WHEN THE DISPUTING IS NOT PRIVATE
BUT PUBLIC

In the foregoing pages, and especially in numbered paragraph 20, I have occasionally made passing reference to public disputations and the like, as opposed to private debates. This has always been in connection with the fact that different rules necessarily apply to public disputations.

In fact, the difference between the two, even as to their goals, is so great that I have actually been using rather loose language when referring to private arguing (what this article is about) as debating. More technically, dialogue between two people for the purpose of establishing the truth of a matter, by strictly reasoned argument, is called *dialectics*. *Debate*, by contrast, is when the debaters are committed to their points of view at the outset, and mean to win the debate, either by proving their argument correct or by proving their opponent's argument incorrect – with a judge or jury, or less formal equivalent, deciding who wins the debate.

The purpose of this appendix is not to teach the science and art of debating, in the technically correct sense of that word, as I have been attempting to teach the science and art of dialectics in these pages. It is simply to note one important area where the rules governing the two are especially different. In order to do this, I am simply going to quote the best treatment of the subject that I know of. It is taken from chapters 20 and 21 of a book called *What Is Liberalism?* by Don Felix Sarda y Salvany, translated by Conde B. Allen PhD., LL.D. – originally published in Spanish back in 1886, translated into English in 1899, and deservedly a best-seller ever since. (I have lightly edited it, for instance to modernise the occasionally old-fashioned English.)

Since the author uses the term Liberalism quite frequently in what follows, it is as well that I indicate here what is meant by that term. Stated as simply as possible: it is (a) the toleration of every sort of error, (b) while *not* tolerating even the *concept* of demonstrable and inescapable truth, and especially of truth that carries with it important duties duties that are inevitably uncomfortable to the undutiful. Under the bogus banner of 'liberty of conscience', Liberalism is the fatally relativistic, self-contradictory creed that *nothing* is objectively true, *other than* the proposition that nothing is objectively true. Now please read on.

★   ★   ★

Granting that error and falsehoods are bad things, to call the public propagators and defenders of them bad is no want of charity.

The law of justice, potent in all ages, can be applied in this case. The defenders of truth and justice of to-day are no innovators in this respect.

We are simply holding to the constant practice of antiquity. The propagators and abettors of pernicious falsehoods have at all times been denounced as well as the falsehoods themselves. There is no sin against charity in calling evil *evil,* its authors, abettors and disciples *bad*; all its acts, words and writings *iniquitous, wicked, malicious.* In short the wolf has always been called the wolf, and in so calling it no one ever believed that wrong was done to the flock and the shepherd.

If the propagation of good and the necessity of combating evil require us to oppose error and its supporters in rather harsh terms, this usage is certainly not against charity. This is a corollary or consequence of the principle we have just demonstrated. We must render evil odious and detestable. We cannot attain this result without pointing out the dangers of evil, without showing how and why it is odious, detestable and contemptible. Christian oratory of all ages has always employed the most vigorous and emphatic rhetoric in the arsenal of human speech against impiety. In the writings of the great athletes of Christianity, the usage of irony, imprecation, execration and of the most crushing epithets is continual. Hence the only law is the opportunity and the truth.

But there is another justification for such an usage. In order to convince the people, we must speak to *their heart* and *their imagination*, which can only be touched by ardent, brilliant, and impassioned language. To be impassioned is not to be reprehensible, when our heat is the holy ardour of truth.

The supposed violence of true rhetoric is amply justified by every page of the works of the great Christian polemicists of other epochs. This is easily verified. St. John the Baptist calls the Pharisees 'race of vipers,' Jesus Christ hurls at them the epithets 'hypocrites, whitened sepulchres, a perverse and adulterous generation' without thinking for this reason that He sullies the sanctity of His benevolent speech. St. Paul criticises the schismatic Cretans as 'always liars, evil beasts, slothful bellies'. The same apostle calls Elymas the magician 'seducer, full of guile and deceit, child of the Devil, enemy of all justice.'

★   ★   ★

But ... 'It is all well enough to make war on abstract doctrines,' some may say, 'but in combating error, be it ever so evident, is it so proper to make an attack upon the persons of those who uphold it?' We reply that very often it is, and not only proper but at times even indispensable and meritorious before God and men.

When Liberals have hurled the accusation of indulging in personalities at our heads, they imagine that we are overwhelmed by the charge. But they deceive themselves.

We are not so easily thrust in the background. We have reason, and substantial reason, on our side. In order to combat and discredit false ideas, we must inspire contempt and horror in the hearts of the multitude for those who seek to seduce and debauch them. A disease is inseparable from the persons of the diseased. The cholera threatening a country comes in the persons of the infected. If we wish to exclude it we must exclude them. *Now* ideas do not in any case go about in the abstract; they neither spread nor propagate *of themselves*. Left to themselves, if it be possible to imagine them apart from those who conceive them, they would never produce all the evil from which society suffers. It is only in the concrete that they are effective; when they are the personal product of those who conceive them. They are like the arrows and the balls which would hurt no one if they were not shot from the bow or the gun. It is the archer and the gunner to whom we should give our first attention; but for them the fire would not be murderous. Any other method of warfare might be Liberal, if you please, but it would not be common-sense.

The authors and propagators of dangerous falsehoods are soldiers with poisoned weapons in their hands. Their arms are the book, the journal, the lecture, their personal influence. Is it sufficient to dodge their blows? Not at all; the first thing necessary is to demolish the combatant himself When he is *hors de combat,* he can do no more mischief.

It is therefore perfectly proper not only to discredit any book, journal or discourse of the enemy, but it is also proper, in certain cases, to even discredit his person; for in warfare, beyond question, the principal element is the person engaged, as the gunner is the principal factor in an artillery fight and not the cannon, the powder and the bomb. It is thus lawful, in certain cases, to expose the infamy of a Liberal opponent, to bring his habits into contempt, and drag his name in the mire.

Yes, this is permissible, permissible in prose, in verse, in caricature, in a serious vein or in badinage, by every means and method within reach. The only restriction is not to employ a lie in the service of justice. This never. Under no pretext may we sully the truth, even to the crossing of a t and the dotting of an i. As a French writer says: 'Truth is the only charity allowed in history,' and, we may add, in the defence of religion and society.

Clifford Harper

THE WORK AESTHETIC

A BRIEF ACCOUNT OF THE DEVELOPMENT OF THE WORK ETHIC, FOLLOWED BY AN EXPLORATION OF A POSSIBLE ALTERNATIVE, WITH REFERENCE TO AN EAST END SAFE-CRACKER

Warren Draper

ETHIC

Work is the refuge of people who have nothing better to do.
— Oscar Wilde

MY FATHER WILL SOON CELEBRATE FIFTY YEARS OF 'retirement'. A lifetime of dodgy-dealings, downsizing and dole has allowed him to live outside the world of work. But despite his relatively early escape from the yoke of wage-slavery and his outspoken contempt for career, he openly admits that it took a very long time to completely rid his mind of the work ethic – for the first 20 years he only felt truly relaxed at the weekends. During the Monday-to-Friday, nine-to-five of the traditional working-week, his thoughts would occasionally be plagued by gnawing little pangs of guilt as the workaday world busied itself around him.

This uneasiness is not unusual even among the most well versed of idlers; that it could hold such sway over my father, a man who had long since realized the [t]errors of *The Job Delusion*, only goes to show the power of the dominant work ethic. Altering, as it has, our evolutionary patterns of sleeping, eating, communication, travel, productivity, shelter and even – for the careerist – mating, it has come to

permeate every aspect of modern life. We would be forgiven for thinking that it was some kind of natural phenomenon; something essential
to our very humanity, like the cerebral cortex or the opposable
thumb – as if evolution were the univers's way of creating the alarm
clock or the Blackberry. But in reality it took many long years of
coercion, suggestion and downright thuggery to prepare freeborn
Homo sapiens for the tedium of the office and the factory-floor.

In order to create wage-slavery it was first necessary to whittle away
those age-old rights and customs which allowed people to gain all that
they needed for basic survival – food, shelter, energy, grazing pasture,
etc. – from the land on which they lived; land which had already been
stolen from the majority of humanity by force of arms, and then kept
from them – as it still is – by force of mythology. Customary rights to
subsistence from the commons were ignored as more and more land
was enclosed in the name of 'improvement' – which may have
'improved' landowners' profit margins, but did little to improve life
for the peasantry (as Simon Fairlie's important essay, *A Short History of
Enclosure in Britain*[1], clearly illustrates). I talked about the theft of the
commons in the last issue of the *Idler*,[2] and will not dwell on the
subject here, but I will say that our dependency on authority – in the
form of corporations, the judiciary and the state (in truth these are
inseparable entities, each a facet of what William Cobbett called 'The
Thing') – is intimately tied to our estrangement from the land.

The invasion of the land was made complete with a subtle, but
equally devastating, invasion of the mind. Communal existence in
rural areas was being undermined by the emergence of what we would
today call a *petite bourgeois* mentality amongst the wealthier, more
powerful sectors of society. Mythologies like *status*, *hierarchy* and
private property have become so ingrained that we are prone to forgot
that they are a consequence of human imaginings which had to be
invented, developed and endorsed – not to mention enforced – just
like any other man-made product. Capitalism could never have
become the Leviathan it is without the adoption of new, anti-social
attitudes. William Cobbett gives us a wonderful insight into this
process and the devastating effects it had on the population:

Reigate, Thursday Evening
20th October, 1825

Having done my business at Hartswood to-day about 11 o'clock, I
went to a *sale* at a farm, which the farmer is quitting. Here I had a
view of what has long been going on all over the country. The
farm, which belongs to Christ's Hospital, has been held by a man
the name of CHARINGTON, in whose family the lease had
been, I hear, a great number of years.

... Every thing about this farm-house was formerly the scene
of *plain manners* and *plentiful living*. Oak clothes-chests, oak bed-
steads, oak chests of drawers, and oak tables to eat on, long,
strong, and well supplied with joint stools. Some of the things
were many hundreds of years old. But all appeared to be in a state
of decay and nearly of *disuse*. There appeared to be hardly any
family in that house, where formerly there were, in all probability,
from ten to fifteen men, boys, and maids: and, which was worst
of all, there was a *parlour!* Aye, and a *carpet* and *bell-pull* too! One
end of this once plain and substantial house had been moulded
unto a '*parlour*'; and there was a mahogany table, and the fine
chairs, and the fine glass, and all the bare-face upstart as any
stock-jobber in the kingdom can boast of. And, there were the
decanters, the glasses, the 'dinner set' of crockery ware, and all in
the true stock-jobber style. And I dare say it has been '*Squire*'
Charington and *Miss* Charingtons; and not plain Master
Charington and his son Hodge, and his daughter Betty
Charington, all of whom this accursed system has, in all likelihood, transmuted into a species of mock gentlefolks, while it has
ground the labourers down into real slaves. Why do not farmers
now *feed* and *lodge* their work people, as they did formerly?
Because they cannot keep them *upon so little* as they give them in
wages. This is the real cause of the change. There needs no more
to prove the lot of the working classes has become worse than it
formerly was. [3]

Let us pause for a moment and consider that last remark – '*the lot of the working classes has become worse than it formerly was.*' Here, writing during the early years of the Industrial Revolution, Cobbett questions another central myth of capitalism, the myth of 'progress'. We are constantly told that we've *never had it so good* and that *progress* will one day create a heaven on earth for all mankind. To deny *progress* is to risk being condemned as a foolish Luddite who stands Canute-like against the inevitable (a sister article to the one you are now reading, entitled *The Shuttle Exchanged for the Sword*, will be published in Volume Two of the very excellent – and refreshingly honest – *Dark Mountain Journal*[4], it covers the history of the Luddites and the ongoing resistance to the *myth of progress*). Technological progress has, without doubt, brought many benefits (and I must confess an absolute admiration for those rare technological geniuses whose vision transcends the narrow confines of the business world – we can only imagine how different the lives of 6 billion humans would be if we had followed Bucky Fuller's 'Critical Path'[5]), but for every beneficial invention there are 10,000 fads designed to distract and entertain. We may have access to a vast and ever-changing mountain of material possessions (although the majority of the world's population aren't even allowed near the foothills), but we are paying a massive physical and spiritual cost for the privilege – as Kirkpatrick Sale observes:

[M]any in the US and throughout the industrial world live at levels of wealth undreamed of in ages past ... Yet it is a statistical fact that it is just this segment that most acutely suffers from the true 'comfortable disease', what I would call affluenza: heart disease, stress, overwork, family dysfunction, alcoholism, insecurity, anomie, psychosis, loneliness, impotence, alienation, consumerism, and coldness of heart.[6]

And that's just the cost to the 'winners' of the human race (make no mistake, we are the victors and beneficiaries of the longest and most savage war in human history), the majority of the human population and the biosphere as a whole has it much, much worse. Recognizing the rough road on which industrial capitalism had embarked Cobbett continued:

[I]f the farmer now shuts his pantry against his labourers, and pays them wholly in money, is it not clear, that he does it because he thereby gives them a living *cheaper* to him; that is to say, a *worse* living than formerly? Mind he has a *house* for them; a kitchen for them to sit in, bed rooms for them to sleep in, tables, and stools, and benches, of everlasting duration. All these he has; all these *cost him nothing*; and yet so much does he gain by pinching them in wages that he lets these things remain as of no use, rather than feed labourers in the house. Judge, then, of the *change* that has taken place in the condition of these labourers! And, be astonished, if you can, at the *pauperism* and the *crimes* that now disgrace this once happy and moral England.

... This is not only the *natural* progress, but it *has been* the progress of England. The blame is not justly imputed to 'SQUIRE' CHARINGTON and his like; the blame belongs to the infernal stock-jobbing system. There was no reason to expect, that farmers would not endeavour to keep pace, in point of show and luxury, with fund-holders, and with all the tribes that *war* and *taxes* created.[7]

In order to best serve capitalism this new *Stock-jobber* attitude had to be accepted by persecutor and persecuted alike. It is no accident that the factories, prisons and schools which were developed during the Industrial Revolution bear a remarkable family resemblance; for it was these institutions, beyond any other, which ensued the success of the dominant puritan work ethic. At first they were brutal places designed to subdue a populace which had previously enjoyed a relatively autonomous and self-sufficient lifestyle. But the anatomy of the human brain makes it ripe for what Plato called '*The Noble Lie*', and soon more subtle forms of subjugation would come into play.

In his *Republic*, Plato describes how a stable stratified society can be created within a couple of generations through the use of a magnificent myth. (In Plato's illustration this is a mythology which states that all men are born of the earth, but are constituted of different kinds of metal – the leaders = Gold; auxiliaries and military = Silver; farmers and peasants = Bronze and Iron – there is some social mobility decided at the time of each new birth in order to keep the various strata from stagnation, but stability is ensured as the 'lie' becomes a deep, unquestionable 'truth' with the passing of time.) The ultra-materialist mythology born in the factories, schools and prisons of capital would become the most subtle and overarching *Noble Lie* in human history.

There were, of course, many liberal reforms regarding factories, schools and prisons, but in his classic work, *Discipline and Punish: the Birth of the Prison*, Michael Foucault describes how institutions with seemingly egalitarian and humanitarian motives would in fact become instrumental in ensuring the widespread submission to authority essential to the success and ongoing survival of the capitalist wage-labour system. In other words, seemingly banal – even beneficial – institutions were ultimately responsible for the domestication of the wider population as a whole. As Foucault observes:

> Historically, the process by which the bourgeoisie became in the course of the eighteenth century the politically dominant class was masked by the establishment of an explicit, coded and formally egalitarian juridical framework, made possible by the organization of a parliamentary, representative regime. But the development and generalization of disciplinary mechanisms constituted the other, dark side of these processes. The general juridical form that guaranteed a system of rights that were egalitarian in principle was supported by these tiny, everyday, physical mechanisms, by all those systems of micro-power that are essentially non-egalitarian and asymmetrical that we call the disciplines.[8]

Foucault shows that prison was simply one aspect of what he calls the '*carceral system*'; the all-encompassing, all-powerful dominant mechanism which created – and automatically re-creates – modern society. He argues that the disciplinary systems prevalent in all capitalist institutions – prisons, schools, factories, companies, universities, the military, etc. – helped to ensure a submissive populace and the ongoing survival of capitalism.

What was then being formed was a policy of coercions that act upon the body, a calculated manipulation of its elements, its gestures, its behaviour. The human body was entering a machinery of power that explores it, breaks it down and rearranges it. A 'political anatomy', which was also a 'mechanics of power', was being born; it defined how one may have a hold over others' bodies, not only so that they may do what one wishes, but so that they may operate as one wishes, with the techniques, the speed and the efficiency that one determines. Thus discipline produces subjected and practised bodies, 'docile' bodies.[9]

The surrender to routine, uniformity, discipline and the clock (which manifested itself as that nagging, uneasy feeling which plagued the early years of my father's 'retirement') is most obvious in prisons, schools and factories, but spend a day observing the patterns of modern life as if you were an outsider and you will see how utterly encompassing the *carceral system* has become. The work ethic, when seen in this light, is nothing short of the domicile surrender of the free-born human animal to the yoke of the industrial machine. It is a perfect system of control because those who display the best aptitude for life under its shadow – in other words those who are most highly domesticated – are those who are most likely to 'succeed'. And the most *successful* in society are also the ones most likely to end up in senior positions within that society, where they will inevitably shape future decisions and further reinforce the *Noble Lie*.

There is no *invisible hand* or *global conspiracy*, just a very powerful *story* that human beings like to tell themselves in order to justify – and maintain – what is a fundamentally insane system. As William S. Burroughs famously observed: 'The aim of education is the knowledge, not of facts, but of values.' The mechanisms and implications of this social filtration are discussed at length in David Edwards' enlightening and life-changing book, *Free to be Human,* in which he highlights the 'necessary beliefs' central to the work ethic:

> [O]ur corporate run economies rely on adherence to a specific framework of ideas for their functioning and survival. [...] First it is important that the majority of people agree that corporate profit maximisation leading to economic growth is the primary goal of industrial society (we are allowed to talk in high terms of freedom, democracy, charity, religious ideals, and so on, but the primary *functioning* goal must be that of maximising corporate

growth) [...] Secondly we should believe (or be resigned to the
idea) that our functioning as 'cogs' within this process of mass
production is the best way of leading a worthwhile, fulfilled life.
Ideally we should believe that 'success' as defined by society is
critical to our happiness [...] [that this success] should be made
possible by conspicuous conformity to the economic system.
Thus, 'success' through status, through conformity should be the
dominant goal. [...] Thirdly, we should believe that mass consumption is the most sensible, sane and realistic means to finding
happiness. [...] Fourthly (and perhaps most importantly), this
system has an interest in our believing that we *freely choose* these
goals. [...] The increased efficiency of this system over the totali-
tarian alternative (of the former Soviet Union for example),
resides precisely in this notion of voluntary participation in, and
(ideally) dedication to, the system of personal gain. In the end,
this system depends on the notion that freedom from coercion is
commensurate with full freedom, that free decisions can mean-
ingfully be made under conditions where the powerful institutions of society have the ability and motivation to manipulate
what we think. [10]

Chris Carlsson expands upon this internalized system of control in his
2008 book, *Nowtopia*:

Capitalism depends on obscuring relationships, fetishising objects, and inculcating ignorance for much of its power. The most
basic relationship at the heart of the system is wage-labour, the
exchange of work for pay. Accepted as normal and proper, this
basic relationship is the daily renewal of subordination to an alien
purpose. In trading our capacities for a wage we simultaneously
give up control over the world our labour is making ... Wage-
labour and consumerism are mechanisms to avoid and nullify
social accountability. Feedback at work consists of pressure to
conform to the company's agenda and to unquestioningly carry
out limited tasks assigned. Negative feedback leads to unemployment, positive feedback is the continued arrival of paycheque.

After work, feedback is limited to banal gratifications of acquisi-
tion and consumption, freed of any connection to ecological
sanity or human effort ... Our characters are shaped by these
narrow options. We obviously depend on large-scale, remote, and
fragile systems to provide for our basic needs (power, water,
food). But we also have a belief system that says each of us
individually should enjoy near total freedom in what we do,
answerable to no one else. As [David] Holmgren sharply notes,
'In a sense, our whole society is like a teenager who wants to have
it all, have it now, without consequences.'[11] A culture that simultaneously glorifies and fears adolescence while promoting shallow
hedonism is perfectly suited to the mass consumerism that under-
pins modern capitalism.[12]

The work ethic not only divorces us from those skills which are
essential to a free, autonomous existence, it also negates our natural,
instinctive creative processes; as the brilliant American anarchist and
free-love activist, Voltairine de Cleyre, showed a century ago:

[T]he one great real idea of our age, not copied from any other,
not pretended, not raised to life by any conjuration, is the Much
Making of Things – not the making of beautiful things, not the
joy of spending living energy in creative work; rather the shame-
less, merciless driving and over-driving, wasting and draining of
the last bit of energy, only to produce heaps and heaps of things
– things ugly, things harmful, things useless, and at the best
largely unnecessary. To what end are they produced? Mostly the
producer does not know; still less does he care. But he is possessed
with the idea that he must do it, every one is doing it, and every
year the making of things goes on more and faster; there are
mountain ranges of things made and making, and still men go
about desperately seeking to increase the list of created things, to
start fresh heaps and to add to the existing heaps. And with what
agony of body, under what stress and strain of danger and fear of
danger, with what mutilations and maimings and lamings they
struggle on, dashing themselves out against these rocks of wealth!

Verily, if the vision of the Medieval Soul is painful in its blind
staring and pathetic striving, grotesque in its senseless tortures,
the Soul of the Modern is most amazing with its restless, nervous
eyes, ever searching the corners of the universe, its restless, nervous hands ever reaching and grasping for some useless toil.[13]

We are, as Erich Fromm observed, *creatures* who evolved to become
creators; we are driven to create, to spend our 'living energy in creative
work'. But the work ethic as it currently exists corrupts – and
ultimately smothers – instinctive creativity. When Picasso said, 'All
children are artists. The problem is how to remain an artist once he
grows up,' he was lamenting that innate spontaneity, originality and
honesty which is lost somewhere on the child's journey through the
carceral system. Perfect-born inventive and inquisitive minds inhabiting
bodies with naturally graceful poise and posture seem to leave school
slumped in every possible way.

This suppression of natural human creativity is a major contributor
to Kirkpatrick Sale's '*comfortable diseases*' of anxiety, depression and
alienation. But at the same time the urge to create is so powerful that it
emerges, regardless of the dominant system, like green shoots through
concrete; manifesting itself in a million magical ways. Here – among
the punks and the permaculturalists and the graffiti artists and the
guerilla gardeners and the pirate programmers and the free ravers and
the outlaw cyclists and the techno-tinkerers and the social-centres and
the off-griders – we are teased with the boundless possibilities of a
new, brighter future for all.

But in order to create an autonomous, stable, open and loving
society we must abandon the work ethic and those other constructs of
the corporate/carceral system – materialism, hierarchy, profit, growth,
progress, etc. – in favour of more human – and more beautiful –
production methods. Work does not have to be a dirty and destructive
four-letter-word (except, of course, for the fact it has four letters), not
if our *work* is first and foremost to *create*. Isn't it time we tried something new? Isn't it time for a work aesthetic?

AESTHETIC

An unfulfilled vocation drains the colour from a man's entire existence.
– Balzac

Unlike my father, who's employment record came to an official end at the tender age of 26, my grandfather's CV reads as if it were advertising spiel written specifically to celebrate the work ethic and *sell, sell, sell* the capitalist dream. Here is a man who dragged himself up from a life of poverty to become a foreman, a clerk of works, a businessman, an architectural surveyor and even chief surveyor overlooking the building of the *Dome of Discovery* for the 1951 *Festival of Britain*. A *real* success story – on paper at least …

In truth my grandfather did all this to escape from wage-slavery. His proudest boast was that 'they haven't printed enough money to get me to work.' He was born into hardship in the East End of London in 1913. As a young man standing 5′2″ on his tip-toes he quickly discovered that reputation and attitude is far more important than physical stature and he learnt to use fear and intimidation to get whatever he wanted – nowadays we'd probably say he was a bit *gangsta*. Going against the advice of his careers officer – and society as a whole – my grandfather turned to crime in the hope that he would escape from the yolk of wage-slavery; his chosen speciality was safe-cracking. Unfortunately he wasn't so good that he didn't get caught. In prison the resident chaplain (who would later become Bishop of Grantham) took a shine to him and advised him to learn a trade – so gramps became a brickie. On leaving prison he started work on a building site. His first day on the job he saw that everyone worked hard except for the foreman, so the very next day he blagged his way onto another building site – as a foreman. During the war he was employed as a Clerk of Works at RAF Station Spanhoe near Uppingham, Northamptonshire – where local farmers gave him back-handers for letting the grass on the airfields grow longer so it could be used for hay. After the war, lacking any qualifications but armed with a new 'posh' persona (a front that proved even more rewarding to him than his earlier *gangsta* attitude), he set himself up as an architectural surveyor. He also created the Draper Brothers building company for his sons which was instrumental in a rather lucrative scam which he ran in association with bent assessors from the War Damage Commission. The Draper boys would place frosted glass in a house to suggest war-time bomb-damage and then apply to the War Commission for work that didn't need doing. The assessor (usually a one-eyed snooker player who had served time in Sing Sing prison – I kid you not!) would promptly sign the job off for a cut of proceeds and the house would get a lick of paint and clear glass in its windows once again. It was the contacts he made during this time which led to him being employed as chief surveyor on the *Dome of Discovery* – even though he couldn't even draw a circle. Luckily for the Dome his incompetence was duly noted and the job was handed to somebody else. This little setback didn't get in the way of him becoming one of the top architectural surveyors in North London – and I'm guessing one of the only ones who did a little bookmaking on the side.

Grandpa was no idling hero. For all but the last 20 years of his life he was a violent drunk whose motives were selfish and ultimately self-destructive. But his refusal to be pigeon-holed and his ability to constantly reinvent himself does illustrate two principles central to the work aesthetic: *diversity* and *adaptability*.

In his 1990 essay, *The Empire of the Rising Scum*, the sadly missed Robert Shea discusses how hierarchical organizations – corporations, governments, academia, the military, religious groups, etc. – are inherently degenerative:

> [T]he more an organization succeeds and prospers, the more it is likely to be diverted from its original ideals, principles and purposes [...] Every combination of two or more human beings has both a useful aspect and a political aspect. These tend to conflict with each other. As the political aspect becomes more and more influential, the organization ceases to be useful to its members and starts using them [...] Why does this happen? Because the better an organization is at fulfilling its purpose, the more it attracts people who see the organization as an opportunity to advance

themselves [...] There are some people who are extraordinarily good at manipulating – organizations to serve their own ends. The Russians, who have suffered under such people for centuries, have a name for them – apparatchiks. It was an observer of apparatchiks who coined the maxim, 'The scum rises to the top.'

The apparatchik's aim in life is to out-ass-kiss, out-maneuver, out-threaten, out-lie and ultimately out-fight his or her way to the top of the pyramid – any pyramid. Appropriately, Russia produced a superb specimen of *Homo apparatchikus* – Josef Stalin [...] It often happens that when a person possesses a particular ability to an extraordinary degree, nature makes up for it by leaving him or her incompetent in every other department. Thus we see owners of baseball teams who lack any understanding of the sport, heads of banks who couldn't balance a checkbook, industrialists whose main industry is riding around in fancy limos, and generals who know more about playing golf with congressmen than they do about fighting wars [...] Unfortunately, the existence of this talent means that every successful organization will sooner or later be taken over by apparatchiks.[14]

Bob offers an interesting solution to this problem ...

One simple way to keep organizations from becoming cancerous might be to rotate all jobs on a regular, frequent and mandatory basis, including the leadership positions. While it may seem wasteful for people to spend part of their time working at jobs they are not particularly good at, and even detrimental to the organization's goals, the healthiest societies do seem to be those that encourage people to do a variety of things – as in pioneer America. A permanent division of labour inevitably creates occupational and class inequality and conflict. As Robert A. Heinlein said through Lazarus Long, 'Specialization is for insects.' [...] Individuals, too, who cultivate a variety of skills seem brighter, more energetic and more adaptable than those who know how to do one thing only. Not all of us can be polymaths, like Leonardo, Thomas Jefferson or Steve Allen, but we can all learn how to do a few more things than we know how to do now, and the adding of skill to skill can be a lifelong and most rewarding process. And, of course, the more self-sufficient we are, the less we will be dependent upon organizations.[15]

Or, as the full Heinlein/Long quote says ...

A human being should be able to change a diaper, plan an invasion, butcher a hog, conn a ship, design a building, write a sonnet, balance accounts, build a wall, set a bone, comfort the dying, take orders, give orders, cooperate, act alone, solve equations, analyze a new problem, pitch manure, program a computer, cook a tasty meal, fight efficiently, die gallantly. *Specialization is for insects.*[16]

Career diversity is not a new idea by any means. In his classic utopia, *News From Nowhere* (a cloth-bound, illustrated, letterpress-printed edition of this manifesto for a more aesthetic way of life should be carried by idle revolutionaries everywhere), William Morris focusses heavily on the fact that his utopians enjoy a wonderfully eclectic working life. The first person Morris meets when he finds himself in a future version of London is a boat-man named Dick. Accustomed as he is to Victorian attitudes (attitudes which our modern society sadly shares) Morris assumes that Dick is working for a wage and that 'boat-man' is his chosen profession. To his embarrassment he quickly discovers that money is obsolete, and when Dick offers to be his guide he finds that the idea of singular employment is equally unfashionable. Morris says that he is worried that he is taking Dick away from his work, to which Dick responds:

'Oh,' he said, 'don't trouble about that, because it will give me an opportunity of doing a good turn for a friend of mine who wants to take my work here. He is a weaver from Yorkshire who has rather overdone himself between his weaving and his mathematics, both indoor work, you see; and being a great friend of mine he naturally came to me to get some outdoor work. If you think you can put up with me, pray take me as your guide.'[17]

Later, on meeting Dick's weaving friend, Morris discovers that everybody's working life is now rich and varied. Morris enquires:

'[S]ince I hear that you are a weaver I would like to ask you something about that craft, as I am – or was – interested in it.'
    'Oh,' he said, 'I shall not be of much use to you there, I'm
afraid. I only do the most mechanical kind of weaving, and am in
fact a poor craftsman, unlike Dick here. Then besides the weaving
I do a little with machine printing and composing, though I am
little use at the finer kinds of printing; and moreover machine
printing is beginning to die out, along with the waning of the
plague of book-making; so I have had to turn to other things that
I have a taste for, and have taken to mathematics; and also I am
writing a sort of antiquarian book about the peaceable and private
history, so to say, of the end of the nineteenth century [...]
[Dick] thinks me rather a grinder, and despises me for not being
very deft with my hands: that's the way it is nowadays. From
what I have read of the nineteenth-century literature (and it is
quite a great deal), it is clear to me that [...] [they] despised everybody who *could* use his hands.'[18]

Work for a 'grinder' has in fact become rather rare; of people working
in a nearby wood the fictional Morris is told:

'Apart from the other pleasures of it, it gives them a little rough
work, which I am sorry to say is getting somewhat scarce for
these last fifty years.'[19]

One of the most interesting conversations in *News from Nowhere* is pro-
voked when Morris asks Old Hammond:

'Now, this is what I want to ask you about – to wit, how you get
people to work when there is no reward of labour, and especially
how you get them to work strenuously?'
    'No reward of labour?' said Hammond, gravely. 'The reward
of labour is *life*. Is that not enough?'

'But no reward for especially good work,' quoth I.

'Plenty of reward,' said he, 'the reward of creation. The wages which God gets, as people might have said time agone. If you are going to be asked to be paid for the pleasure of creation, which is what excellence in work means, the next thing we shall hear of will be a bill sent for the begetting of children.'

'Well, but,' said I, 'the man of the nineteenth would say there is a natural desire towards the procreation of children, and a natural desire not to work.'

'Yes, yes,' said he, 'I know the ancient platitude, wholly untrue: indeed, to us quite meaningless. Fourier, whom all men laughed at, understood the matter better.' [Fourier was the only major socialist thinker of the nineteenth century to insist on 'the necessity and possibility of making labour attractive.']

'Why is it meaningless to you?' said I.

He said: 'Because it implies that all work is suffering, and we are so far from thinking that, that, as you may have noticed, whereas we are not short of wealth, there is a kind of fear growing up amongst us that we shall one day be short of work. It is a pleasure we are afraid of losing, not a pain. [...] [A]ll work is now pleasurable; either because of the hope of gain in honour and wealth with which the work is done, which causes pleasurable excitement, even when the actual work is not pleasant; or else because it has grown into a pleasurable *habit*, as in the case with what you may call mechanical work; and lastly (and most of our work is of this kind) because there is conscious sensuous pleasure in the work itself; it is done, that is, by artists.'[20]

Morris, of course, was himself an artist of such high degree that his influence is still with us today. His own life story and industrious creativity illustrates the possibilities offered by the adoption of a more diverse working life. When Morris passed away at the tender age of 62 it was remarked that he died having 'done more work than most ten men.' He was a writer, designer and craftsman who achieved success in an incredible number of fields, including ceramics, stained-glass, painting, embroidery, printing, fabric and wallpaper design, typography and book design, poetry (for which he was most famed in his own lifetime), prose and illuminated manuscripts, to name but a few. He was completely self-taught and if an art or craft that interested him was no longer practised he would himself resurrect it by studying ancient artefacts and medieval guidebooks. Morris utterly personifies Shea's 'polymath', and he does so for the simple love of art.

Indeed it is *art* – both as the human reproduction of aesthetic beauty, and as 'simple' craftsmanship – which led Morris to become a socialist in the first place; as he himself observed:

> [It] must be remembered that civilisation has reduced the workman to such a skinny and pitiful existence, that he scarcely knows how to frame a desire for any life much better than that which he now endures perforce. It is the province of art to set the true ideal of a full and reasonable life before him, a life to which the perception and creation of beauty, the enjoyment of real pleasure that is, shall be felt to be as necessary to man as his daily bread, and that no man, and no set of men, can be deprived of this except by mere opposition, which should be resisted to the utmost. [21]

As an artist Morris dreamt of a world where people would be free to create, and to freely enjoy the creations of others. Peter Kropotkin's anarchist philosophy had similar motivations, although, as a geographer, he wanted everyone to have an equal access to scientific method and the joys of scientific discovery:

> He who has once in his life experienced this joy of scientific creation will never forget it … and he cannot but feel with pain that this sort of happiness is the lot of so few of us … if scientific methods and leisure were not limited to a handful of men. [22]

This desire for freedom, openness and accessibility in *all* human endeavours is reflected in modern times by the growth of what has been described as the *Open Everything* movement; an offshoot of the *Open Source* revolution. The term Open Source was originally used in computer programming to describe the practice of keeping the 'Source

Code' of a programme – that which is written by human programmers in a human-readable programming language – freely accessible and open to anyone who might want to correct or improve the software or otherwise alter it to suit their specific needs. Open Source software is usually created and maintained by a vast network of people and anyone can sell or freely distribute their own adapted versions of the software as long as the source code remains open. The opposite to this is 'proprietary software', where, as the name suggests, for reasons of profit the software is designed in-house by a closed team of programmers (though the art of programming is such that few modern applications can be created solely – from scratch as it were – by a single company or individual) and sold under license; it is deemed illegal to alter the software or, of course, to use it without said license.

The success of Open Source software, and the expansion of the Open Source philosophy, has encouraged the free and open exchange of ideas, skills and knowledge necessary for the production of other vital technologies. One famous example is Vinay Gupta's[23] 'Hexayurt'[24] a simple, but strong and long-lasting, emergency shelter built from cheap, locally available materials. The plans for the Hexayurt are freely available online[25] and people are constantly adapting and refining the original design. An entire Hexayurt village was created at the 2010 Burning Man Festival and Hexayurts have since been built to aid relief work in Haiti.

Commercially there are strong parallels between Open Source methodology and the Guild System. As a collective endeavour Open Source creativity is self-regulating because shoddy programming (craftsmanship) and naff software (product) reflects badly on the community as a whole, likewise in a Guild system bad workmanship reflects on every other member of the Guild. Regular *Idler* readers will be familiar with the Guilds and there is little need to expand upon the concept here – those who would like to find out more about the possibilities they offer a post-industrial world would do well to consult Arthur Penty's 1906 masterpiece, *The Restoration of the Guild System*.[26]

The enclosure of human knowledge has proved as devastating and disempowering as the enclosure of land itself, and so the newly emerging *Open Everything* movement may prove to be vastly more important than anyone dare yet hope. But open access to knowledge must be matched by an equally free and open access to the means of produc tion. As well as being an advocate of the Guild System, the aforementioned Arthur Penty was also a *distributist*. Developed and promoted by Catholic thinkers like G. K. Chesterton and Hilaire Belloc, distributists believe that the ownership of the means of production, rather than remaining in the exclusive control of the state, corporations and/or wealthy individuals, should be spread as widely as possible among the general populace. They believed that the land, knowledge, tools-of-production and other vital resources should be co-owned by the local community so that everyone had access to that which was necessary to make a living without being indebted to a central state, corporation or private third party. Distributism offers greater freedom and equality than either capitalism or state-communism because it respects private property and individualism, but also guards against the menace of centralized power and extremes of wealth or poverty. Modern technology now makes it possible to produce a whole range of vital products – including many items which were formerly considered too specialized or complex for local production – using smaller, localized workshops. Now, more than ever, it is possible to return to a network of decentralized cottage-industries (each self-regulated by the Guild system) as our main system of production (something which I expand upon in the aforementioned sister article to this, *The Shuttle Exchanged for the Sword*).

Open Source principles – and the formation of an Open Guilds – practised by a diverse network of cottage industries (working to a rhythm that suited their own needs rather than the demands of capital) would be central to a society dedicated to the work aesthetic. As for *what* should be created, we would do well to return to that most Olympian of aesthetes, William Morris, who famously advised:

If you want a golden rule that will fit everything, this is it: Have nothing in your houses that you do not know to be useful or believe to be beautiful.

By extension anything we ourselves produce – the fruits of our own labour – should also be proven useful through application and/or be believed beautiful by producer and consumer alike. Taking Morris's maxim to its logical conclusion, it would also be necessary to avoid all other employment that is itself contrary to these ends or may in some way aid the needless production of the useless (including that which is of negative use – i.e. that which is destructive to life on Earth) and/or the ugly.

So let us dream for a moment, as Morris did before us, of a perfect future society. A place where people are encouraged to swap and change jobs as often as they please so that no vocation or desire remains unfulfilled; where free and open access to knowledge and resources allows people far greater levels of autonomy and self-sufficiency; a fairer, decentralized, distributist economy where wealth is measured by utility and beauty rather than crass status or cold hard cash; a place where decisions are made through the application of reason rather than hierarchy or force of arms – or indeed force of numbers; and where cloth-weaving, print-making, music-composing mathematicians get to punt boats on the crystal clear water of the Thames.

This may ever be a dream, but that does not mean that we ourselves cannot live in accordance to the work aesthetic right here, right now, in our existing everyday lives. The obstacles we face are cultural, rather than physical, bonded as we are by the '*mind forg'd manacles*' of the work ethic. But as Epicurus said: 'To live under constraint is a misfortune, but there is no constraint to live under constraint.' Our lives are songs that are yet unsung – why not turn them into a symphony.

Do whatever your heart would have you do – *make pictures, take pictures, pour pitchers, write scriptures, right wrongs, sing songs, stitch thongs, weave wonders, feed wanderers, punt gondolas, build scooters, programme computers, pedicab commuters and match-make suitors* – but never feel guilty for those moments when you're heart is happiest doing nothing at all.

Be useful. Be beautiful. Be free.

Notes

1. Fairlie, S. 2009. *A Short History of Enclosure in Britain, The Land*, Issue 7.
2. Draper, W. 2010. *Common People, The Idler, No.43 Back to the Land*. Idler Books.
3. Cobbett, W. 1967. *Rural Rides*. Penguin Classics.
4. http://www.dark-mountain.net
5. Fuller, B. 1981. *Critical Path*. Hutchinson & Co.
6. Sale, K. *Five Facets of a Myth*. www.non-fides.fr/?Five-Facets-of-a-Myth
7. Cobbett, W. 1967. *Rural Rides*. Penguin Classics.
8. Foucault, M. 1979. (Sheridan, A., translator) *Discipline & Punish: The Birth of the Prison*. Vintage Books.
9. ibid.
10. Edwards, D. 1995. *Free to be Human: Intellectual Self-Defence in an Age of Illusions*. Green Books.
11. Holmgrem, D. 2002. *Permaculture: Principles & Pathways Beyond Sustainability*. Hepburn, Australia: Holmgren Design Services.
12. Carlsson, C. 2008. *Nowtopia: How Pirate Pogrammers, Outlaw Bicyclists, and Vacant-Lot Gardeners Are Inventing the Future Today!* AK Press.
13. de Cleyre, V. 1910. *The Dominant Idea. Mother Earth*, Issue 5. http://praxeology.net/VC-DI.htm
14. http://bobohea.net/empire_of_the_rising_scum.html
15. ibid.
16. Heinlein, R., Vassallo, D.F. (illustrator). 1978. *The Notebooks of Lazarus Long*. New York: G.P Putnam's & Sons)
17. Morris, W. 1993. *News From Nowhere and Other Writings*. Penguin Classics.
18. ibid.
19. ibid.
20. ibid.
21. Morris, W. 1894. *How I Became a Socialist. Justice*.
22. Kropotkin, P. 1989. *Memoirs of a Revolutionist*, cited in *Mutual Aid: A Factor of Evolution*. Black Rose Books.
23. http://vinay.howtolivewiki.com
24. http://hexayurt.com
25. http://www.appropedia.org/Category:Hexayurt_project
26. http://www.strobertbellarmine.net/books/Penty – Restoration_Guild_System.pdf

Bron Jones

IDLE HANDS

A BRIEF HISTORY OF WORK

Mark Vernon

THE WORK OF A PHILOSOPHER WOULD SCARCELY BE called work by most people: 'Nice work, if you can get it', they might think. Fair enough! – except that the philosopher would also observe that there is really no such thing as 'work', in the singular, anyway. There are, rather, an enormous variety of ways in which people can be said to be working. Moreover, that range of occupations only grows. It is an arresting thought to remember that in ancient Rome, say, there were only about 30 common tasks for which people were employed – artisans mostly, like shoemakers and potters. Today, the number of jobs people might do has risen to about 30,000. Such is the success of the division of labour.

The diversification of work carries several implications for any consideration of what good work might be. For example, work that is a blessing to one person will inevitably be a curse to another. 'There are in work all grades, from mere relief of tedium up to the profoundest delights, according to the nature of the work and the abilities of the worker,' observed Bertrand Russell. Alternatively, recall Adam Smith's chilly description of the pin factory: 'One man draws out the wire, another straightens it, a third cuts it, a fourth points it, a fifth grinds it at the top for receiving the head: to make the head requires two or three distinct operations to put it on ...' Etc., etc. And Smith hadn't visited today's factories in southern China.

So whilst the division of labour is not a bad thing per se – being a key generator of wealth, to make just one obvious comment in its favour – it has raised a spectre that haunts modern work, namely that it can be alienating, to use Karl Marx's word. 'The proletarians have nothing to lose but their chains,' he continued. You might think that a little extreme. However, there is truth in the observation that for some, work is deadly and probably always will be. With more wit, George Orwell echoed the sentiment when, in *Down and Out in Paris and London*, he wrote:

> A beggar, looked at realistically, is simply a businessman, getting his living, like other businessmen, in the way that comes to hand. He has not, more than most modern people, sold his honour; he has merely made the mistake of choosing a trade at which it is impossible to grow rich.

So the first contribution from any philosophy of the concept of good work is sobering. At the very least, there is a monumental task ahead of anyone who seeks to ensure that most work can be called good. That noted, the history of what various thinkers have written about work throws up a number of rich ideas as to what good work might be.

The discussion goes back at least to the ancient Greeks – though they tended to think that it was the practical consequences of work rather than work itself which was good. Hesiod, the poet who wrote around the time of Homer, urged his followers not to 'let wicked strife persuade you, skipping work, to gape at politicians and give ear to all the quarrels of the marketplace': you need to work to fill your barns with grain. Similarly, in the Bible, it might be said that God's work during the mythical six days of creation led to the day of rest upon which God looked out and then saw that 'it was good.'

Historically, then, there is an ambivalence around the process of doing work – which is reflected in the origins of the word. The French *travail* stems from the Latin *tripalium*, an instrument of torture made from three sticks. Similarly, one Greek word for work, *ponos*, means sorrow; the Latin *labor* implies drudgery; and the German *arbeit*, adversity. Thus too, when Adam and Even were thrown out of Eden, Adam was condemned to till the soil, for creation was no longer simply good.

To put it the other way, the ancients tended to think that work was necessary: presumably Plato and Aristotle worked hard on their philosophy, as much as Pericles and Alexander did on their conquests. However, what was demeaning was to be forced to work. Hence the fear of being captured and sold into slavery. What aristocrats like Plato, Aristotle, Pericles and Alexander exercised was choice: they could work as they willed.

In between slave labour and industrious aristocrats were working artisans – stone masons, shoe makers, carpenters and the like. They had a skill that was valuable and even personally rewarding. But still, they were bound to exercise the trade in order to earn a living, and more-over at the behest of customers. It was not bad work like a slave; but it didn't enjoy the full freedoms of chosen activities either. These 'middle workers', no doubt, had ambivalent feelings about their employment – good days and bad days, we might say. It was ever thus. However, this flags up a factor that must be part of any conception of good work: some degree of choice. Richard Reeves noted one aspect of this in his book *Happy Mondays*: people do not mind working long hours so long as they have a say in when they work that overtime. Elements of choice must be built into the good working day.

Ideas have shifted across time, and in the ambivalent associations of the word 'work' – not least at the Reformation. In the sixteenth cen-tury, emerged a powerful and new notion, that work is a vocation. People should do it to the best of their ability as an offering to God. The difference from the ancients is that it is not just the products of work that are good – grain for the barn, and the like – but that work itself could be called good.

Luther wrote: 'The works of monks and priests, be they never so holy and arduous, differ no whit in the sight of God from the works of the rustic toiling in the field or the woman going about her household tasks.' No longer could priests and monks claim that they alone were responding to a 'higher calling'. We certainly agree with him to this day, in relation to the farm labourer: unions would not be possible without such an underpinning philosophy. Whether or not we have embraced his progressive ideas about housework is another question entirely. However, Luther highlights a second key element in good work. For work to be good, it should be valued by society, which is partly what it means to call work a vocation.

That said, the Reformation developed a further idea that has informed much of what we make of work today. It was that to be out of work is to be at moral risk. 'The devil will find work for idle hands to do,' Morrissey sang – almost directly quoting a Reformation proverb. Henry Ford echoed the same sentiment if in mass industrial guise: 'There is no place in civilization for the idler. None of us has any right to ease.' Hence, to this day, unemployment is viewed not only as an economic failure but as a social threat: any work is better than no work, be it good or bad.

The adulation of work for work's sake reached its zenith in the purple passage in praise of work written by Thomas Carlyle in *Past and Present* (1843):

> For there is a perennial nobleness, and even sacredness, in Work. Were he never so benighted, forgetful of his calling, there is always hope in a man that actually and earnestly works; in Idleness alone is there perpetual despair. Work, never so Mammonish, mean, is in communication with Nature; the real desire to get Work done will itself lead one more and more to truth, to Nature's appointments and regulations, which are truth.

But not everyone agreed with this idolizing of work. John Stuart Mill, for one, objected to it: it is not work per se that is good, but the object of work that may or may not be good. He was picking up again on the older, consequentialist idea of the ancients: 'Work, I imagine, is not a good in itself,' he argued. 'There is nothing laudable in work for work's sake.' Rather, good work is that which enables the individual to reach his or her fullest potential. But this raises a third element that's important in our notions of good work. If work enables us to reach our potential, then work also becomes caught up in our quest for meaning in life. If work is part of our greater flourishing as human beings, in what way is it meaningful?

The meaningfulness of work has been interpreted by modern philosophers in different ways. For Hannah Arendt, it is shown in a distinction between labour and work. Labour is what animals do. It is the struggle for survival, it is not freely chosen, it is tantamount to slavery. In work, though, the human animal is able to respond to more than just basic biological needs and create something of greater significance. The craftsman and the artist engage in types of activity where this is seen most clearly: they make something, that has market value, but the primary purpose for making it is in the pursuit of a higher goal than merely to secure a sale – perhaps self-expression or to create an object of beauty. According to Arendt, any work that is to be meaningful is engaged in transforming the natural world to satisfy and realize such wider human needs and ends. But real life, actual work, is not always so ideal.

In truth, the search for meaningful work has also made things more complicated. As Lars Svendsen points out in his book entitled *Work*, today the task is to find your 'true self' at work. Thus, if people do not find one job fulfilling, they change it – and do so with increasing rates of churn: the job for life that was once a blessing would, perhaps secretly, be regarded by many today as a curse. This is good work as shaped by individualism – though it is perhaps worth remembering that whilst individualism tends to have a bad press today, its roots stretch back to the Reformation too, and Luther's concern to value everyone's contribution. But it also makes for conflicts, between who you feel you are and what your work makes you.

An obvious conflict is when an individual's moral values clash with the ethics of the organization for which they work. It's the phenomenon of someone having to hang their private beliefs at the office door alongside their coat. Maybe work requires them to treat customers in ways they'd find unacceptable at home. Maybe they have wider worries about the impact of the company's activities upon the environment or in the developing world – the company that exploits poverty stricken labourers further down the supply chain. Good work will seek to address these concerns and close the gap; it will have an ethos.

But with the best will in the world, this highlights another tension within the conception of good work. If the workplace is supposed to be the locus of individual meaning, it is invariably sometimes going to disappoint. For, in fact, work does not exist to serve workers alone. And its ethos will to some degree be compromised. The efforts of the workers must serve other interests – those of shareholders, customers, bosses. Thus, we are caught in a crux. Work risks becoming one of those parts of life where we seek fulfilment but never quite find it, because it can never quite deliver on our search for personal satisfaction.

There's a common way round this, or rather a way that organizations might seek to sideline the difficulties. You see it when organizations attempt to offer modes of fulfilment for employees that, while located at work, extend beyond the goals for which they're employed. Take the office that installs showers so that staff can cycle to work, or the company that builds a gym or does a deal with a health club for reduced corporate membership. Such 'perks' are not only doing their bit to fight the nation's collective flab. They suggest to employees that working here is good for them.

The maverick economist E.F. Schumacher, who had a deep criticism of capitalism as a whole, contributes something else to the discussion. He strongly objected to the idea that the worker is a cost item, which the employer will ideally seek to reduce to a minimum – if not do away with altogether, by automation. For the employee, this turns work into a kind of sacrifice: they give up their leisure and receive a fee in compensation. Such thinking, according to Schumacher, signals notions of bad work.

It treats the goods that employees produce as more important than the people who produce them. It regards the activity of pure consumption as more important than nurturing the creative capacities of humankind. All in all, it substitutes the human for the subhuman. He wrote, 'to organize work in such a manner that it becomes meaningless, boring, stultifying, or nerve-racking for the worker would be little short of criminal; it would indicate a greater concern with goods than with people, an evil lack of compassion and a soul-destroying degree of attachment to the most primitive side of this worldly existence.' Conversely, good work would provide employees with a chance to develop their faculties, appreciate the value of working with others in a common task, and work on products and services that themselves contribute to the betterment of their lives. In short, good work is good for you.

As an aside, 'the value of working with others in a common task', which Schumacher highlighted, might be manifest in another way, namely in having friends at work. Aristotle had noted that nothing contributes to the happy life more than good friends. Indeed, human beings are creatures for whom every other good thing in life would count as nothing if they did not have friends with whom to share them. So friends at work are as important for wellbeing as anywhere else.

The point has been underlined by the research of Tom Rath. In his book *Vital Friends* he uses research to show that people who have a best friend at work are seven times more likely to be engaged at work. They also have fewer accidents, better customers and show more innovation. Close friendships at work boost employee satisfaction by 50 per cent as well. He recommends that companies design offices to include spaces in which people can enjoy their friendships even when they are not working on something together — a coffee shop or spacious foyer. The necessity of friendships at work also requires bosses to lead by example: to be friendly with everyone, if not exactly friends with everyone, and to ensure that the company culture is one that doesn't expect staff to be proving themselves productive every moment of the day. It will pay off: another one of Rath's findings is that people with friends at work tend not to look for employment elsewhere or seek higher pay packets.

Let me draw some threads together. If our brief history has shown anything, it is that any sensible conception of good work will be conscious of its limits. To state the obvious: work is not the whole of life. Good work requires the time and energy to enjoy the good life elsewhere. Echoing again some of the themes of the ancient Greeks, the happiest workers will enjoy a certain freedom in relation to their work: they will have a life apart from work, a hinterland, other concerns. Holidays are not just time off work. Good work will certainly imply a cap on hours. At the very least, it will cultivate a climate in which time off work is not disdained. But then, we find ourselves caught up in another bind. For are not the boundaries between work and leisure now thoroughly fuzzy too?

'Knowledge workers', for example, are heralded as particularly fortunate since their work is 'flexible'. This is said to contribute to their wellbeing since, say, it allows mothers, and possibly some fathers, to work *and* do the childcare. There is little doubt that women and men gain from being able to work whilst also being fully involved in raising their families. However, it would be wrong to believe that flexible working is without its own stresses.

One interesting manifestation of this is shown in the fact that whilst the number of hours people work has fallen in recent decades (though perhaps not in recent years), there is a sense that work has never been more pervasive. The risk is that work is always on the minds of those working from home and the like. They exist in a semi-permanent state of being logged onto the office intranet. It is not just that the boundaries between work and leisure have become blurred, but that work has invaded leisure. If the home office is only a few yards from the sofa, it might never be out of your mind for more than a few minutes.

This could have much to do with the research which shows that well over half of employees suffer from stress at work, well over a third from depression, and close to a quarter have panic attacks. Alternatively, a recent British Social Attitudes survey reported that 77 per cent of full-time women and 67 per cent of full-time men would like to be able to spend more time with friends. The paradox is that these figures are worse than those twenty-odd years ago, when flexible working was less widespread: then only 62 per cent of women and 49 per cent of men made the complaint. It is not hard to find statistics that paint a picture of sickness not success in relation to apparently good, because flexible, work.

But perhaps the problem rests not so much at the office door as at the front door. For if there is a concept of good work, and it depends in part on our leisure, then we need a concept of good leisure too. And that is up to us. No boss can help us with that.

To put it another way, perhaps the fundamental problem we face is that we are losing our ability to enjoy time off because we never quite power down. We're like our computers, which we don't turn off but prefer to leave on standby. In *The Time Bind*, Arlie Russell Hochschild shows that less than 10 per cent of workers want shorter hours, 65 per cent want to keep things about the same, and 25 per cent want to work longer hours.

So one final part of the challenge of good work might be not so much that work has invaded leisure, but that we have come to think of our leisure as itself being a time for work-like effectiveness and efficiency. As those Reformation puritans had it: idling is of the devil. People rush from work to pick up the kids, feed them, get to their evening class, feed themselves and then collapse into bed. The weekends are planned with a great sense of urgency. Vacations are no longer days to do nothing, but to do everything that there is no space for otherwise – decorate the house, catch up with family, see the world.

Friedrich Nietzsche spotted the tendency over 100 years ago. In *Beyond Good and Evil* he opined, 'Industrious races find it very troublesome to endure leisure; it was a masterpiece of English instinct to make the Sabbath so holy and boring that the English begin unconsciously to lust for their work- and week-day.' The prophet of Germany saw us coming: commuters on Monday morning glad to be getting back to the office, for the rest.

Alice Smith

THE MORE THE MERRIER

Matt Bullen

POLYAMORY is defined as 'The practice, state or
ability of having more than one (sexual) loving
relationship at the same time, with the full
knowledge and consent of all partners involved.'

THE START OF OUR OWN ROAD TO POLYAMORY SMELLED,
as we'll see, of citrus. Polyamory can be a practical way to structure a fulfilling, original and inexpensive way of living. This
might or might not involve much sex, but it almost always teems with
colour, creative scheduling, conviviality and feeling. It brings together
more people who love each other, who can help each other and who
can help care for any children in the group. While at first glance the
energy and communication often involved seem not to fit with the idle
life, all that effort is exactly equivalent to the exertion involved in *any*
process that one decides is worth the candle. After all, creating a winter
garden or cleaning homebrew equipment take monitoring and effort,
but that's just fine if one wants to be doing those things and enjoying
the benefits.

First, a bit of our story:

In the centre of the fenced front garden of a cottage in New Zealand
is a lemon tree. It yields big, contented lemons all year. My wife and I
would chase our little boy around and around it, evening after evening,
ducking down among the giggles to pick up a fallen fruit. A family of
exactly three, contained and adrift, owning little else than stacks of
vitamin C.

It was a welcome plateau of stability, having skipped from one temporary home to another since leaving Seattle and our jobs months earlier. We had come to NZ without work offers, carrying what we had not sold or given away. After a while we invested the little money we had in a down-payment on this cottage in the Waikato. Our toddler son loved it; loved the lawns, the lemonade, the horses and pigs grazing nearby.

But geography was about to split me from Vera for several nights each week. She was set to spend a lot of time teaching at a university in Auckland, almost three hours to the north. She would be staying by herself, an attractive woman going through a time of excitement and stress, surrounded by thousands of bright, cute people. I would be alone in the countryside, looking after our boy.

She and I, it seemed to me, should talk. Any sensible couple would: even we, who had been married and utterly monogamous for well over a decade, could see that logistics might now open a sustained fracture into which sexual desire and the plain need for company might creep.

We had our talk, and then several other talks on the heels of it. Result: for the first time in our relationship, we gave each other permission to have casual sexual encounters with other people. As the odds for such sport were heavily in her favour, and I was doing little paid work, I had plenty of evenings alone after our lad went to sleep to think further about what our new arrangement might mean for our relationship. Two-thirds thrilled and one-third lonely, down among the dark paddocks of dairy country, I thought about how she might be spending the night in the city. Why were we okay with our agreement? How okay were we? Why was I mentally cheering her on, agog to hear any good war stories when she returned? This went on for many weeks. What I began to notice was that the energy I was putting into coming to terms with our sexual potential, and with the possibility that she might at any given moment be enjoying with someone else what I was used to her getting only from me, was where I *wanted* to be burning a good amount of my mental and emotional calories. Exploring closeness and satisfaction was, to me, worth the outlay. Why devote most of one's inner life to fretting about charts, product (horrid compound usage), miles per gallon, plasma screens?

Here's what happened about our sex deal: neither of us did

anything, at all. Not an iota. Not once. We didn't during this time, and
we didn't later in the year when I decided to move back to Seattle with
our son, to re-establish our lives there and to wait for Vera to finish her
Auckland contract and return to the US. However, perhaps curiously,
when we regrouped in Seattle the next winter and Vera and I decided
to keep the agreement in place for a while longer, we *did* each have sex
a few times with other people. Of course we were discreet for the sake
of our child. This period lasted a couple of months. It was fun. It was
not polyamory.

Then we met Terisa, Scott and Larry. They came to one of the
cheap and cheerful cocktail parties we threw each month at our North
Seattle apartment. Terisa lives with the two men, who are both her
partners of many years. She met Scott first. Later, he introduced her to
Larry. The guys are not involved with each other.

Terisa and I had a talking point from the off: the English accent she
feigns for her role in her online polyamory comedy series *Family* (I
would soon join her as her co-writer on the show, one of the earliest
and most stable pit-props of our relationship). I am from England, and
her accent was so good that I genuinely did not know that she was
really American, brought up in LA. She thought I was teasing her
when I complimented her, and that moment sealed one of her most
enduring tributes to me: 'Matt, you are so full of shit'. This exchange,
by the by, also flinted the spark of mischief between us that would
ignite one of the most tapestried and glorious loves of my life.

Once Terisa and I had established our shared professional interest in
writing, we soon started dating and making love. We also found that
we were able to get on well as pals. These strands interplayed, wove in
and out, curveting off each other or muttering along famously.

Soon afterwards Vera started going out with Larry, Terisa's husband.
At first this led to a couple of classic quasi-farcical moments, such as
Vera and I texting each other at daybreak from respective bedrooms at
the triad's house, asking politely who was going to pad downstairs to
make the coffee.

This state of affairs was, in Terisa's phrase, all very convenient. Vera
and I would spend a night or two at their house each weekend, most of
the time spent making and editing *Family*, working in the garden, or

cooking and eating as a group. Scott would join us often to chat or eat: sometimes he would head out for an evening with his own girlfriend of the time. We were careful to make sure that our son had his own room and that we entered and left our partners' bedrooms while he slept.

But something else was starting to develop. As months passed, we found that the core romantic liaisons were sprouting other relationships and benefits: other kinds of love, if you like. Vera and Terisa became good pals, lunching and doing dance class together. Our seven-year-old learned editing skills sitting on Terisa's knee at her computer suite; editing that was valuable not just in the filmic sense, but as a general ability critical to crafting all manner of creative work. Larry and Scott would also pitch in with our lad, helping with maths homework or bantering. Vera and Larry toiled hard to develop produce patches at the triad's home: as I write there is a huge bowl of their ripening cherry tomatoes a few feet from my desk. I baked bread and made soups for the group. And *Family* continued to act as a cementing force for all of us. I helped to write it, our son had an acting role in it, Vera catered and assisted. Larry was already executive producer, Scott a director of photography. Terisa directed and orchestrated the whole thing on a shoestring budget, with a cast and crew of up to 20 people per episode. It was a relentlessly creative time, an awful lot of fun and cost little. We also began to attract the attention of media from *Newsweek* to Canal+ TV France. (Egotistical side note: can you imagine my satisfaction, as a skinny English boy, in talking to the French nation about how to love women?)

More recently, Terisa has started to collect our boy from school once or twice a week to take care of him for a few hours, giving Vera more freedom to earn part-time cash teaching ballet. This childcare arrangement was, in turn, made possible by our moving to an apartment three minutes from the triad's house. It costs less than our old apartment, and we can nip to each other's home to drop off a loaf or to pick someone up on the way to the huge local charity shop where we buy most of our clothes.

I could go on effusing about this part-Pop-Larkin, part-Bob-Carol-Ted-Alice, part-Lord-Ickenham scene. But people tend to want to know if there really is as much joy involved as I have begun to outline. The answer: yes. The context: polyamory also takes pretty much constant maintenance, and involves the occasional flashpoint scene that could strip the paint off the eyes of Mars. Living polyamorously is a bit like getting into the SAS: myths aside, and above all, you have to want to do it and to be able to focus way, way beyond initial illusions. To stretch this simile further, you have to be able to function well as your own person and as part of a group, sometimes parachuting into one of these two camps when you'd far rather be left in peace in the other.

Do we fight, do we get on each other's nerves, do we get jealous? After all, Dr. Pepper Schwartz opined in a recent KOMO News piece that 'it is not in most people's capacity to love multiple people at the same time, much less all live together as a happy family.' The answer is: certainly there are tensions and jealousies. For example, as a family we all tend to be a little over-solicitous of each other's feelings. This can lead to problems. Terisa and I have just worked through a set of mis-understandings stemming, on the one hand, from my trying to second-guess everyone else's wants rather than just stating my own and, on the other, from her over-sensitive reactions on occasions when I *have* just bluntly stated my mind. These two inclinations were feeding off each other unhealthily, so we had to do some surgery. Now we're better.

As to sexual jealousy, we sometimes feel it and we strive to work through it. Often we replace it with 'compersion'. This is not really the antithesis of jealousy: rather, it is a feeling of pleasure that someone you love is enjoying themselves with someone else. Why should anyone think this so very suspect or delusional? If Vera calls me from a dance conference and says she is taking a walk along a sunny beach, I might get a twinge if I am in rainy Seattle but my overall feeling is 'Great, sweetheart!' Similarly, if she spends a vivid night with Larry, I am pleased for her. She is a human female surging with wants, fears, juices and hormones. It does not detract from our love if she gallops some of these with another man. It just doesn't. We might be at the centre of each other's universe, but we're not always in the middle of same. So deal.

A good tip, if *you* are contemplating how you might deal with

jealousy, is encapsulated in a section title of Dossie Easton and
Catherine A. Liszt's book *The Ethical Slut*. That is: 'Go For The Ick'. In
other words, cut to what is really making you feel anxious and queasy.
Is it the thought of your partner looking into someone else's eyes, or a
fear of being dumped, or giggled about, or what? The nearer you can
get to the core, the more clearly you can see yourself: and that is a
good – though scary – place to be. Moreover, I advocate sharing your
exploration with your partner. It can be quite wonderful to be sharing
a bottle of wine together, talking around the forest of your insecuri-
ties, and suddenly to find yourself in a clearing where you can say with
conviction something like 'Fuck, that's *it*. I'm scared that you'll shout
things out to *him* at orgasm that I've only known you utter to *me*!'
There. Was it that dread an admittance?

Besides, Larry is fond of pointing out – and he's quite right – that
time jealousy is a more significant factor. Right now, Terisa and I are
emerging from a difficult patch during which she spent almost all her
time with someone new. They were working together and became
infatuated with each other. She freely admits that her time management was poor. At every turn she had a choice of who to be with, and
at every turn she chose this other chap. It hurt me, and others. But
that's just how she is sometimes. She has done it before and might do so
again. As it happens, our relationship came out of this period stronger,
tested in the furnace. I understood her behaviour and its context.
We're still together, all the strands of our connection intact.

Such episodes are not uncommon in poly lives.

It comes down to this: while each polyamorous set-up is as unique
as a snowflake – not all, for example, are charged with the hot stink of
sex, as Ted Hughes almost wrote – they all involve more central people
than does a monogamous relationship. And the more players there are,
the richer the whole garment and the greater the need for fine knitting
and labour. An example is what had clearly started to develop between
Terisa and me. What had been allowed to begin because of a deal
between Vera and I about one-night fun had rapidly mutated way
beyond that. Terisa and I had fallen in love, and that was not an agreed
outcome of the original arrangement. But what I felt for both women,
aided by the various allegiances developed and by the Vera–Larry axis,

made it worthwhile for us all to work on the reality. In line with several
of Morin's (1999) observations about successfully adjusting to non-
exclusivity, we all had a reservoir of goodwill, little lingering resent-
ment, and felt similarly powerful and autonomous.

Speaking of power, Jim Fleckenstein, quoted in Helena Echlin's
2003 *Guardian* article on polyamory, observes that modern polyamory
has often been driven by women: 'Increased financial independence
means that women can build relationships the way they want to.'
Clearly, the girls are often on top.

So, is polyamory *enviable*? Put it this way: when I go through our
challenging times, I usually ask myself whether I would want to be
living any other way or spending time doing anything else. No. Our
son is happy and healthy. We all get on, even when the six of us
descended on the UK for a hectic vacation. We are doing our best to
maintain an inventive work schedule that suits each of us. I love my
wife, with whom I share a history of companionship, adventure and
humour. She is a ballet educator, with great legs, who can and does
out-dance anyone in Seattle's Capitol Hill nightclubs. My girlfriend
Terisa and I work hard to shape half a dozen script drafts over a couple
of days and afterwards, when we collapse into bed, I literally have to
catch my breath when I see her long, naked back as she twists round to
switch off the bedside light. Although here's some full disclosure: yes,
I fancy them both rotten and like to express this at any given opportunity, but most of the time I am more likely to be found in the local
library with our son while Vera is watching Larry's violin rehearsal; or
to be fretting over whether Terisa has refilled her keychain pillbox
with migraine pills. That's more like the workaday love we all know,
right?

Polyamory is great, and it is tempting. But there is one cautionary
point I would make above all. Unlike *Generation Game*-style endeavours such as joining one's spouse for a one-off pot-throwing class or
archery lesson, polyamory (or even swinging) is not something to be
tried lightly. Ducks need to be corralled into a row, and anyone involved has to be searingly honest about what is likely to please or to
disturb them. Otherwise, I almost guarantee shock and/or sadness.
Indeed, I would advise not trying just in order to try, but to try with

the full intention of succeeding. And *that* takes preparation and compassion. And courage.

If my family and I have any influence, via our living more or less openly and in the media, I would like it to be that we help other people get to a stage at which polyamory can be aired as a relationship option as comfortably as organic food or alternative medicine are now aired – in their spheres – without blushes or blinks.

Polyamory acknowledges our ability to love, to fancy, to share, to live collectively. And because it helps to satisfy those needs, it also helps us to live idly.

Lots of loves to you.

WILD FOOD WILD FLOW

HOW I GAVE UP BUSINESS AND GOT MY FINGERNAILS DIRTY INSTEAD

Robin Harford

> Man is not himself only...
> He is all that he sees;
> all that flows to him from a
> thousand sources...
> — Mary Austin

OUR CULTURE DEEPLY FEARS THE EARTH, FOR WE KNOW what happens when we take ourselves away from this so-called civilization, and return to the primitive, the primal ... we change.

Our masters do not like us to change, for we become difficult, unruly, unlicensed ...

> Those who go into wilderness, into Nature that has not been tamed, are no longer under (arbitrary) human law, but under the all-encompassing, inevitable law of Nature. They go out from under human law. They are no longer citizens, they are not orderly, they are not civilized – they are outlaws. When you go into wilderness, something happens, something that civilization does not like. (That's why they cut it down, you know).
> — Stephen Harrod Buhner

It is early on a cold autumnal morning, and I am at the estuary squatting down among the plants. It is too early for most people to be out. I sit alone, watching my breath mist out from my nostrils.

I am aware of the landscape around me, shift down a gear, and the stream of my thinking goes quiet. I prefer, instead, to keep the focus on my body, to sense how it responds to subtle fluctuations and signals around me.

Canada geese arrive. Bird calls sound the alert when I start to move, then die down again. I am seen, no longer, as a threat. And so I sit, absorbing the landscape and wait.

At some point I feel the urge to get up and start to move. My body is relaxed, my senses heightened. By staying present with my body, I walk slowly, observing what is around me.

It is at moments like this that I am happiest. The modern world with its deadlines, schedules, hyperactivity and linear way of living no longer exists. Instead a timelessness embraces me. I am no longer a passive observer looking at the land, but instead am immersed in it, feeling and sensing my interrelationship with it.

As I amble through the estuary I gather food – wild food, feral food. Plants that have adapted to their environment over millennia, plants that feed my bones with their nutrient-dense goodness. No vegetable, home grown or bought, can match this. Within a short while, I have gathered enough food to last my family for three days. The kitchen will, once again, be overflowing with Nature's bounty.

Some call wild food, free food. I do not see it as such. There is no such thing as 'free' in Nature. Everything has a price, not necessarily a monetary price, but definitely a price. I pay the price of energy expended to harvest plants, the price of sacrificing countless hours to learn which plants are edible. Ultimately I pay the price of shedding my old, former self.

From 1999 to 2004 I was a gung-ho, adrenaline-fired, go-getting internet marketing consultant. I was brought in to destroy and lay waste to the marketplace, to make my 'paymaster' top dog and annihilate the competition. And I was very good at doing it. I was riding the wave of the Internet bubble, and getting paid handsomely for it. But the price was huge. I paid with my soul, my happiness and my freedom.

Nearly seven years ago a new service came online that everyone was talking about – Facebook. So, being such a cutting-edge kind of guy (or so I thought), I went to complete my profile, and froze. It wanted me to list my interests. I simply could not think of one single interest other than 'Marketing'. For five years I had spent seven days a week, ten to twelve hours a day 'Working the Net'. I had taken a single three-week holiday in all that time. I knew nothing else.

A deep realization came over me – who the hell was I?

Something had to change!

It took a while to untangle myself from my business, to wind everything up and walk away. But I did it, and the resulting journey has taught me more about myself and how the world works (outside human constructs) than anything conventional wisdom dictates. This was an education through my heart, not studied in academia, business or the schoolroom. It was a lesson unveiled. By immersing myself in Nature I started slowly to re-emerge, to rediscover who I was (and am).

Many thought that I was mad to walk away from my business, but something inside me was calling: a deep quiet voice from the past, from times when I was young and carefree. I pined for the old freedom I remembered in my bones – the world of my childhood – bounding through the woods and streams, getting muddy and worn out, eventually to fall on the earth, lie still, listen, look and breathe the scent of the soil.

Nowadays I am a forager and introduce people to the 'edible landscape' around them and under their feet. I do not charge a fixed price for the walks and courses I run (unless I am teaching with someone else), and instead receive donations. Many cannot understand how I can support myself on such a business model, but what Wild Food, Wild Flow has taught me is that life always provides.

Plant knowledge is not a commodity, something to be sold to only the elite and those who can afford it. It is knowledge that needs to be open to all, irrespective of their status in life or ability to pay. It's a simple principle, 'take what you need, give what you can'.

You see, plants are only one gateway. You could, if you were so inclined, take any aspect of Nature, and discover for yourself an ancient, wild world. Don't be afraid to go and meet the Wild Redeemer. Through the simple act of engaging and wanting to meet as many plants as possible, dreams and memories long lost have come flooding back into my consciousness – wonderfully joyful memories of being in 'The Great Outdoors'.

As a boy of twelve I owned a natural history book that taught me how to watch nature – everything from tracking badgers to gathering the hedgerow harvest. Sadly, I could not remember the author or its title. One vivid image suddenly came to mind. It was a line-drawing, showing the importance of wind direction when stalking deer. This image seemed to haunt me. I kept seeing it over the course of about a week. This was when I realized I was changing. I had started to spend much of my time outdoors, away from the computer and thought the image was simply an association, reminding me of how I had been when a boy.

But then that damn charity shop turned up!

I was walking down to my town, and on the outskirts I passed a charity shop I had not been in before. Without thinking I stopped dead in my tracks, and back-stepped towards the door. I was telling myself to go and take a look at the clothes section, and so I went in.

For some reason I found myself in front of the books, and, without thinking, pulled out and opened the first book that I laid my fingers on. There was the exact line-drawing that had been nagging me previously. A chill ran through my body. This was definitely the same book, different edition, but the same. And so began my journey into exploring Wild Flow.

★   ★   ★

> It is not the brain that thinks,
> but rather the heart.
> – Hildegard von Bingen

Nothing in life is static. Nothing in Nature is separate. It is easy to think of a single plant as isolated and on its own. In truth, a plant is part of everything else. A plant has a relationship with the other plants around it and in community with it.

Everything is related to everything else and there is a constant flow between all species. By delving deeper into this interrelationship, we knock on the door of mystery, opening ourselves up to deeper, more subtle aspects of life.

I am beginning to trust that certain processes work, without even being able, necessarily, to understand them. By reconnecting to the landscape through my body and feelings, I get a sense and appreciation of Wild Flow. Our culture teaches us to work with our heads. We learn to interpret experiences using our reason. This is back to front. The key to opening the door to Wild Flow is through the heart. The heart is an organ of sensory perception, and is often overlooked in dominant culture. Instead, we are forced into logical, rational activities, cutting ourselves off from our sensual, signal-receiving body. When this happens the inherent trust in Life, and ourselves, is usurped.

No longer are we encouraged to trust our senses, but are taught to look outside of ourselves, to another authority. And so the world of experts, specialists, bureaucrats, politicians and gods descends upon us.

The cultural script dictated by organized religion, in cahoots with government, enforces the belief that our bodies are evil, what we feel is corrupt and that we cannot trust ourselves. The uncivilized feel, the civilized do not.

Yet it is through the very process of cultivating sensory awareness that Wild Flow starts happening. The simple act of slowing down, and focusing on the heart, is all that is needed to welcome it in.

There are no magical incantations, no shamanic journeying involved. It is about letting go. By releasing the need to micro-manage every aspect of life, we learn to become Zen surfers, following the wave of life, wherever it takes us. We gently navigate the currents and experience the things we want out of life, never clinging to anything, and never being totally in control. For how can we control that which is wild?

Wild Flow teaches that abundance, in its vast diversity, exists all around us and is a natural state. Only frightened people live by grasping, grabbing and hoarding. Sahlin, in his essay 'The Original Affluent Society', from his book *Stone Age Economics*, writes: 'Free from market obsessions of scarcity, hunters' economic propensities may be more consistently predicated on abundance than our own.'

So what is this abundance Sahlin writes about? Contemporary society has so much more material wealth than hunter-gatherers, who barely had any material objects to speak of. They would carry only what was essential to survive – a means to make fire, carry water, catch animals, build shelter and so on. Give a nomad a precious gift and he will treasure it dearly, for about 24 hours, after which he may look around for a discreet place to leave it. Everything has to be carried, so anything superfluous to daily survival is discarded.

Nomadic cultures are believed to be primitive, in a negative sense. Yet they intimately know the landscape they walk through, and trust that it will provide for them. When they catch or gather a large amount of food, they call other communities together and share the bounty, in celebration, instead of making it last a few days. This is not the action of a frightened people, who believe in scarcity. Rather, it is a trust that the land will always provide.

A similar way of viewing the world is espoused in the Biblical passage, Matthew 6.25–6.26:

> Therefore I say unto you, take no thought for your life, what ye shall eat, or what ye shall drink; nor yet for your body, what ye shall put on. Is not the life more than meat, and the body than raiment? Behold the fowls of the air, for they sow not, neither do they reap, nor gather into barns, yet your heavenly Father feedeth them.

I'm no Christian, but the attitude that all will be provided can be found throughout many religions. These are rare snippets of wisdom against a plethora of rules and laws.

Wild Flow is akin to the Buddhist begging bowl. A monk will go out into the world with nothing and humbly accept alms. His bowl is a symbol of non-attachment to material possessions. The monk merely receives from the world. He places no price, value or judgement on the things the world chooses to drop into his bowl. Yet this simple practice also teaches the monk to trust life, to accept that all is well, and that his needs are always met. This can be very hard to understand for those of us brought up in the West. In our world we always want more.

So where does the heart come into all this?

Ask indigenous people where they exist in their bodies, and most point to their heart region. Ask the same question of any European, and more than likely, the majority will point to their head.

This simple shift of awareness in the body, as to where we experience the world, elicits a fundamentally different way of living life. Doc Childre, in his book *The Heartmath Solution* states:

> Many ancient cultures, including the Mesopotamians, the Egyptians, the Babylonians and the Greeks, maintained that the primary organ capable of influencing and directing our emotions, our morality and our decision-making ability was the heart; and they attached enormous emotional and moral significance to its behaviour.

Traditionally the heart has been seen as an organ for pumping blood, but this reductionist viewpoint has recently been challenged, even by science itself...

Armour and Ardell, in their book *Neurocardiology*, claim that there are at least 40,000 neurons (nerve cells) in the heart. In fact, certain crucial sub-cortical centres of the brain contain the same number of neurons as the heart. So the heart is now being considered an organ of perception. Studies have shown that it constantly feeds signals into the brain, and processes information from its own internal environment, as well as from the outside world.

★　★　★

How did our heart–brain mode of cognition get forgotten? Throughout Europe, from the fifteenth and up until the end of the nineteenth century, country dwellers were slowly moved off the land. The rich and powerful started to enclose the Commons, turning it into private property. This move had the effect of cutting our sensory bodies off Nature. Take people away from being close to the land, then force them into cities to work in factories and workhouses, and you create conditions where every signal the body receives is lost or ignored. But

Nature is fighting back, demanding to be heard again.

> I am afraid of cities. But you mustn't leave them. If you go too far
> you come up against the vegetation belt. Vegetation has crawled
> for miles towards the cities. It is waiting. Once the city is dead,
> the vegetation will cover it, will climb over the stones, grip them,
> search them, make them burst with its long black pincers; it will
> blind the holes and let its green paws hang over everything.
>
> – Jean-Paul Sartre

★　★　★

I am on a track, walking slowly. My body relaxes down, as I slip into
sensing the landscape. It is a simple process, and one that is the cornerstone for experiencing Wild Flow.

To sense the land yourself, stop for a moment and stand up. Gently
bring your awareness to your heart region. Start feeling it, sensing it,
allowing your breath to slow down. As you do so, relax the focus of
your eyes and hold your hands out in front of you. Now slowly move
them horizontally out to the side. Keep watching your fingertips as far
back as you can while still looking straight ahead. If you have done this
correctly, you will most likely be looking 180 degrees around you.
Normally our focus is very narrow. This process expands it outwards.

Maintain your awareness and start sensing, with your body, what is
happening behind you. Slow down and breathe. Now start walking,
observe your breath, what you 'feel', listen to all the sounds, smell the
wind. Your monkey mind may become calm, or resist by screeching
and turning up the volume. It depends on how much you give into the
process of letting go.

It takes a fair amount of focus to do this practice effectively, but over
time, due to the openness of observing the world, you may start to
notice subtleties often missed when you looked from a narrow head-
centric perspective. Life starts shining. Events may cross your trail,
subtle opportunities that take you into hitherto unknown experiences,
if paid attention to and followed.

On occasions these flow-states can defy logic. Let me give you an
example.

Recently I had an idea that I would like to offer wild food courses at campsites. I wanted to lead late-afternoon forages, and on returning home everyone would get together and cook a community feast around a fire. It was partly a way to give campers something to do, but more importantly, a great way to engage folk with the landscape and spread the plant knowledge to as many people as possible.

And then one morning my partner mentioned that she would like to stay in a modern Roma caravan. I put both ideas on the back burner, not being able to see clearly a way to actualize them.

That very same afternoon I received a phone call from an organization (http://www.caravanserai.info) in Cornwall that was running a sustainable food and art event during August 2010 at Treloan campsite on the Roseland Peninsula. They wanted a forager to teach wild food to the campers, and asked if I would be interested in coming along. They mentioned that they could not pay me, but could accommodate me and my partner for three nights in a modern Roma caravan, in exchange for a couple of two-hour wild food sessions, followed by a community cook up over an open fire.

Welcome to Wild Flow! Where payment comes in many more ways than cold hard cash.

This is just one small example of Wild Flow, there are many more that happen. So why do these kinds of 'opportunities' show up in my life?

I see it as a direct result of shifting my focus about money away from tunnel-vision, wanting only a fixed price, and instead moving into Wild Flow.

Foraging has taught me to trust the abundance of the land and of life. It's a metaphor for living, and this is what the plants have to teach us. That through mindfulness we can experience, maybe only momentarily, the joy, beauty and bounty that is right here, right now, all around us at all times.

Karolin Schnoor

NARROWBOAT LIVING

Paul Miles

I'VE BEEN LIVING IN A FIELD FOR MOST OF THE SUMMER. Cows wake me in the morning, with their bellowing and rhythmic tearing at grass or, if they're feeling adventurous, my strawberry plants.

As the nights have grown cooler, the evenings and mornings are wreathed in mist. In the half-light, cattle float through the vapour and ducks flap, quacking, towards me as I lean outside to greet the day. Sometimes, I hear the faint thrum of traffic on a distant motorway but the nearest road is half a mile away and that is just a minor one. I carry my provisions – in panniers on my bicycle – across the field, dodging fresh cowpats, to my home.

By day I swing in my hammock while white willows rustle in the wind and reflected sunlight dapples the wooden roof above me. Walkers pass by and smile.

In what structure have I been enjoying this idyllic, bucolic life? Not under canvas, in a cabin or a caravan, not a stick shelter in the bushes or a more substantial treehouse but on a steel boat with big side-doors that open to the sun and breeze. I live on a narrowboat, a peculiarly British vessel, with an interior just six feet wide. When a friend who used to live on one described it 'as such a big space' I didn't know what she meant. Now, after my first summer on my first boat, I realize. The experience is like camping and I feel as if all of the outdoors is mine to enjoy. For days on end I have been moored on a stretch of the Oxfordshire Canal in the middle of a meadow with the River Cherwell meandering through the bottom of 'my' wonderfully main-tenance-free garden. At the other end of the field, near the tiny road, more conventional homes – cottages of bricks and mortar – line the opposite bank of the waterway and a 200-year old bridge arches across it.

In two centuries from now, the combustion engine and axles having long been superseded by an even faster means of transportation, will the tarmac motorways revert to quiet byways on which people travel for leisure or on which they live, in old-fashioned motor homes, re-joicing in the historic quaintness of service stations and overpasses? Will holidaymakers pootle about in articulated lorries, their containers converted into cosy cabins, charmed by the slow pace of 70mph? I think not. But the canals offer us a glimpse back in time to a world where 'fast' is a brisk walking pace. The Oxfordshire Canal, finished in 1790, was one of the first to be built in Britain, dug by hand, as they all were, by teams of men. It was designed by civil engineer James Brindley, whose method was to follow the contours of the land hence the canal meanders along the gentle valley, hugging the river's course. Later, engineers decided that speed was more important – that the shortest route was a straight line – and so tunnels and cuttings and staircases of locks became more common. This new, smooth, fast, 4mph transportation of cargo – from iron ore and coal to pottery – brought huge economic growth and a decade of 'canal mania', with rich and poor rushing to invest. It was the dotcom bubble of its day and by the early 1800s there were some 5,000 miles of navigable inland waterways in Britain. Then the bubble started to deflate when the new technology of the railways steamed ahead. Not all cargo needed to be moved faster though and trade survived for a century or more. Working boats – pulled by horses and later with diesel engines – were lived in by those who worked them: whole families sharing a tiny cabin which they decorated with fancy plates and bright paintwork of roses and exotic fairytale castles. By the 1950s, cargo carrying had all but died out and the final death knell came with the severe winter in 1963 when the canals froze solid, trapping boats in the ice. Today, it is mostly leisure boats that pootle along the remaining 3,000 miles of inland waterways. If it hadn't been for the pioneering work of engi-neer and philosopher, Tom Rolt, who was born a century ago last year [2010], then even more of the canal network would, today, be con-creted over; turned into roads, buried under shopping malls or choked with nettles. In 1939, Rolt, with his wife, Angela, was perhaps the first to cruise on the canals for leisure. He was seeking to understand our increasingly mechanized civilization from which, although he was an accomplished engineer, he felt alienated. He wanted an '"island"... withdrawn from the headlong flight of "progress"' from which he could observe the modern world. He wrote about his travels in his book, *Narrow Boat*, in which he chronicled encounters with the last few horse-drawn working boats, the boat men and women whose 'life is stripped of all the complex comforts with which we have surrounded ourselves at the price of contentment'. He was dismayed by the amount of traffic in towns and, in Banbury, from where he set off, he decried 'the chain-store mongers who have defaced the ancient houses with their chromium and plate-glass shop fronts ... solely [for] the aim of money-making.' As my boat and I headed northwards out of Banbury, after a summer in the meadows to the south, I wondered what Rolt would think of the shopping centre and car parks that line the canal today and of the ancient houses that are still defaced.

I didn't cast a backward glance. I was off, continuously cruising, as the Rolts had done decades earlier, off to be a water gypsy. With a British Waterways licence, I can moor more or less anywhere on the canals for up to two weeks at a time. Urban or rural, riverside or canal-side, in marinas with plug-in electricity, CCTV, wifi and supermarket deliveries or in bucolic isolation with no phone signal, solar- and wind-power, firewood to chop and mushrooms to pick – I can sample them all and still look out the same window from the same room. Location, traditionally the most important factor in choosing where to buy a dwelling place, is no longer the deciding issue when you live on a boat. You are free. Free to roam with your home, to travel *not* dwell. You can find your inner nomad and explore whether you prefer country or city, solitude or company, self-sufficiency or convenience, northerners or southerners. You can go anywhere. Well, almost and unlike living on a boat at sea, the shore is only ever a wade away and, unless you venture onto the rivers, there are no tides or currents to contend with. New marinas are being built, providing 3,400 new mooring spaces since 2006 with 400 more planned. There are more boats on the waterways now – over 31,000 – than at the height of the

Industrial Revolution. British Waterways estimates that about 10 per cent of these are lived on. Many owners are retired but others include artists, poets and mobile yoga teachers. Me? I'm a writer and photographer and can work anywhere as long as I have reasonable public transport links and internet access – thanks to my mobile broadband dongle. I've also done a few weeks' manual work in a boatyard to 'learn the ropes'. My colleagues were all 'live-aboards', escapees from the rat-race. They work with hire-fleets in the summer and spend the winter cruising the canals at leisure.

On the canals, nature takes centre stage. Even in the towns and cities, the shopping-trolley-filled, graffiti-lined waterways are homes to ducks and swans that make nests of our human detritus, and to herons that stand on rubbish-strewn banks, motionless, waiting to spear a fish. But, under the flyover and over the railway line and on past the sprawl of suburbia, out in the countryside, with the smell of cattle and the caw of crows, ragged in the big skies, is where I prefer to be on these highways of liquid silver, gliding past blood red hips and haws and under arthritic oak trees. Pheasants, with a panicked call like a rusty engine refusing to start, explode out of the trees. Kingfishers whistle as they dart in an arrow-straight line, like a startled flying fish, over the surface of the water in a flash of brilliant turquoise. Long-tailed tits, their tails ticking as if they were needles on the dials of my engine, gather on hawthorns. Rolt too was charmed by the birdlife: 'Coot and moorhen fled to the shelter of the rushes with a furious commotion of beating wings, indignant clucking and frantically paddling feet. Swans sailed by with an air of aloof, slightly offended dignity, while every now and again a heron would wheel away, borne up with effortless grace on great grey pinions,' he wrote.

No wonder so many narrowboats are named after birds. There are countless vessels called Kingfisher or Heron. My boat came with a nonsensical name, Malteazer, a misspelt confectionary. It could have been worse. There are many punning names, Meander (sometimes with the joke rubbed in as *Me and 'er*) is popular. Or it could have been an embarrassingly pretentious name painted boldly above the gunwales: Carpe Diem crops up a lot and I've seen more than one Festina Lente, or a name a touch too whimsical, like Dreamcatcher, or too feminine and personal, such as Patricia. I don't like the convention of boats being considered female. Sturdy male names, such as Albert or Edward seem more appropriate to a steel boat, if any gender needs to be assigned. Whatever I choose (I've considered Midsummer – as I moved in on Midsummer's Day – but wonder if it's a tad twee?) I'll bear the superstitions in mind. It's bad luck to change a boat's name while it's still in the water and so is best to rechristen your vessel (and fill in the paperwork) when it's out of the water. Once you have renamed it, you make a toy model, emblazoned with the old name, set fire to it and set it afloat. Perhaps it's easier to stick with the given name?

But the name should be your last consideration when choosing a boat on which to live. After budget (second-hand boats in good condition start at about £30,000), length and ratio of interior to exterior space is probably your main consideration. A 57ft boat can cruise the whole canal system, anything longer – up to 72ft – won't be able to cruise some of the northern canals. A 'cruiser' stern has sociable outdoor space, so you and a few friends can stand by the tiller as you steer the boat along the canal but the downside is you lose out on interior space. I chose a 57ft traditional stern boat that has ample storage space inside but it gets a bit crowded if more than one other person wants to join me at the tiller. There are 3,000 miles of towpath and riverbanks as my outside space though, plus the boat's roof and a small area at the bow.

Then there are other features to consider: the age, make of hull, quality of steel, engine, type of toilet, interior layout, windows ... It's worth spending some time trying out a variety of boats and speaking to other boaters to work out your requirements.

I had wanted a narrowboat that would reflect my environmental ideals: solar-powered propulsion that is quiet and emissions-free, a vegetable and herb garden on the roof, a composting toilet. There are a tiny number of solar-powered boats on the canals. I saw one recently, Naiad, the water nymph; 'bringing peace to the inland waterways' was painted on her water-lily-decorated side. There was a bank of solar panels on the roof and three young women with Pre-Raphaelite hair and long, hand-knitted jumpers, sitting in the bow, facing the sun.

They had been born on the boat, they said. They reminded me of a line from Keats: 'Foster-child of silence and slow time.' They were now moving Naiad to the new owner as she had just been sold. I was a few months too late. The solar panels provide enough charge to the 1.5 ton battery bank to provide up to 30 miles of quiet cruising a week. Another silent, low emissions option would be to have a pedal-powered boat. There's at least one on the waterways. It has a fibreglass hull light enough to move without too much effort. The man who invented the mechanism for its propulsion – directly turning the propeller with the action of pedalling – is working on a pedal-powered, tug-style raft that could push heavy, steel narrowboats through the water. I wondered whether a pedal-powered battery bank that could be charged up with a daily cycle on an exercise bike would be an option but he's not keen on battery banks. Well, they are full of pollutants and rare earth metals, so it does negate some of the environ-mental benefits. In the end, I decided I should be more pragmatic and reconciled myself to the fact that at least I could probably use biodiesel from waste vegetable oil in my engine, but, so far, I haven't been able to organize this and most engineers try desperately to dissuade me. In the meantime, with two solar panels providing my domestic electric-ity, at least my carbon footprint has shrunk from one the size of a Yeti to that of a mouse. I have vegetables and strawberries growing on my roof, which the cows have enjoyed, and the composting toilet will have to wait until I've saved up nearly a thousand pounds. Yes, boat toilet technology costs, ahem, shit-loads of money. (A 'Separret' boat toilet that separates liquids and solids and has a small fan to assist dehydration can be yours for £780, not including installation.)

As for location, if you don't intend to be nomadic, cruising the net-work continuously, moving on every two weeks at least, then it's a good idea to find a suitable permanent mooring – either in a private marina or by the towpath – before buying.

While it means you can easily move if you don't like your neigh-bours and you need never pack for a holiday again – you simply relocate your home – there are downsides to your residence being so mobile: it can disappear when you're away for one. Once, on a tele-graph pole by the towpath, I saw a handmade poster. 'Stolen' it said, in

big letters, with photographs of a smart, new vessel and the distressed
owner's name and contact number. The name of that boat? *Que sera
sera*. Well, that was tempting fate. Other potential problems are mostly
technical. It is the integrity of the hull that is most important. If that
fails your home will sink. A hull survey before purchase is always recommended. A recommendation I didn't follow myself as Malteazer
had had a full survey two years previously and, barring a major colli-
sion that had resulted in unseen damage below the waterline, I didn't
imagine much could have changed. I had the boat taken out of the
water to have the hull blacked – a process that slows corrosion – and an
expert friend reassured me that all looked fine but I sometimes wish I'd
had the full professional survey with ultrasonic measurements to the
nearest millimetre to reassure me.

But the boatmen and women of old managed without such
gadgetry. Sometimes it seems that the more variables we can measure,
the more worries we're bound to have. The canals exemplify a meeting
of eras, as if they are a portal to distant, simpler times. Watford, for
example, is a nexus where Roman road, canal, railway and motorway
all come within a few feet of each other. As trains whiz by, traffic roars
and, trumping them all, an airforce fighter jet breaks the sound-barrier
overhead, narrowboats chug slowly through the locks. The people
steering them – live-aboards and holidaymakers – have time to stop
and chat.

Those heading south have just come through Crick tunnel, nearly a
mile-long dark, dripping, intestine of a monster that swallows you up
and seems to take forever to digest you. There is no illumination of any
kind in canal tunnels and, travelling at the grand speed of 3 mph, the
journey takes 20 minutes. In the middle of this Stygian subterranean
passage, the darkness is almost overwhelming. Alone, under the hill,
with the throaty putt-putt of the engine and the dim light of my head-
lamp diffusely lighting the way, I sorely regret reading that this
tunnel's roof has collapsed in the past. Although I've been through
tunnels much longer, never have I yearned for the passage to end quite
so much. It's a cliché I know, but now I realize the significance of the
'light at the end of the tunnel' like never before. It finally takes shape in
the distance, a white arc in which I can make out some greenness and

shape. It becomes a tree and, behind that, what looks like the arch of an old brick bridge. A bird flies past. There is sunshine. Now there is enough daylight reflecting inwards to give texture to the dark, dripping crescent of brick walls. They no longer seem menacing but beautiful, like the scales of a snake, turned outside in. When I emerge into the cool day, I begin to wonder whether enduring dark tunnels may be worth it for the joy that comes with the daylight at the end? I've been far more than six feet under and now I feel reborn, surrounded by nature, under the eternal weightlessness of our pale skin of sky. I see everything afresh – the sun sparkling on the water, flame colours of autumn, a bobbing wagtail – and I take a deep breath.

SPACE EXPLORER

Wilko Johnson

I SUPPOSE IT BEGAN WITH A TOUR OF AUSTRALIA WITH IAN
Dury and the Blockheads. The flight out was a long one – an Arab
gentleman died during the first leg of the journey and our plane
was diverted from Abu Dabai to Bahrain. They told us that fog had
prevented a landing at Abu Dabai (I believe they are often troubled by
pea-soupers out there in the desert) but I saw this dead body wrapped
in a British Airways blanket being shunted out of the luggage bay and
driven off on one of those luggage vehicles – perhaps it's a form of
burial like the Tibetan 'Sky Burial' where they take the corpse into the
mountains, chop it up and leave it for the vultures to devour – only
here they put you into the airline luggage system and you're never seen
again.

Anyway, what with one thing and another, this flight took a long,
long time. To while away the hours many of us resorted to self-
medication of various kinds, and by the time we got to Melbourne we
were thoroughly cured, not only that but severely jet-lagged too. I had
never believed in jet-lag, but I experienced it then – and it's great! If
you could buy it I would definitely keep a stash for special occasions.
There's a speedy rush and you want to do everything at once – everybody's walking up and down the hotel corridors in the middle of the
night – then suddenly you feel this immense weariness, a lethargy that
almost pushes you into the floor – you gotta lie down! But as soon as
you do you get some more great ideas and you've got to go and tell
somebody...

Thus it was that I was in the hotel bar explaining some stuff to the
other guys when I realised that it was night time.

'Different stars!' I said and went flying off to the hotel roof. A swimming pool. I got one of those reclining chairs and lay back to witness this spectacle – and wow! The stars really were different! There seemed to be many more of them and lots of them were brightly coloured and furthermore these coloured ones were in motion – the whole sky was alive. Then I realized that I was seeing fireflies which were attracted by the swimming pool lights. This was a bit of a disappointment but I continued with my observations and gazed up at constellations I had never before seen in the night sky. The edge was taken off this by the realization that I didn't know what the sky at home looked like. The only constellation I could ever identify was the Plough – which is of course not a constellation; it's a shape made by the brightest stars in Ursa Major. But anyway, I could see it wasn't up there and that was the only difference I *could* see – I tried to find the Southern Cross but I couldn't and by then the great tiredness was coming upon me, so I made my way back to the bar to report my findings.

And there Astronomy rested for some years.

My interest was rekindled by another trip to the antipodes. I had been booked to tour New Zealand with a rhythm and blues road-show – going out there on my own and working with NZ musicians. During the weeks before I was to go down there my thoughts turned once more to the southern night sky. Not wishing to repeat the debacle of that first night in Melbourne, I decided to go this time armed with some knowledge. I didn't however start learning to identify the constellations – no, I was preoccupied with this problem – *is the Moon upside-down in New Zealand?* It's a difficult piece of reasoning and none of the books of Astronomy I consulted had anything whatsoever to say on the topic. I thought and thought about it – sometimes I tried standing on my head to try and work it out but I couldn't come to any firm conclusion. I would have to go and see.

This of course meant familiarizing myself with the face of the Moon as it appears in our skies. I began to look at the Moon.

The Moon is an awesome and magnificent thing – not only is it woven deeply into the human psyche in myths and legends and beliefs but it is a tremendous object in itself – in fact it occurred to me that the Moon is the most familiar object in the universe. Every single human being who ever lived with eyes to see has gazed upon it – Pharaohs and cavemen, savages who worshipped it; the great intellects of Ancient Greece who tried to measure it; Newton, Einstein, everybody in this room. Everybody has stared and wondered at that thing … Future ages will gaze at it when we're gone – weather permitting.

Anyway, by the time I set off for New Zealand I had a clear picture of the face of the Moon. When I arrived in Auckland it was the time of the new moon (which means the Moon is dark and not visible). Over the next couple of weeks it would be waxing into a full moon. In fact the skies were cloudy during this time and I didn't get a glimpse.

These gigs we were playing were often in ballrooms attached to hotels. This is rather good because you can stay in your room right up until show-time and then pick up your guitar and walk across to the gig and afterwards, when you come off stage soaked in sweat, you are just minutes away from your luxuriously appointed bathroom. You don't even bother to take your guitar off – you just walk across to the hotel with it. You feel a bit silly if you pass anyone in the hotel corridor – walking along with a Fender guitar round your neck, it's impossible to be casual. I mean – what a pose!

So one evening after a gig I am walking with my guitar across to the hotel. I turned a corner and there was the great shining disc of the full Moon. And it was upside down.

When I returned home, I continued to look at the night sky whenever I could. I learned to identify the planets. I knew that the bright object then in the south at midnight was Jupiter, and one night I took a pair of very cheap binoculars belonging to my young son and pointed them at the planet. Oh! I could see a tiny but distinct orange disc and strung out on either side of it were four pinpoints of light that were orbiting moons. To see by such simple means another round world with its attendant satellites was a revelation; what emotions must have gripped Galileo when he witnessed this very sight and understood that it meant that the Earth was not the centre of all things – that these tiny lights would shatter mankind's universe? I bought a good pair of binoculars and looked at Jupiter every clear night – the four Galilean moons orbit the planet quite rapidly and appear in constantly changing formations – sometimes one or other of the moons would be invisible, eclipsed behind Jupiter, sometimes all four would be shining brightly, strung out like beads on either side of the orange Jovian disc. Of course I also looked at the Moon discerning the crinkly mountain ranges and craters. My binoculars even showed me that the bright planet Venus goes through phases from crescent to full like the Moon. I would see many more things through these binoculars but they could not show me the wonder of wonders that I wanted most of all to see – the rings of Saturn.

At the millennium time we moved to a house with a garden which gave access to a larger area of the sky and computer-driven telescopes became available – their electric motors can exactly track objects as they travel from their rising in the east to their setting in the west and computers can point the telescope with a whirring robotic action at any target at the touch of a button.

My first telescope was a small five-inch one (this denotes the diameter of the concave mirror used by such 'reflector' telescopes – 'scopes using glass lenses are called refractors). It was easy to carry the telescope in one hand and the tripod in the other out to the garden when darkness fell. After the telescope was assembled and switched on it would automatically begin to take its bearings and point at a bright star – this would then be centred manually and its position entered – once two stars had been located in this way the computer could extrapolate the position of any object in the sky.

This alignment procedure, although necessary, carried its own dangers ... I try to live a quiet life, attracting no particular attention from my neighbours, my paranoia convincing me that they watch me night and day so I try to keep cool. But when the telescope was lining up it would always pick a star that was hidden behind a leaf or branch – now there is a procedure for dealing with this but I used my own methods – I would physically remove the offending leaf or branch. As you can imagine this involved a fair amount of leaping and grasping and I could not help but wonder what the insomniac neighbour staring out of her window at 3 a.m. would have made of this.

Anyway, at this time Saturn was rising just before dawn – a bright star over the housetops. I decided to wait for a couple of weeks until Saturn was higher in a dark sky before taking my first look ... But one morning I was just packing up for the night when I saw that star rising. The batteries of my telescope had run down so the computer could not be used to find the planet. Looking through the eyepiece I made a couple of random sweeps.

Suddenly it flashed across the field of vision – less than a second it was in my view but it was Saturn; Saturn perfect, the image tiny but sharp and clear, tilting to show the unmistakable rings. In that brief moment all my expectations of the planet were fulfilled and the kick of that first glimpse stays with me. In time I would have larger telescopes which show the division in the rings and their shadow on the pale surface of the planet. I would gaze on this view for hours sometimes, telling myself 'That thing exists – it's really there'. If you were told to create something beautiful from two basic geometric shapes, who could have conceived of such a thing? Yet there it hangs in the night sky; impossibly beautiful and at the same time ... obvious.

My little telescope developed a fault after a while and the shop said they couldn't fix it and would give me my money back. I was having none of this and asked what was the next step up towards a real grown-up telescope.

And so it was that I took possession of a twelve-inch Meade LX200. This was big and it was heavy – there was no chance of carrying it back and forth from the garden – in fact the instruction manual contains the following advice: *Two or more people should always be used to move the telescope. Disregard of the above warning could result in serious injury or death.* Grim pictures of my friends finding me one morning beneath the telescope like a squashed hedgehog.

But my house has a flat roof! What else was there to do but haul the thing aloft? I made sure there were plenty of helpers and we all survived.

The best plan with a large telescope is to set the thing up and then leave it permanently in place – this avoids the necessity of aligning it every time. It also means that the telescope must be protected from the elements. I kept it covered with tarpaulins for a while, but this was not very neat or reliable. Eventually I made a fitted cover for it using tarpaulin and plenty of gaffer tape. This cover took the form of a six-foot high green condom, flared at the base to accommodate the tripod.

When darkness fell I would emerge from my trapdoor, pull off the cover and there was my telescope ready to go. There was a problem when I had finished – it was impossible to reach up and simply put this long condom over the telescope, and I adopted the method of getting inside the thing, putting it over the 'scope, then crouching down and crawling out from underneath. This was awkward, and on frosty nights when the cover was frozen stiff, something of an ordeal. My paranoia also gave rise to fears that those same neighbours who had observed my antics pulling leaves off trees would look out of their windows and see a six-foot tall green alien stumbling about on my roof before engulfing the telescope.

Eventually I decided to house my (now massive 14-inch) telescope in a dome. This dome is made of fibreglass, delivered in pre-fabricated sections. It consists of a circular wall with a domed roof that turns on a roller track. I built the cylindrical lower section myself, but needed assistance to lift the revolving dome into place. For some days I would go up to the roof and stand inside the topless dome like a child in a playpen. Still wishing for complete discretion, I decided to thwart the curiosity of my neighbours and complete the construction under cover of darkness. That way, the dome would appear one morning without commotion and hopefully pass unnoticed.

Round about this time I took up cycling and at first I practised riding around at three or four o'clock in the morning when the streets were deserted. On one of these early expeditions I rode up the street that runs parallel to mine. There is a gap between two houses on this street where you can look through to the back of my house and I wanted to see how conspicuous my dome was. I rode slowly along looking for the place – 'This is it – no, the next one ...' By the time I found the spot I was riding very slowly – I saw the dome – it was huge and shining white in the darkness – my astonishment was interrupted by the realization that I had slowed down too much and was actually going to fall off. It's really hard to fall off a bike without making a noise – basically you've just got to fall without flailing about and so I did – in slow motion I toppled – the side of my face made contact with *terra firma* and somehow seemed to keep on falling so that my cheek was ground into the pavement. I made not a sound. I got up and looked around – the street was dark and silent and no one had witnessed my mishap. I pushed the bike home.

I've got another story involving astronomy, cycling and Newton's first law of motion ...

I had been up all night making my observations and the morning was breaking so I switched off the telescope and went downstairs. That's the astronomy bit. I had a cup of coffee then found that I needed some Rizlas. It was broad daylight by then but still very early and no one about and I set off on my bike for the 24-hour shop. In the shop I thought I might as well buy some provisions so I got milk and bread and so on and for some reason a jar of marmalade. The man put these items in one of those extraordinarily delicate blue plastic bags. This was already stretching as I walked out of the shop and I was forced to gather the whole bundle in my arms. In doing this the top burst off of the marmalade and it began pouring down my front. I was still in view of the shopkeeper so I kept walking steadily until I was out of sight. I disposed of the marmalade jar – most of its contents were soaking into my shirt – and mounted my bike. The bag had disintegrated, so I balanced the groceries in the crook of my arm and set off. When I reached the top of my street my arm was aching so I stopped and transferred the pile of items to my left arm. Now my street is on what we in Essex are pleased to call a hill – that is, it declines from the horizontal by a few degrees, so I could free-wheel the last leg of my journey. So I go sailing down the street ... I'm accelerating ... here comes my house ... at this point I realize that using my right hand to control the bike means that I can only operate the front brake. The cyclists among you will appreciate the peril I was in. A couple of dabs on the brake emphasized this. My house is racing towards me – what could I do? The voice of reason would have said, 'Drop the groceries – they're gonna hit the ground anyway' but I had reached my house and jammed on the brake. Newton's first law of motion states that an object will continue to move in a straight line until acted on by a contrary force. The bike was operated on by the brake and experienced a sudden deceleration while I continued in a straight line over the handlebars and ended up sprawled on my back in the middle of the street with the groceries strewn about me. As I said, it was broad daylight but still very early ...

I looked around and found that once again I had escaped unobserved, but at any moment one of those inquisitive neighbours could look out and my credibility would be damaged beyond repair. I got to my feet and gathered up my bike and the scattered groceries. I was in some considerable pain – in fact I believe I was actually whimpering as I dragged myself indoors – I lay on the floor for some time before realizing that I had forgotten to buy the Rizlas.

My current telescope is a 14-inch reflector – as well as the onboard 'go-to' computer, it is equipped with sat-nav to determine its exact location and time. The images it produces are quite strikingly clear even though I live in a very light-polluted town. Images of the Moon are splendid – the best time to look at the Moon is when it is a crescent – then the features on the Moon's surface, craters, mountains and so on, cast long shadows and appear really three-dimensional. With a full moon, the sun is shining directly down on the Moon – it is noon on the Moon – and there are no shadows so it appears quite flat like a sepia photograph. But when the conditions are right, panning the telescope across the Moon is like flying over it – you get to know different localities and fantastic landscapes can be seen in great detail. Other planets also show observable detail – you can see the frozen ice caps white on the red planet Mars, the red coloured stripes and Great Red Spot of Jupiter, and of course the rings of Saturn. It's difficult to drag your eyes away from Saturn; but it's not always in the sky. You can turn your attention to more distant objects such as nebulae. These dim and hazy objects are either dust clouds in our own Milky Way galaxy or are themselves galaxies – congregations of billions of stars, each flying apart from one another as the Universe expands, separated by unimaginable gulfs of empty space. When you look at them you are looking deep into the past, because the light forming the image you see may have taken millions of years to reach us here on Earth. The famous Andromeda galaxy (the most distant object that can be seen with the naked eye) – is two million light years away. What you are seeing is M31 (Andromeda Galaxy) as it was two million years ago, and of course the people up there are looking two million years into the past when they look at us – a world before the rise of humanity: their descendants will be seeing us in two million years, by which time we'll be gone. Of course they can't really see us (no matter how many eyes they've got) but I'm convinced the galaxy – and the Universe – is full of worlds inhabited by intelligent beings. The terrible thing is we can never know each other: 'HELLO THERE, HOW ARE YOU?'... two million years go by ...'ALL RIGHT, HOW'S YOURSELF?'... another two million years pass before we hear that reply; civilizations have risen and fallen in the time it takes just to be civil. This problem of space and time also renders the whole idea of extra-terrestrial visitors arriving here in their flying saucers to spend ten minutes freaking out some farmer in Kansas unfeasible if not downright risible. Having said that, I must admit to having had occasional Close Encounters of my own ... For instance, Telescope House (my favourite supplier of Astronomical hardware, an old-established and respected institution) has a subtle strangeness ... Once I was visiting their premises in the heart of the Kent countryside when I asked to try some binoculars – I had some difficulty getting the images to coalesce. (Why is it that whenever somebody in a movie looks through binoculars, even in this twenty-first century, we are immediately and without fail presented with a point-of-view shot through a horizontal figure of eight shape – have binoculars never arrived in Hollywood? Has nobody there ever dared to tell the FX people that, with the possible exception of The Lone Ranger, nobody looks out on the world in this crude double-barrelled manner?) Anyway, the boffin soon put things right by setting the eyepieces at the correct distance apart for my eyes: this led to reminiscences of a customer who had been unable to obtain suitable binoculars *because his eyes were much too far apart*. Plainly a Neptunian.

Now if the cosmos contains large numbers of intelligent life forms, given the billions of planets where such evolution is possible, then some of them must be of a higher order of intelligence than human beings – but just how clever can you get? The human race is the cleverest species on this planet and here and there and from time to time it produces individuals like Leonardo, Shakespeare, Newton and Einstein. These people, much more clever than the average, are nevertheless perfectly normal human beings in every other respect – from this we can postulate a planet where the average individual possesses intellectual powers that equal those of Earthly geniuses, and of course the *clever* bastards there would be clever indeed, although pitiful dunces compared to the denizens of yet a third planet. And so it goes on, this line of reasoning, until it brings us to Cleverness Central where civilization, the arts and sciences have been brought to such a pitch of perfection that it's a shame we will never know anything about it.

Meanwhile back on Earth, my dome has more than paid for itself, by keeping my telescope safe from wind and weather and ready at a moment's notice to lock on to any object in the night sky – sometimes, when clouds are drifting overhead, I take a rest from the telescope and look out over the sleeping rooftops of the neighbourhood – but I don't see an Essex suburb, I see a small community of survivors from a space-ship disaster in some uncharted region of the galaxy where it is my duty to watch night after night for signs of the rescue ships. I have recently wallpapered the interior of my nocturnal watchtower – a heavy maroon paper embossed with a floral pattern. It's like being in a yurt, and when rain is beating down on the sealed roof, it's a good place to be – especially if you've got some biscuits.

BIRTH OF A NOTION

A THOUSAND AND ONE WAYS TO FORGET YOUR SELF

PENNY RIMBAUD

'Let's be the generation that makes future generations proud of what we did here.'

Barack Obama.
12/01/11 – Twitter – http://OFABO/sbkkHna

$1 | WHY SHALT THOU NOT?

OUR COMPLICITY WITH THE GOVERNANCE OF MAMMON

'And the Lord came down upon Mount Sinai, to the top of the mountain, and the Lord called Moses to the top of the mountain, and Moses went up. And the Lord said to Moses, "Go down and warn the people, lest they break through to the Lord to gaze and many of them perish."'
Exodus 19.

Proclaimed as they were by a third person who I do not believe was or is the Divine, and who by the simple expedience of replacing the 'thou' with the common 'we' might have at least existentially presented us with some kind of an imperative, the Ten Commandments are on the one hand once-removed from first person engagement, and on the other are just another second-hand hand-me-down. In any case, as I shall set out to prove later in this essay, this matter is further complicated by the fact that the first person is in itself a second, which is not exactly to say that it does not exist, but it is to say that if it does exist, it does so only as an illusion.

The sound of one hand slapping.

That these denials of our primary biological urges are seriously put forward in the Commandments as the basis of 'morality' is nothing short of a gross travesty against intellectual rights. Notable amongst these is the unique feature of human consciousness which gives us the ability and right to say 'no'.

THOU SHALT NOT
LEST THOU ART,
or at least might become so.

If it were a truly consensual imperative that we should not kill, there would be no killings, but, equally, **THERE IS NO WE.**

If it were a truly personal imperative that I should not kill, I wouldn't kill, but, equally, who the hell is

I?

IMPOSED MORALITY IS NO MORALITY AT ALL, INDEED, IN THE TRUEST SENSE IT IS DEEPLY UNETHICAL.

In whatever way you might choose to look at it, the Commandments aren't an imperative, they're orders, barked by a third person into the ears of an abstract second who, unless we rise to the bait, quite simply cannot exist. And this is to say nothing of the God from whom it is claimed these absurdities emanated.

Yes, we certainly can, can not.

If Moses wanted to play blind man's bluff, that's entirely his business and, equally, if he wanted to play at being God, fine, but given the scale of that god's later mythic misdemeanours with his ill begotten off-spring, any one of us should have had just cause to further doubt HIS word. But few of us did.

HE GAVE US HIS ONLY, AND THEN GOT OUT THE HAMMER 'N' NAILS.

In the great 'thou shalt not' there is no engagement whatsoever with the first person, in which case, what the fuck has it got to do with me? In this particular equation, thou is not I and I am not thou and ne'er the twain shall meet.

SO, I SHALL KILL IF I WANT TO BECAUSE, QUITE SIMPLY, I CAN. THERE AIN'T NO ONE GONNA TELL ME OTHERWISE.

Like it or not, I, and, indeed, any one of us, has the potential to kill, and many (if not most) of us do, albeit existentially. From the mouths of anyone who cast a vote in the last general election or who espouses the platitudinous virtues of Western democracies, 'not in my name' is pure self-delusion.

Oh, they certainly can chant cant.

The outright slaughter of the 'other' is a day-by-day reality to which all of us turn a blind eye that we might reap the benefits. 'More tea?' This is the nature of our complicity: the obligatory blinkers of the capitalist system.

Since World War Two, the largest democracy on the planet, America, with the wholesale support of the oldest, Britain, has slaughtered millions upon millions of people in the name of democracy. Millions more have been maimed, mutilated and tortured. Few have been democratised.

'Their names.' Smash, bang, wallop.
'Give us their names.' Twist, pierce, spike.
'Their fucking names.' Punch, force, tighten.

EXTRAORDINARY RENDITION?

You ain't fucking joking,
the script's already written.

'Okay, sarge, pass me another, this one's done for.'

The slave ships of Empire and the cattle trucks of the Third Reich are in every sense ideologically matched by the juggernaut sheep transporters of the meat industry: same 'otherness', same process.

Bah, bah black man...

The joke of electro-convulsive therapy, practised on those who can stand no more, was borrowed from the abattoirs of Italy where pigs were stunned before being slaughtered: all in the name of compassion.

ZAP!!

THIS LITTLE PIGGY HAD NONE.
What passing bells indeed.

The streets of the New World Order are paved with 'thou shalt kill'. How else is Mammon to feed its parasites while still feeding itself? This is the Reichstag of tribal community, the WTC of global unity: the benchmark beginning of so many ends.

THE WAR TO END ALL WARS IS A PROVEN OXYMORON.

Applying the law of the conservation of energy (if only ironically), there is almost certainly a statistical correlation between the number of civilian deaths in any given insurgence and the volume of resources to be extracted from that insurgency. It is, after all, the very meter by which insurgency is justified (but never initially professed as). More than any-thing else, it is the price of oil which governs our day-to-day costs. However, and whatever the price to us, it is a cost more dearly carried by those innocent civilians mown down in its procurement. In all matters of extraction, from oil to diamonds to uranium, it is never the 'us' who pays the true price, but the 'them'.

THEM, THE OTHER, ALWAYS THEM
which by definition cannot be us.

The very lubricant of our everyday lives is not oil, but the blood of oil.
Each turn of wheel and whine of cog is a death toll.

And is it not now mooted that water could be the next front-line?

THE VERY TEARS OF HEAVEN.

$2 | BOMB OR BURGER?

WE ARE ALL VICTIM TO MAMMON'S RAPACIOUSNESS

Out of the mouths of babes
and sucklings there flows a
terrible bile:
the insanity of pre-ordainity:
the bane of consciousness.

THOU CANST YET THOU SHALT NOT.

Oh, Beelzebub, that I might know thee now.

And on the meadowed banks of the Rubicon I shall lay thee down to squirm that we might indulge in heresy or plait each other's hair to make of the hangman's noose a better daisy chain. And there we gag and choke on fetid torpidity, our sluggish souls neutralized by whim. 'Oh thee I love,' I whisper whilst tightening the stranglehold.

But where the ferryman?

Laying claim to an illusory divine right, the social elites command that thou shalt not kill, while at the same time giving licence to us and others like ourselves to commit killings of further others, all in the name of the deity of choice, that being the thinly veiled alter-ego of religious connivance.

IN GOD'S NAME.

Thus spake the executioner,
the hangman and the judge,
the general, the politician,
the president and the priest,
the compliant public and the platitudinous
Ten Commandments.

ALL CONFIRMED
BY THE PSYCHOPATHY
OF THE CRUCIFICTION.

Now, to claim that the deceitful lies of an illusory God have been equalled by those of an equally illusory democracy is not as absurd as it might at first seem. If God sent Moses down a hill to tell us all not to kill (a commandment which to this day the chosen tribes appear to have had a great deal of difficulty in conforming to), then democracy, while subjecting us to the illusion that we have some choice in the matter, applies the same commandment while manifestly disobeying it in its endless wars and resultant killings: all in the cause of enforced democracy. And yes, of course enforced democracy will, on the surface, appear to be a contradiction of terms, yet there is no democracy on earth that has not been created through force of arms. Was the UK united peacefully? Ask the Irish.

ONE MAN'S ISLAND
IS ANOTHER'S KILLINGFIELD.

Moral laws are exactly that: confinements firstly of action and secondly, and more importantly, of genuinely considered, authentic thought. But how can thought be either considered or authentic, and by what agency? Taking the Cartesian line that as 'I the thinker' I am able to claim existence as my own, considered thought is consummately easy. However, question for one moment the source of that I (which presumably does something or other prior to the thinking) and the equation falls upon singularly rocky ground. What (or even who) is the I that gives rise to the I who we believe ourselves to be?

Being so completely divorced from commonality, indeed from any form of real society, the Cartesian I is eminently enclosable. Without an I isolated in time and space, there can be no enclosure either psychic or physical. And therein lies a clue to the only true escape route:

e = mc² = a pathway to infinities

Modern physics operates before and after the strictures of enclosure in the same manner in which the pre-Cartesian I operates before and after the strictures of imposed morality.

BEFORE AND AFTER.

We are born of beauty, temper and light,
and know no other way.
Then what travesty is this
which casts our force
or decides upon our superficiality?
Divorced from the infinitive root of existence,
we are as surface,
powerless even against ourselves.
Confounded by essence,
we become mere sacrifice,
a portrait of victimhood.
Convinced by this folly,
we persist as if permanence might be made of the flux,
or granite quarried from the very air that we breath.

Oh, for certain I know the nature of solidity
which is not the illusion of immovable mountains,
but the reality of symbiosis.
I know that matter is indivisible
even whilst inhabiting invisibility.
There is no separating place nor place of separation,
for always there is infusion and confluence
so profound that we are for ever contained,
before and after birth,
throughout life,
before and after death.

Clearly, the Cartesian I is in itself a third person masquerading in the first and, thus prescribed, is at once removed from the authenticity necessary to the creation of any true moral imperative. In short, being no more than a frail extension of another, deeper force, the Cartesian I is nothing but a construct (read 'delusion') upon which further constructs can be layered by those who share those delusions.

ЯОЯЯIM, MIRROR, ON THE WALL, HOW COME I'M NOT THERE AT ALL?

Hence the Western States (read 'the elites') are able to present as 'democracy' a form of governance which in fact is nothing but a crude combination of meritocracy and plutocracy which inevitably gives rise to hegemony. Now, if ever there was a woolly mask designed to be drawn over our eyes, democracy must be its brand name. That way we not only act like sheep, but get to look like them as well.

OH, LAMBS TO THE SLAUGHTER, YOU SODDING CHRISTS.

THE GRAND ILLUSION OF CHOICE.
You make it, they'll take it.

Born as we are into a 'nation', which in most cases defined its operational parameters many centuries ago, what choice do any of us have over the form of indoctrination to which we will be subjected and from which we will abstract what we come to believe is our 'person'. It is no choice of ours which national prides and prejudices are implanted in us and to which most of us remain compliant throughout our lives. Even our names are given to us as a form of de facto. Yes, that's right, Christian names are a form of seal: an official stamp of approval. However, what choice did any of us have over which religion it was that we were subjected to? Those who later wish to truly eradicate such small-minded cults of superstition from their consciousnesses will have a hard job on their hands. I know, I've been there. Such matters as these run deep in the very fibre of any culture and, whereas on a personal level they might be questioned and, indeed, largely negated, on a social level they remain solid as the rock of ages which, of course, is precisely what we have been told they are. Central to all this is the question of governance. Within democratic nations, democracy is accepted by most of the people who suffer its strictures as a fair and civilized political system (read form of control). We are informed by others like ourselves that this is a 'representational' form of government, and that our vote and our voice are essential to its correct functioning. We are told that the choice is ours in much the way that the giant supermarkets are keen to inform us that their interests are ours. However, just as democracies can claim that it is the peoples' vote which gives them the right to act as hegemonies, so supermarkets justify their monopoly through platitudes concerning customer choice. Most of us know full well that this quite simply is not true. What vote gave Tony Blair the right to wage an illegal war against Iraq, and what choice does the customer have as high street retail outlets are systematically undermined by the avariciousness of the supermarkets? But still we persist in subscribing to the illusion. Yes, of course reforms will be made to accommodate our concerns, particularly if they are put forward in the form of resistance, but this is merely circumspection by those in power to ensure continued voter/customer control. Tesco's will 'go organic' in much the way that governments will 'go green', but, rather than real change, this is incorporation which, by design, undermines the strength of resistance and thus, by degrees, of concerns. So, while claiming to be of and for the people, democracy is in fact the antithesis of people power: a surrogate dictatorship of the masses by the masses instituted by the same elite cadres who by one means or another rule the world. This spectacular sleight of hand, which makes possible a totalitarianism whose governance depends upon the licence given it by those whom it oppresses, would as much have impressed Houdini as it would Hitler himself, and never mind the 'heils'. This is the greatest con in political history and, what's more, with none of the chutzpah of the Nuremberg rallies.

THAT MAN IS LAUGHING.
OFF WITH HIS HEAD.
MALICE IN BLUNDERLAND.

The juggernauts roll. The meat racks buckle beneath the weight. The executioner wears the mask of reason. The trapdoor opens. The hungry hordes are ready to devour (and, so, be devoured). All in the name of other.

GOD, QUEEN, COUNTRY AND THE SHAREHOLDERS.

How manifest the lie & how incorporate the being of it.

Working on the sound premise that there quite simply is no such thing as inherent morality, what, beyond the absurd trinity given above, is it by which we might meter our lives?

THOU SHALT NOT WHEN, MANIFESTLY,

THOU CANST.

Is it really good enough that the very core of our being is encased with a set of preconditions which, for all their possibly good intentions, deny us any serious consideration of the key questions of existence?

THOU HAST NOT BEEN CORRECTLY DEFINED. HENCE THE RULE OF NUMBERS.

If for no other reason, I am a vegetarian because it is easier to be one: it quite simply disengages me from what should, to any thinking being, be a difficult moral conundrum. However, nothing at all is proved by this, after all, Hitler was also a vegetarian.

MAKE MEIN RARE.

I have also throughout most of my life followed the principles of pacifism while, contradictorily, giving tacit support to a fair number of liberationist movements to whom pacifism would be an anathema. And yes, biblically speaking, the assassination of Tony Blair would have been no bad thing given the horrific damage that his avowed 'faith' continues to wreak.

THIS IS THE FAITH OF SICKNESS
WHICH PINS 'MINE HOLY'
TO THE CROSS,
WHICH KNOWS
NO REPENTANCE,
WHICH IS BLIND
TO COMPLICITY,
WHICH KNOWS ONLY BLAME
IN ITS PITIFUL SIMPLICITY.

Following the Nuremberg Trials, the unrepentant Nazi elite, at least those who had not taken the comfortable option of suicide, were hung for their crimes against humanity. Would it perhaps be so very wrong to offer Blair a length of rope that he might also take the comfortable option rather than suffer the slow strangulation of his unrepentant duplicity? Or would it be so very wrong to practise the poetics of history that the ice axe might strike again in an act of divine retribution? And while we're about it, how about George Bush, Barack Obama, blah, blah, blah…

YES
YES
YES

in my name,

but, but, but ...

$3 | CONFIRMING THE RULE OF THUMB

THE FIRST AND LAST SUPPER – EATING FROM MAMMON'S PLATE

D'YA EVER SEEN A PIG SHOOT A PIG? D'YA EVER WORN THE MASK OF REASON?

The only reason that the ruling elites are happy to kill and eat animals as opposed to humans is that, in the interim, humans might be useful to them as a workforce in the factories and killing-fields of their making.

It was that behemoth of democracy, Winston Churchill (he who first advocated the bombing of civilians and the construction of concentration camps), who proposed that one million 'degenerate British citizens' be sterilized or put into labour camps.

One little piggy ate roast beef...

Whereas the ruling elites suffer no problem whatsoever in orchestrating mass genocides, they have the audacity to command that we shalt not, whilst at the same time licensing any number of us to do so, not, of course, in their name because, this being a democracy, they can claim that it's in ours. Wow, now there's a conundrum.

Most products in any supermarket, and in particular the 'luxury' items, have at some time or other been procured and/or sanctioned by force of arms. They are, in fact, death pickings.

Finger bre aking good.

Being a particularly effective WMD in the battle for global supremacy, AgriWar, as practised by the US Pentagon and, by proxy, all other Western democracies, is the silent but deadly tactic of enforced impoverishment.

FOOD NOT GUNS.
ANYTHING YOU CAN DO,
THEY CAN (UN)DO BETTER.

On September 11th 2001, 3,000 citizens of the US, the most powerful nation on the planet, died in what we are assured was a terrorist attack. If the total number of deaths by starvation throughout the world in that year were divided into a daily average, the result would be 23,000 persons. The vast majority of these would have been citizens of the least powerful nations on the planet, many of these most certainly being those from which, through the ministrations of AgriWar, resources, human, vegetable and mineral, are ruthlessly exploited by the democracies of the West, of which the US is undoubtedly the most insatiable. Whereas the events of 9/11 led to almost unanimous cries for justice and revenge, the death by starvation of nearly nine million persons during that year will have been dismissed by most pundits in the West as being the unfortunate result of some form of 'natural' disaster. Given that one in three Americans 'suffer' from obesity, this being the natural result of excess, is it not only natural that America with its all-powerful military/industrial complex should claim the monopoly on world resources? They are, after all, only looking after their own. Meanwhile, over half of the world's population is starving. This is, of course, a disaster, but, as any one of us who is prepared to listen will know, it is a perfectly natural one. Oh, it's a cruel business this nature, which, I guess, brings us to the one million dollar question:

In the Nazi death camps, did those who died not in the showers, but from overwork, cold and hunger, also die a natural death?
JUMPING JACK FLA$H, IT'S A ...

So yes, of course thou shalt not kill when thou canst so easily just leave people to die their own deaths and, whilst we're about it, isn't death by asphyxiation also perfectly natural?

WARead 'killing'

WELL, IT'S HUMAN NATURE INNIT?

$ $

NIGGER IN THE WOODPILE.
A brief survey of survival.

Imagine a situation in which for no other reason than to ensure their future, mutual supremacy, five bullies in the school playground gang together to see to it that while they remain free to practise their reign of terror, no other kid (potential bully or not) will be allowed to even get a look in. However, rather than acknowledging (even to themselves) that this is nothing but self-interest, and whilst continuing to bully everyone around them, they insist that this is to protect the other kids in the playground from being bullied. And who, one might ask, is in any position to say different? It is, in short, a protection racket.

In early August 1945, the US launched the biggest terrorist attacks in the history of mankind: Hiroshima and Nagasaki, in which over 200,000 people were liquidated in a flash while many hundreds of thousands more were left to die slow, painful deaths through the effects of radiation. That Japan was already at that time prepared to negotiate a surrender was of no consequence at all to those who launched the attacks. Their purpose was to demonstrate to the world at large their absolute supremacy in the field of terror (later to be euphemistically termed as 'collateral damage'). Since that time, the world has been held in a nuclear thrall where 'if?' is no longer a sensible question. It is 'when?' that rules supreme in global consciousness. The fact that this supremacy was later paralleled by Russia, France, China and Britain led to the creation of the NPT, the Nuclear Non-Proliferation Treaty designed by the nuclear gang of five to prevent further nations from joining in the fun. Perhaps not surprisingly, the existing gang are the five nations whose membership of the United Nations Security Council is permanent. That's some security! Players outside the gang of five are India, Pakistan, North Korea and, although no one really likes to talk too much about it, Israel. Well, they've got problems of their own.

If the events of 9/11 were an act of terrorism whose iconic imagery has seared its way into the global psyche, what of those mighty glowing mushrooms which, over 50 years ago, sucked away the very breath of it? Since that time the world and its people have never breathed free. Stifled by fear, our consciousnesses numbed into indifference, we sit and wait. Under that constant threat, what else are we to do? If we are ever to be rid of this suffocation, either there must be unilateral nuclear disarmament, or any and all nations must be left free to develop whatever weaponry they take a fancy to, and bugger the consequence. Until such time as this is achieved, and for all the glitzy gewgaws of commodity culture (we could, after all, choose to drown in Pepsi), there can be no real freedom for any one of the seven billion inhabitants of Planet Earth. On the other hand, through the disarmament of the Cartesian I ...

$$

In 2010, the world's biggest arms manufacturer, BAE Systems, paid £276m to 'settle' investigations by the British Serious Fraud Squad and the US Department of Justice.

PEACE AT ANY PRICE.
Well, at least that's settled.

At the end of 2010, BAE's operating profits were 'down' at £982m.

Everyone's got their price.

Property owned by Tony Blair is valued at around £14m.

'Like Judas of old, you lie and deceive,
a world war can be won, you want us to believe.

You fasten all the triggers for the others to fire,
then you sit back and watch while the death count gets higher,
You hide in your mansion while the young people's blood
flows from their bodies and is buried in the mud.
Let me ask you one question, is your money that good,
will it buy you forgiveness, do you think that it could?
I think you will find when your death takes its toll,
all the money you made won't ever buy back your soul.

And I hope that you die and your death will come soon,
I'll follow your casket on a pale afternoon,
and I'll watch as you're lowered onto your deathbed
and I'll stand over your grave 'til I'm sure that you're dead.'

'Masters Of War', Bob Dylan.

The second amendment of the American Constitution gave the citizens of the US the right to bear arms not for the shooting of gooks, nor for surreal mass killings in shopping malls, but for the simple expedience of being able to protect themselves from their own government should it become tyrannical. Erm, so?

Meanwhile, at a conservative estimate, the civilian death count caused by the current invasions of Iraq and Afghanistan stands (or, rather, lies) at around 900,000 mostly nameless persons, and never mind the dogs and goats: if not in your name, in whose?

THE SHAREHOLDERS
GOD, QUEEN, COUNTRY.

There's a cute kind of poetry here. BAE's operating profits stand at nearly £1,000,000,000 while the Iraq/Afghanistan civilian death toll stands at almost 1,000,000. That's a neat £1000 per body, pre-tax. But then, to be fair, it wasn't solely BAE product which was instrumental in these conveniences of collateral, and neither were these the only killing fields supplied by them, so let's call it a cool £500 per body and have done with it.

THE WAGES OF WAR.
CHEAP AT HALF
THE PRICE.
Go get 'em, Barack.

The carnage of 9/11 has become a benchmark justifying the continuation of terror policies which have been the key to governance since the beginning of civilization[sic]. For each one of the 3,000 deaths of 9/11, 300 Iraqi and Afghanistan civilians have been slaughtered in what, by no other name, is pure revenge.

THREE HUNDRED EYES FOR AN EYE.
So who's looking?

While the Athenian elite pontificated over the roots of civilization, the slave class, resigned as they were to the abject, confirmed both essence and substance: 'these are placed and thus must stay'. And this is named philosophy, and we are in irons.

OH, BUT NIETZSCHE ROSE TO GREAT HEIGHTS
(THAT HE MIGHT THEN BE CRIPPLED).

The second amendment of the American Constitution gave the citizens of the US the right to ...

KERBANG!!

The carnage of 9/11 has become a ...

KERASH!!

BAE puts a smile on the face of its shareholders whilst in Baghdad ...

KERIST!!

The bankers defend their right to bonuses ...

oh, for fuck's sake.

Yoh, man, we're the generation that'll make future generations proud of what we did here, and if they ain't proud, well then, we'll tan their motherfucking hides.

$4 | A WINTER'S TALE

BEYOND THE GRASP OF MAMMON

Of essence and substance, there is none. It is all a matter of attitude, or is it infinities we seek? So charmed we are by grace. Then, also, might I see this as complaint or criticism, and hurry fleet-footed to the screeching temple (like any other fool). I've lived at times beyond doubt, but that was always paralleled by a sense of lost discovery and, bit by bit, my horizons would fade. Oh then, let the tables be turned, let magnificence become its shadow that we might rise again.

And halfway up the mountain, just below the snowline, I came face to face with grace wearing the face of fate, and pretty she was too. 'Oh, Angel,' I whispered, my breath forming hieroglyphic betrayals of desire, 'that we might walk together awhile. But first, are you one or two?' 'I am both as one,' she replied in a tongue I barely understood, adding, 'but are there maps for this journey?' I wondered whether she had somehow read the clouds, seen the distant grimaces in the landscape, the whirl and frisk of combination. Or perhaps it was some strange abacus of mind that played its geometries. 'Full circle, my love.' I smiled, knowing that within this there was neither beginning nor end, yet sensing all the same that a diagram had been planted in faraway lands. And then the wolf howl, the ice cascade and the tremble of forbidden avalanche. 'Now, quick, beyond,' in unison, 'in one, as one.' Below, I could see the moraine, proof of a permanence (albeit one that had been created from lack of it), confirmation of solid ground. I'd climbed before in places like this, panting against nerve and energetics, but never before had chanced upon so testing a hold. My palms were wet, my mouth dry, my head thumping. 'We are no strangers here,' she smiled as if in an effort to reassure me. 'Then onward,' I cried, and then echoed from dark crags. And so we climbed, foot by careful foot, up and into the snowfield. Massive cornices hung above us. Eagles circled silent in the huge air behind us. There seemed to be nothing else.

How white that memory is, how strangely blank. Yet was that not the unwritten book of silence, the tablets in waiting? Of course, one day this shall be, but for the moment, oh, but for the moment. Was my companion aware of this, clinging to my sleeves that I should not be ether in so wild a place? Not once had I asked her name, but already we were bonded, bound in a profound nakedness. There was nowhere to go but beyond. No question to ask: grace wearing the face of fate.

$5 | DESCARTES' GREAT DUMB-DOWN

THE CREATION OF MAMMON IN OUR OWN IMAGE

Despite whatever claims might be made by the academics, reason is not fact, and no amount of peer reviews will make it so. Descartes' *cogito ergo sum* might appear to some as being well-reasoned and, indeed, to most others as fact, but it is nothing of the sort. Certainly it is a fact that, as Cartesian individuals, Enlightenment thinkers were able to develop the premise to give rise to the enclosures, the Industrial Revolution and, indeed, democracy itself. If there is no I isolated in time and space, then there can be no limitation placed upon it: definition is all. The slave is his own greatest manacle.

I THINK THEREFORE I AM:
ONE MAN,
ONE VOTE,
and never mind the 'selections'.

Which was, after all, just another way of saying *arbeit macht frei*, but that was only if you'd been unlucky enough to have bought into the conceits in the first place or, later, to have been brought into them. All of this, of course, having singularly unpleasant Darwinian undertones. Spurious notions like 'the survival of the fittest' completely ignore the natural symbiosis underlying all existence and the complex complicities inherent within all interchange; animal, vegetable and mineral.

Jesus died for a gamut of sins,
and they weren't all his own.

As long as we cling to the Cartesian premise, we will remain bound to Enlightenment mechanics; that which sees the world and its inhabitants as disparate forces bound only by competitiveness and its resultant conflict.

MINE'S **BIGGER** THAN YOURS
even when yours is mine,
you fuckarse.

Hence the aggressive posturings of everyday social interaction. Hence the wholesale acceptance that profit is more important than people. Hence the cults of specialization, exclusivity and celebrity. Hence the hallowed temples of the corporations, those who have made global theft into a virtue, rape into love and money into a god as unattainable as any that ever existed.

> Moonlight in Dubai, ski-slopes in a desert's sun, a Mecca and Jerusalem: the very heart of Mammon. This, then, the soul of the beast, the wholly unholy capital of the unholy feast. Dubai, playground of the social elites: misanthropy in marbled boardrooms, sodomy on silken sheets. Sheikhs and princes, cabbages and kings taking a slice of their favourite things: string of pearls in a one to one, diamond-studded dildos to spice up the fun. Despots and dreamers taking a pinch, shysters and schemers out for every inch. Tycoons and magnates pulling cheap tricks, greasing their palms whilst oiling their pricks, forcing their way up glistening thighs, then sealing the deal on cocaine highs. Botox babes with peekaboo bras, Errol Flynn contenders propping up bars. A-list celebs playing it cool, silicon chicks playing the fool. Movie stars and their constellations, Big Brother no ones and their aspirations. Surgical miracles smothered in glitz, with an army of servants to pick up the bits. Mercenaries, hit-men and arms-dealing whores discussing the profit to be made out of wars. Intelligence agencies comparing notes with lobbyists and PR men forcing the votes. Journos, paparazzi and media hacks spewing out fiction and calling it fact. Mafia moguls and Masonic lords with toxic handshakes and cancerous words. Political giants and admen gimps prostituting resources with pornographic pimps. Dubai: the conspiracy of wealth confirmed hour by hour in the blood-splattered corridors of absolute power.

BABYLON REVISITED.

Wealth-driven scum encircled by a poverty ridden slum. 65 per cent of the population of Dubai are itinerant workers, many of them illegal: the pathetically poor attracted to the preposterous rich that they might pocket some miserably miniscule part of that gross excess. This predominantly rural peasantry, stripped from the security of their own lands with the cruel cynicism once reserved for the slave barons, are lucky if they can earn as much as £200 per month, which wouldn't even pay the cost of a flight out of that hellhole. Those who are lucky are forced to live in pathetic hovels eking out some kind of an existence. The less lucky ones are forced to grovel in the streets where they are seen as mere shadow. Is it any great wonder that hovel and grovel are so Shakespearian in tragic rhyme? These are the detritus, the infinitely replaceable nobodies upon whose sub-existence the entire capitalist system is based. These are those who thou shalt not kill, but whom, with absolute impunity, you may impoverish to the point of death and, if necessary, beyond. These are today's 'huddled masses yearning to be free', but there is nowhere for them to go but damnation or desert.

DUBAI – DO OR DIE.
THE TEARS OF MISS LIBERTY
FALL ON BARREN GROUND.

This, then, is the ultimate betrayal of everything that is humanity: Mammon's creed of greed which places us against our neighbours that we might remain passive as they are mowed down in their millions through the inexhaustible cupidity of global capitalism.

Buy, buy, buy, buy, buy,
BYE, BYE.

On a scale unparalleled in the history of human(un)kind, commodity culture[sic] as orchestrated by the global elite has succeeded in enslaving not only those who serve it from afar, but also those who it likes to call its own. What should be ours has become theirs, yet still we rush to the temples to tighten our manacles. Still we prostrate before the poll box that we might be branded. Still we bow down to their authority: the specialists, the exclusivists, the celebrities.

OINK $ OINK

In the great scriptures of the New World Order, dissent is condemned as a social illness, its victims being jailed in institutions of oblique torture while their jailors chant platitudes concerning our greater welfare.

FOR OR AGAIN$T?

THE INCANTATION OF MAMMON, THE MANTRA OF MADNESS.

However, in the (non)society of 'I the thinker', welfare is something which is given not as a social service, not with grace, not as a right, but with miserly reluctance and, more often than not, stifling conditions.

THE STRUCTURAL ADJUSTMENT PROGRAMMES OF THE PSYCHE.

S.A.P. BUSINESS IS ($)CRAP BUSINESS.

Nature is to be tamed, mountains vanquished, tides turned. Equally, that arrogance can seep into the narrative of those who would aspire to oppose these conditions. The greenest of environmentalists are every bit as likely to take the 'I the thinker, I the saviour' line as any erstwhile imperialist.

'Oh, but only MAN can save the world of HIS imaginings.'
And in that there is quite possibly a distorted kind of a truth.

If we have become so deluded as to believe that we can control life, then inevitably we will believe that as much as the negative results are ours and ours alone, then so also must be the positive. But, rather than engagement, this is removal.

I^a THINK THEREFORE I^b AM, YET I^b IS NOT I^a.
A GOAT DOES NOT PROVE A SHEEP.

Descartes' ergo was the Faustian tryst from which stemmed Freud's metastatic definition of ego. And now, as post-millennium individuals isolated in time and space, we quite literally can't exist without it.

I THINK THEREFORE I HAVE ONLY MYSELF TO BLAME:
The dragnet of twentieth-century psychoanalysis.

Cartesianism is, then, the essential ingredient of egotism, for, without the I^b as defined and isolated by Descartes, the ego, as later defined and isolated by Freud, simply cannot exist.

I^b AM ERGO EGO IS.

Given that the source entity, I^a, is not the same entity as I^b, it would seem perfectly reasonable to further suggest that I^b is every bit as insubstantial a construct as Freud's ego. There is no question, then, that both the ego and I^b are dependent for their existence on the source I^a. Indeed, it could argued that Descartes' I^b and Freud's ego are in essence one and the same or, conversely, that whereas I^b is once removed from I^a, Freud's ego is twice removed unless, of course, I^b is Freud's ego, nothing more, nothing less. Either way, none of this offers solid enough ground upon which to build any kind of authentic existence:

THE INSUBSTANTIAL CONFIRMING ITSELF THROUGH THE INSUBSTANTIAL.

Nietzsche's heroic attempts to grab Descartes by the balls and to make something positive of all this by postulating *der übermensch* failed only in that it was just too much to ask of those addicted to the moral strictures of 'I the isolated thinker'.

FOR AS LONG AS ONE MAN IS HELD IN SERVITUDE,

NO MAN SHALL BE FREE.

THE DREADFUL TRUTH OF SUB-EXISTENCE, THE DOUBLE BIND OF CARTESIANISM.

Ultimately, it took Einstein to break the Cartesian thrall with his physics, Picasso wth his cubism and, later, Sartre to pounce upon the philosophical implications, before the ergo and its ego were at last conclusively challenged.

I THINK THEREFORE I BLAME DESCARTES.

BEHIND YOU, LOOK BEHIND YOU!!!

The essentially indefinable forces of nature are the unavoidable forces of life and, indeed, the only true fact of it. These natural forces should not and, indeed, cannot realistically be measured against the negative projections made possible only through human consciousness. This is not the yin yang law of opposites as promoted by the mystics, nor the rule of balance as practised by the BBC. The natural world, which by nature must include all human activity, is at this very moment in perfect accord. This is not a moral judgement, it is a fact, and it is a fact quite simply because it could be no other way: each moment, each moment, each moment by moment, not in the horizontal, temporal trajectory of the Cartesian universe, but in the multi-layered, infinitive multi-directionalism of the quantum multiverse. So, at last, we have reached this moment not as individualized entities bound by time and space, but as manifestation of absolute symbiosis. There is no other way.

ABSOLUTE CHOICE IS NO CHOICE AT ALL.

LIKE IT OR NOT, WE SIMPLY ARE.

WE SHALL KILL IF WE DO.

Whereas, to exist at all, any human construct must have its opposite (black/white, light/shadow), attempts to apply this rule to nature are quite simply fatuous. In nature, by nature, there can be no separation, no this or that, for the interdependence of symbiosis defies the specific in manifesting the whole.

Love is all or love is not at all.

Like love, evil is a human construct practised only by humans, but whereas the nature of love is reflected within the absolute interconnected nature of the symbiosis, evil in itself contains not one element of it.

LIVE – EVIL

Thus, paradoxically, while attempting to stand in direct opposition to the interdependence of the symbiosis, evil is completely contained by it, connected to it, dependent upon it and, thereby, conceptually nullified by it.

In divine contradiction of the alchemic,

TO BELIEVE IN EVIL IS TO PRACTISE IT.

BE SURE THY SINS WILL FIND THEE OUT.

Hence, whereas love can reasonably be described as a force of life (of its nature), evil, being solely a human construct confined to human practise, can only be defined as perverse human imaginings, not only divorced from life, but profoundly anti-life.

THIS IS THE RIGHT TO SAY NO

DEFILED.

THEN THOU SHALT NOT, FOR IT IS ONLY IN YOUR IMAGININGS OF SELF THAT YOU MIGHT.

THIS IS THE IMPERATIVE.

THIS IS THE MORALITY.

I defy thee to exist beyond it.

FINI

IDLE MARKET

IDLER BOOKS

BRAVE OLD WORLD (Hamish Hamilton) Signed hardback copy.
Mr Hodgkinson's latest book. A literary and practical guide to husbandry,
in calendar form. Illustrated by Alice Smith, and typeset by Mr Brett.   £16.99

THE IDLE PARENT (Penguin) Signed paperback copy.
by Tom Hodgkinson. 'A godsend to parents,' *Sunday Times*.   £8.99

THE IDLER'S GLOSSARY (Biblioasis)   £12.95
by Joshua Glenn and Mark Kingwell. US book which is destined
to become the *Devil's Dictionary* for the idling classes.

THE BOOK OF IDLE PLEASURES (Ebury)   £10.99
edited by Tom Hodgkinson & Dan Kieran with fine illustrations by Ged
Wells. A sumptuous hardback anthology of pleasures that aims to prove
the best things in life really are free. 'Lovely book,' Mark Radcliffe, Radio 2.

HOW TO BE FREE (Penguin)   £9.99
by Tom Hodgkinson. 'Essential!' *Time Out*. Signed paperback copy.

HOW TO BE IDLE (Penguin)   £9.99
by Tom Hodgkinson. Signed paperback copy.

**WE WANT EVERYONE: FACEBOOK
AND THE NEW AMERICAN RIGHT** (Bracketpress)   £7.95
by Tom Hodgkinson. Describing the political ideology of the
founders of Facebook. Signed limited edition. Bracketpress pamphlet
with letterpress printed cover. Third edition.

THE IDLER BOOK OF CRAP HOLIDAYS (Boxtree)   £5.00 (rrp £10)
edited by Dan Kieran. Readers' accounts of their worst holidays in the sun.

**ON THE VISIONARY WORK AND REVOLUTIONARY
LIFE OF AN IDLE IDOL: WILLIAM MORRIS** (Bracketpress) £25.00
by John Mitchinson. Letterpress printed essay with frontispiece by
Edward Burne-Jones and Kelmscott borders, hand-bound limited edition.

IDLER BACK ISSUES

WORK WORK WORK No.3 – January/February 1994   £8
Bertrand Russell, Charles Handy

SKINT No.24 – September/October 1995   £8
Keith Allen, Louis Theroux, Charles Handy

MAN'S RUIN No.25 – Winter 1999   £15
The first book-format Idler, featuring Louis Theroux's Sick Notes, Will Self,
Howard Marks, Adam and Joe, and Ken Kesey

THE LOVE ISSUE No.30 – Summer 2002   £10
Louis Theroux meets Colin Wilson, Johnny Ball on Descartes, Crap Towns, Devon
Retreat, Chris Yates interview, Marchesa Casati

WAR ON WORK No.35 – Spring 2005   £10
Keith Allen's A to Z of life, Raoul Vaneigem interview, Jeremy Deller's Folk Art,
Dan Kieran's Seven Steps to the Idle Life, Chris Donald, Peter Doherty
and more Crap Jobs

YOUR MONEY OR YOUR LIFE No.36 Winter 2005   £10
Mutoid Waste Company, Edward Chancellor on credit, Penny Rimbaud,
Jay Griffiths, A Hitch Hiker's Guide, The Guilds, Chris Donald

CHILDISH THINGS No.37 – Spring 2005   £10
Childcare for the Lazy, Michael Palin, Bertrand Russell, Free Range Education,
Running Away to Join the Circus

THE GREEN MAN No.38 – Winter 2006   £10.99
Stephen Harding on why doing less is the way forward, Richard Benson tries to sow a
meadow, In conversation with Jamie Reid, John Michell on Cobbett, plus ukulele special

LIE BACK & PROTEST No.39 – Spring 2007   £10.99
Penny Rimbaud on The Meaning of Life, Jay Griffiths eats missionaries for breakfast,
Ronald Hutton, Green Gartside, L. A. Rowland explains why we shouldn't bother
going to university

CARNAL KNOWLEDGE No.40 – Winter 2008   £10.99
Damien Hirst cover, Esther Perel on the sex drought, Neil Boorman, Nick Lezard,
Michael Bywater, Sarah Janes and Kevin Godley

SMASH THE SYSTEM No.42 – Summer 2009   £18.99
The first hardback Idler, bound in cloth. With essays by Alain de Botton,
Penny Rimbaud, Paul Kingsnorth and many more. Interviews with Oliver James,
Jaz Coleman and Youth.

BACK TO THE LAND   No.43 – Summer 2010   £18.99
Featuring interview with David Hockney and Ian Bone. Essays from John-Paul Flintoff, Matthew De Abaitua, Tim Richardson, Simon Fairlie, Joanna Walsh, Boff Whalley.

IDLER CLOTHING

T-shirts are £20 and are available in XL, L and M and in girl's fit L and M. Designs include Snail, Work Kills, Do Less, Smash the System. Hoodies are £45 and feature the Idler Snail. All designed and produced by Ged Wells. Send cheque and size and we will choose design. Or check on the website for availability. Colours and designs change constantly.

IDLER SUBSCRIPTIONS

UK subscription	£40.00
Europe subscription	£50.00
Rest of the world subscription	£60.00

New subscribers will receive a hand-printed personalized card welcoming them into the Grand Order of Idlers

Go to www.idler.co.uk and order online, or write your order and send with a cheque payable to 'The Idler' and send it to:
The Idler, Mail Order Dept.,
81 Westbourne Park Road, London W2 5QH

You must include post & packing costs as follows:
Issues 1–24: £1.50 per issue.
Issues 25–34: £2.75 per issue.
T-shirts and hoodies: £2.50 per item.
For European Community, add 50%.
For rest of the world, add 100%

A downloadable order form is available from the Idler website
www.idler.co.uk

THE IDLER ACADEMY

of Philosophy, Husbandry and Merriment

BOOKSELLER AND COFFEEHOUSE
*serving fine coffees and teas, cakes and simple lunches
ginger beer, lemonade, dandelion & burdock*

DEALERS IN BOOKS BOTH OLD AND NEW
*Specialists in old textbooks, Grammars, Classics,
English History and Literature, Classical Studies, Husbandry,
Fashion, Anarchist Literature, Science*

CLASSES, COURSES AND SYMPOSIA

Competence is at the foundation of happiness.
– William Cobbett

81 WESTBOURNE PARK ROAD   LONDON   W2 5QH
OPP. THE WESTBOURNE   TEL: 0207 221 5908
Call in for a timetable, or visit: www.idler.co.uk/academy

ART & FASHION ≠ INDUSTRY

ETSY.

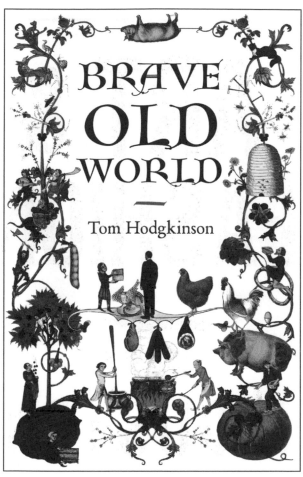

A Practical Guide to Husbandry
or the Fine Art of Looking After Yourself

Containing a calendar showing what to do in the garden
and smallholding, urban or rural, and when;
also showing the principal feast days.

To be published by Hamish Hamilton on the 7th July 2011
Available from all good booksellers. ISBN 978-0241143742

GWYNNE'S GRAMMAR

INTRODUCTORY GRAMMAR NOTES:

DEFINITIONS, EXPLANATIONS AND ILLUSTRATIONS

OF THE PARTS OF SPEECH

AND OF THE OTHER MOST IMPORTANT TECHNICAL TERMS

OF GRAMMAR

N. M. GWYNNE

"A most improving pamphlet from Mr. Gwynne."

Published by Idler Books and available to purchase in person at
The Idler Academy or order online at: www.idler.co.uk

THIS CRIPPLED FLESH
A BOOK OF PHILOSOPHY AND FILTH

A NOVEL BY **PENNY RIMBAUD** ILLUSTRATED BY ALICE SMITH

"… this immature collection of pointless varying text fonts and sizes and
repeated sentences – which equates to wasted page space; ultimately
this proved to be an entire waste of trees, time & effort."
– Pagan Ronnie, Amazon.co.uk, 28.10.10

ISBN: 978-0-9566184-0-5 · Free UK P&P direct from www.bracketpress.co.uk

AN ADVERTISING MESSAGE TO ALL READERS

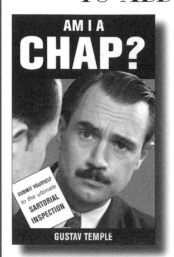

THE POLITICS OF ENVY

The New Banalists Orchestra

MANIFESTO

We, the New Banalists, have formed an orchestra to proclaim our manifesto:

TASTE IS A FORM OF PERSONAL CENSORSHIP

DENY THE POLITICS OF ENVY

TECHNIQUE IS A REFUGE OF THE INSECURE

SHADOW WAR

John Sinclair   Mark Stewart   Youth   David Tibet   Zodiac Youth

I. MAMMON — PENNY RIMBAUD
Poet-provocateur Penny Rimbaud attacks the god of greed Mammon.
It's business as usual for the pin-strip parasites. Hear the arms dealers laughing like hyenas.

2. POLITICS OF ENVY — MARK STEWART
Dissident maverick mindfucker Mark Stewart attacks the economics of genocide.

3. REALITY IS A CONSTRUCT — ZODIAC YOUTH
Boxer Bukowski poet reconditions and explodes his Zodiac killer myth;
an accident waiting to happen ...

4. CONSPIRACY BORN — DAVID TIBET
Gnostic Acrostic and Coptic scholar David Tibet deals in strange currencies.

5. TESTIFY — JOHN SINCLAIR
MC5 magus, White Panther founder; the myth that is John Sinclair
delivers his testimonial to the bohemian ideal.

6. SEATTLE — YOUTH
The Joke that is Youth comes of age (with an excerpt from Kommune).
A parable for this age of treason.

Free download

To download your free 'Politics of Envy' album send an e-mail to:
catchingfire@me.com

Produced by Youth · Mixed by Michael Rendall

OUR NEEDS FEED THEIR GREED.

What do you call a hegemony
headed by global corporations
sanctioned by a plutocracy
yet feigning to be a meritocracy?

WESTERN DEMOCRACY.

Serving the exclusive interests of the Global Corporations, yet under cover of the names of all those who through the ballot boxes endorse the tyranny, Western Democracies are currently waging vicious, illegal, armed interventions across the globe, with particular concentration on Islam.

Stretching from Morocco in the West, to India in the East, Islam is the new Iron Curtain, harbouring irresistible resources while at the same time preventing easy access to those of even greater value in the as yet 'untamed' territories of black Africa: the future killing-field of commodity culture. Capitalism's lust for global domination will only be satisfied when the children of Islam and Africa have been made, if necessary at gun point, into passive consumers: 'make poverty history' (with emphasis on the 'make').

EXCUSE ME, BUT ...

2011. Who are the 'Libyan Rebels', and who or what do they represent? Beyond the self-evident malevolence of pure revenge, why are they being 'supported' by Western Democracies in their attempts to overthrow the governance of Muammar Gaddafi? And, more to the point, why is no one talking about it? Then, on the other hand, why didn't the same 'standards' apply when, in 1984, the British miners sought to overthrow the intransigent despotism of Margaret Thatcher? All for one, and one for all: the serpent eats its own tail.

$ $ $

This, then, is the New World Order. Like morality, politics are defunct. Our personal complacency over these matters is matched only by our social impotency.

POSTSCRIPT

Leading environmentalists are giving assurances that the next generation of nuclear power stations will be safe while, at the same time, we are informed that the United States Air Force is using 50 per cent biofuel in its bomb attacks on Libya. Yes, it's a green world.

— Penny Rimbaud, April 2011.

IDLER BOOKS

81 WESTBOURNE PARK ROAD   LONDON   W2 5QH

Idle Limited Reg. No. 5897340

A CIP catalogue record for this book is
available from the British Library

I

Editor Tom Hodgkinson
Typesetting Christian Brett
Art Editor Alice Smith
Proof Reader Nancy Campbell

The views expressed by the contributors
do not necessarily reflect those of the editors

The type used is Monotype Bembo Book designed by
Robin Nicholas and complimented with ITC Golden Cockerel Initials
by Richard Dawson from original designs first created by Mr Gill in 1929

Printed by the MPG Books Group, Bodmin and King's Lynn

ISBN-13: 978-0-9548456-2-9

www.idler.co.uk